The Quest for Good Governance

Why do some societies manage to control corruption so that it manifests itself only occasionally, while other societies remain systemically corrupt? This book is about how societies reach that point when integrity becomes the norm and corruption the exception in regard to how public affairs are run and public resources are allocated. It primarily asks what lessons we have learned from historical and contemporary experiences in developing corruption control, which can aid policy-makers and civil societies in steering and expediting this process.

Few states now remain without either an anticorruption agency or an ombudsman, yet no statistical evidence can be found that they actually induce progress. Using both historical and contemporary studies and easy to understand statistics, Alina Mungiu-Pippidi looks at how to diagnose, measure, and change governance so that those entrusted with power and authority manage to defend public resources.

ALINA MUNGIU-PIPPIDI teaches democratization and policy analysis at the Hertie School of Governance in Berlin. She chairs the European Research Centre for Anti-Corruption and State Building Research and is Chair of Policy Pillar of the EU FP7 five-year research project, ANTICORRP. Professor Mungiu-Pippidi has served as an adviser on issues of governance measurement and anticorruption to the European Commission, UNDP, Freedom House, NORAD, and the World Bank, among others. She is is also a popular op-ed writer and the author of two film documentaries: *Where Europe Ends* and *A Tale of Two Villages*, screened by the BBC.

The Quest for Good Governance

How Societies Develop Control of Corruption

ALINA MUNGIU-PIPPIDI

CAMBRIDGE
UNIVERSITY PRESS

University Printing House, Cambridge CB2 8BS, United Kingdom

Cambridge University Press is part of the University of Cambridge.

It furthers the University's mission by disseminating knowledge in the pursuit of education, learning and research at the highest international levels of excellence.

www.cambridge.org
Information on this title: www.cambridge.org/9781107113923

First published 2015

A catalogue record for this publication is available from the British Library

Library of Congress Cataloguing in Publication data
Mungiu, Alina.
The quest for good governance : how societies develop control of corruption / Alina Mungiu-Pippidi.
pages cm
Includes bibliographical references and index.
ISBN 978-1-107-11392-3 (hbk) – ISBN 978-1-107-53457-5 (pbk)
1. Political corruption–Prevention. 2. Public administration–Corrupt practices–Prevention. 3. Government accountability. 4. Transparency in government. I. Title.
JF1525.C66M8 2015
352.3′5–dc23 2015010006

ISBN 978-1-107-11392-3 Hardback
ISBN 978-1-107-53457-5 Paperback

The research for this book was funded in part by the European Union Seventh Framework Research Project ANTICORRP (Anti-corruption Policies Revisited: Global Trends and European Responses to the Challenge of Corruption grant agreement number 290529). The views expressed are solely those of the author and the European Union is not liable for any use that may be made of the information contained therein.

This book is the first from Cambridge University Press related to the ANTICORRP project (www.anticorrp.eu).

Alina Mungiu-Pippidi (2015) The Quest for Good Governance

This project is co-funded by the Seventh Framework Programme for Research and Technological Development of the European Union

Contents

Figures

Tables

Abbreviations

ACA	Anticorruption agency
ACI	Anticorruption interventions
ANTICORRP	Anticorruption Policies Revisited: Global Trends and European Responses to the Challenge of Corruption
BDP	Botswana Democratic Party
CoC	Control of Corruption (World Bank)
CPI	Corruption Perceptions Index
CSOs	Civil society organizations
DPP	Democratic Progressive Party, Korea
EITI	Extractive Industries Transparency Initiative
EQI	European Quality of Government Index
EU	European Union
EVS	European Values Survey
FCPA	Foreign Corrupt Practices Act
FDI	Foreign direct investment
FIFA	International Federation of Association Football (Fédération Internationale de Football Association)
FOIA	Freedom of Information Act
GCB	Global Corruption Barometer
GDP	Gross domestic product
GNI	Gross national income
GRECO	Group of States against corruption (Council of Europe)
HDI	Human Development Index
IACC	International Anticorruption Conference
IAACA	International Association of Anticorruption Authorities
ICAC	Independent Commission Against Corruption, New South Wales, Australia
ICRG	International Country Risk Guide

IMF	International Monetary Fund
ISD	Indices of Social Development
KMT	Kuomintang
KOF	Index of Globalization (ETH Zurich)
MCC	Millennium Challenge Corporation
MP	Member of Parliament
NGO	Non-governmental organization
NORAD	Norwegian Agency for Development Cooperation
NUTS	Nomenclature of Units for Territorial Statistics
OBI	Open Budget Index
OECD	Organization for Economic Cooperation and Development
PPP	Purchasing power parity
PRS	The PRS Group, Inc.
QoG	Quality of Government Institute, University of Gothenburg, Sweden
UN	United Nations
UNCAC	United Nations Convention Against Corruption
UNDP	United Nations Development Program
UNESCO	United Nations Educational, Scientific, and Cultural Organization
USAID	United States Agency for International Development
WEF	World Economic Forum
WGI	Worldwide Governance Indicators, World Bank
WVS	World Values Survey

Acknowledgments

This book was born out of sheer frustration. I started as one of the many young people who had been involved in a 1989 revolution and who then went on to study in a great Western university. Upon my return and, still early in my life, I took up public office, only to discover that any public policy is irrelevant in an environment where corruption is the norm and where heavy prices are paid by the whistle-blowers, not the bribers.

In 2003 I won my first important EU research grant, with which I organized a survey in five Eastern European countries to explore and test the insights I had gathered from my public sector experience. A first resulting article, which analyzed the survey results, argued that bribery was only a small part of postcommunist corruption, and that the particularistic allocation of public resources was the main governance norm and the main driver of politics (Mungiu-Pippidi 2006a). It was on this basis that I planned what seemed at the time a highly successful anticorruption campaign that I organized in my country (Romania), and which received praise in World Bank textbooks and mainstream international media. My 2004 anticorruption campaign worked marvellously, as should always be the case with research-grounded reforms: it toppled a corrupt government leading in polls, made anticorruption the number-one issue on the public agenda and empowered reformers in grand style. But more corruption followed just as anticorruption was taking hold. Only ten (hard to bear) years later am I finally running out of names on my "black" wish list, as I watch every day on the internet news of jailed top Romanian dignitaries. I have my own private, although incomplete, virtuous circle.

My second corruption article, "Corruption: Diagnosis and Treatment," published in 2006 in *Journal of Democracy* (edited by The National Endowment for Democracy and The Johns Hopkins University Press), proposed a new theoretical framework to study corruption. It argued that particularism was the "default" governance regime and that ethical universalism could be reached only after long and quite exceptional state-building. It also contended that political competition in new democracies was mostly a competition to spoil public resources. Corruption is thus bound to increase after democratization and can decrease only when sufficient civil society control develops that can be sustained over time (Mungiu-Pippidi 2006b). I owe many thanks to Michael Johnston and Bo Rothstein for their generous promotion of this article as a new paradigm setter. Also Tom Carothers, Claus Offe, Larry Diamond and Mark Plattner in the democracy studies community were enthusiastic supporters of anticorruption in the final stage of democratic revolution and encouraged me over the years to pursue this further. The *Journal of Democracy* remained the privileged testing ground of my ideas, and I owe thanks to editors, reviewers and readers who helped me advance my ideas through several articles. The New School journal *Social Research: An International Quarterly* published the core historical argument that I took six years to develop, as "Becoming Denmark: Historical Designs of Corruption Control", in its special corruption issue (Mungiu-Pippidi 2014).

So how can a state captured by private interests evolve into one operating on the basis of ethical universalism? This became the key question of my seminar on good governance transitions at Hertie School of Governance in Berlin, which has always been short on successful cases to study, although not on students. I had to add historical case studies to be able to present more "achievers," and I always felt very close to my graduate students from countries who insisted that their country "was not there" yet. I felt the same about my own. In 2011, the Norwegian Agency for Development Cooperation (NORAD) commissioned the Hertie School of Governance to write an analytical report to explain the modest results of the first generation of anticorruption instruments supported by international donors and propose a new generation of evidence-based reforms. The report warned of exaggerated ambitions and modest results, as its first working title, "Chasing Moby Dick across Every Sea and Ocean," indicated. Fredrik Eriksson, then with NORAD, deserves thanks for the enthusiastic advertising of new theoretical insights that he claimed to have spotted in the report. The title we had to give up as too pessimistic for the development community. Instead, the report was called "Contextual Choices in Fighting Corruption: Lessons Learned, NORAD, Report 4/2011" and its main structure and argument became the core of the present book. The views and opinions expressed in the report did not necessarily correspond with those of NORAD. The agency graciously agreed that some of the work I initiated there is used here in a more developed form.

I also owe thanks to the Trust for Civil Society in Central and Eastern Europe (CEE Trust), the Open Society Institute Think-Tank Fund, Balkan Trust for Democracy, Freedom House, Black Sea Trust, Stanford's Center on Democracy, Development, and the Rule of Law, the European Institute at Oxford University, and the International Democratic Forum in Washington DC for the support they have given me over the last fifteen years to develop anticorruption experiments, test them and report the results. I also want to thank New School for Social Research, the Journal of Democracy, NORAD and Barbara Budrich, the publisher of the EU FP7 ANTICORRP Anticorruption Report Series for publishing in advance bits and pieces of what would later become chapters of this book. In 2011, the European Union Seventh Framework Project awarded me and my colleagues 'ANTICORRP', the largest social science EU Framework Project grant at that time, 10 million Euros. Its title, "Antibody" in English is manifest in itself of how I saw the cure of this particular disease – not by using particular medicines, but by empowering natural immunity.

Historians Mette Frisk Jensen (for Danish history), Andrei Pippidi (for intellectual history of ethical universalism) and Guy Geltner (for Italian medieval city states) gave me great advice and guidance. My research team at Hertie School deserves special thanks, in particular Aram Khaghaghordyan with his invaluable help on editing, Roberto Martinez Barranco Kukutschka for his dedicated work on graphs and tables, and Ramin Dadasov for his relentless updates and improvements to our statistics.

Researchers and practitioners from all over the world brought great contributions to our three-year-long seminar "Transitions to Good Governance" which helped document this book: Drago Kos, Chris Walker, Monica Macovei, Francesca Recanatini, Alena Ledeneva, Donatella Della Porta, Alberto Vanucci, Richard Rose, Mark Pieth, Masa Loncaric, Bianca Vaz Mundo, Ana Carolina Sponza Braga, Michael Weinhardt, Angelica Pulido Solares, Aiste Skardziute, Maira Martini, Fortune Agbele, Mariam Gabedava, Dainius Velykis, Kristof Kleemann, and Mihaly Fazekas. I also owe many thanks to all the academics, civil servants and journalists who patiently received me in South Korea, Chile, and Uruguay.

Finally, all non-governmental organizations and individuals who worked with me to develop anticorruption coalitions and civil society anticorruption projects in Albania, Romania, Moldova, Kosovo, Serbia, Croatia, Ukraine, Slovakia, Czech Republic, Poland, Russia, and Central Asia are entitled to my gratitude and solidarity for their endless and frequently unrewarded efforts.

1 Understanding control of corruption

Why corruption is worth studying

Tarek al-Tayeb Mohamed Bouazizi was a twenty-seven-year-old Tunisian street vendor who set himself on fire on December 17, 2010, in protest at the confiscation of his wares following an accusation by officials that he was trading illegally and evading taxes. That street vendor's action started the fires of the Tunisian Revolution and then the wider Arab Spring, and he was instantly cast as a hero by the global anticorruption community – after all, then-President Zine El Abidine Ben was a typical corrupt leader with a wife who had built herself an unauthorized villa at the Carthage UNESCO heritage site. While the people who disassembled her villa with their bare hands could not have been asked to look at the situation objectively, perhaps the global anticorruption community should still try to do so.

The hero of the Tunisian Revolution was in fact avoiding taxes, like most small traders in poor countries all around the world. He saw himself as acting legitimately against a state that had done so little for him and his family, while President Ben Ali and his wife prospered. The state could have argued that since people such as Bouazizi had never paid taxes, there were insufficient public resources to offer them much in the way of education or healthcare. It might turn out that the money spent on Ben Ali's villa and other spoils was insufficient to provide healthcare and education for all those in need who were either not earning enough to pay taxes or considered it unnecessary to do so. In other words, beyond the paradigm of predator and victim – two parts with ideally cast actors in this particular circumstance – what seems to be the problem in the Tunisian situation is the absence of an agreed social contract between these actors, avoiding both corruption and tax evasion. Only such a contract would give development a chance.

Does such a social contract exist today, after Ben Ali's demise? Are other democracies in the world, more mature than the Tunisian one, doing better? Judging by the grass-roots protests in India, Ukraine, Bulgaria, Turkey, and Brazil, one gets the feeling that people are genuinely fed up with governments controlled by rent seekers trying to enhance crony capitalism and inequitable development. The term "corruption" has grown to include all unaccountable public spending. In summer 2013, a fifty-year-old man in Rio de Janeiro held up the poster, "New Hospitals, Not New Stadiums," protesting against what he and others saw as "corrupt" public spending in advance of the FIFA Soccer World Cup. He said proudly to the media, "I was here in the 1980s. Then we were demanding democratic elections. Now we want better public healthcare and education. We work hard, we pay our taxes, but we get nothing back in return" (Young 2013). Like many other Brazilians, he wanted Brazil to stage the World Cup, but on this occasion he and others were struck by the hard truth that to host such an event, a parallel country, from stadiums to hospitals, must be created corresponding to the standards demanded by FIFA, while he and everyone else are left in the "old" country, the one without standards and where "anything goes." For this generation of the third wave of democratization, yet another chapter needs to be opened to complete a democratic revolution, a chapter that will cover the elimination of such double standards, of privilege, of what they call the "corruption" of their political leaders. Now that a relative majority of countries holds elections and more citizens than ever before are involved in choosing their own governments, it is more and more difficult to explain why good governance remains such a scarce benefit while corruption seems to flourish in new democracies.

Many scholars and policymakers dismiss these widespread perceptions of corruption across the world as being based on "misperceptions." But why then do we find consistently that a high perception of corruption is frequently associated with low public expenditure on health (e.g., hospital queues in Brazil) and education, but high on various infrastructural projects (from Brazil's expensive World Cup to Ben Ali's grandiose and empty mega-mosque in Tunis), reduced absorption of assistance funds (see HIV funds for South Africa or EU funds in Greece and Romania), low tax collection (if all EU states would control corruption at the same level as Denmark, they would collect twice the EU budget in one year, ending the eurozone crisis), and low participation of women in both the labor market and politics (Mungiu-Pippidi 2013a). Leaving aside the complex relationship between corruption and development and its reverse causality problems (corruption may hinder development, but in poor countries that do not pay their policemen or doctors at all or only insufficiently, direct payments by citizens as bribes fund such services directly), evidence exists of some indisputable negative consequences of corruption; once again pleading for a holistic approach to the control of corruption. For instance, high corruption is associated with massive brain drain, as the best educated flee to more meritocratic countries, ultimately further subverting their own country's investment in education and finally development itself (Ariu and Squicciarini 2013; Mungiu-Pippidi 2013a). Corruption on a national scale thus creates disincentives for hard work and integrity: in a 2013 survey of 88,000 Europeans, only in Northern Europe did a majority agree that, for the most part, advancement in their public or private sector is based on merit (Charron 2013). This suggests the mechanism by which corruption is detrimental – through the subversion of fair competition: from admission exams into schools to public sector employment; from a biased allocation of public funding to an unequal treatment of taxpayer funds – thus generating social loss and high opportunity costs. Perceptions of corruption are grounded in such negative experiences, although few respondents have any direct evidence of corruption. Of course, economic hardship enhances sensitivity to such issues, but the negative consequences of corruption on brain drain, gender equality, competition, equal access to public resources and public spending are sufficient to warrant the new wave of attention and bad press it has recently received.

The definition of corruption is controversial in academic debate and the broader world, simply due to the very different ends of defining corruption by lawyers, voters and economists. Everyone agrees that any corruption involves some undue private profit (for someone) due to abuse of an entrusted public authority. The opposite of a corrupt authority seems to be universally agreed upon, or we would not find that more than 150 countries have already signed the United Nations Convention Against Corruption (UNCAC), which came into force on December 14, 2005, committing signatories to a certain universal set of governance standards. In Articles 7 (public sector) and 9 (procurement), the treaty spells out the modern principles of efficiency, transparency, merit, equity, and objectivity as the only accepted governance norms. It also goes far beyond the criminalization of bribery or influence trading, stating in Article 1c that it will "promote integrity, accountability, and proper management of public affairs and public property." This puts an end to moral relativism in the area of governance. The UNCAC, together with the International Covenant on Civil and Political Rights (adopted in 1966, signed by 167 governments by 2011) and all related treaties and conventions, signal that the world now has universal governance norms that sovereign countries have willingly adopted and that should be implemented. That also means that citizens of those countries now have a legal basis to demand better governance. The angry crowds in the street are therefore well within their rights to demand corruption control, but this particular public good seems very hard to deliver.

How people understand corruption

In the 2013 Global Corruption Barometer (GCB), commissioned by Transparency International and by all accounts a typical public opinion poll on corruption excepting its size (the largest of its kind, with 114,000 respondents in 107 countries), nearly two-thirds of participants expressed their belief that favoritism (contacts) gets things done in the public sector and more than half think that vested interest groups and not the public interest drive government actions. In contrast, a (relatively) more modest 27 percent reported having paid a bribe in the last twelve months. As with the anticorruption protesters interviewed by media in the streets, these respondents also seem to think that bribery is only the tip of the corruption iceberg. In fact, evidence in recent years from multiple survey sources would be contradictory and incomprehensible unless we were to accept that the general population when asked to assess corruption offers its assessment of its society's capacity to enforce public integrity and fairness, rather than reporting on individual experiences of corruption as legally defined in criminal codes. The answers that respondents give to surveys on corruption are filtered by the respondents' assessment of whether corruption control in general succeeds or not in their own country to endorse fair competition and social advancement based on merit, which has come to be their main expectation of governance. There is remarkable consistency across attitudes: low trust in government goes with high perception of corruption among officials, a general perception that the law does not treat everyone equally and that favoritism rather than merit explains social advancement. Over 50 percent of

GCB respondents believed that corruption had increased in the last year, and for every nine people who consider national anticorruption strategies ineffective, only one thinks that they work. In most countries in the world, the majority of citizens do not believe they enjoy corruption control: hence the growing frustration we see on the streets, from Brazil to Turkey.

People grant a far broader meaning to what pollsters call corruption than lawyers do, which can be described quite systematically. Firstly, as already mentioned, we find that societies that perceive high levels of favoritism and corruption also believe that merit has little to do with social advancement and success in life. The correlation between these two perceptions reflects the overall capacity of a society to enforce merit and honesty versus connections or privilege, thus granting a holistic view of the country's performance. Perceptions are important as they reflect popular experiences in all aspects of school, career, and public life, exposing the mechanism of advancement in society and the way the state operates. The data from the GCB 2013 show remarkable consistency within national perceptions, as perceived corruption and the incidence of bribery are significantly associated with the importance of connections for getting things done in the public sector, and the belief that big interests run the government (see Table 1.1).

Secondly, in nearly every survey we find a large gap between corruption victimization (having been asked for a bribe) and perception of corruption (assessment of how many public officials are corrupt), despite the two being significantly associated (bribe givers perceive even more corruption than the rest). Ninety percent of the GCB 2013 respondents who assessed the bureaucracy of their country as corrupt had not experienced bribery directly. In order to fill this gap, we simply have to "top up" the experience of bribery with other experiences of corruption, notably favoritism on the basis of particular connections, which is highly correlated to the perception of corruption of public officials (see Table 1.1).

Thirdly, national perception of corruption is associated in regression analysis with factors other than bribery, with structural factors such as religion or development being very important in the first case (Treisman 2000) and circumstantial factors very important in the second. In other words, different factors matter at collective rather than individual level, explaining the gap. Richer or less educated individuals

Table 1.1 *The faces of particularism*

VARIABLES		% of respondents who think that personal contacts are important/very important to get things done in the public sector	% of respondents who think that the government is to "a large extent"or "entirely" run by a few big interests	% of respondents that have paid a bribe at least once	% of respondents who consider public officials/civil servants as "very corrupt" or "extremely corrupt"	Perception of corruption of public officials/ civil servants (weighted average)
% of respondents who think that personal contacts are important/very important to get things done in the public sector	Pearson Corr.	1				
	Sig. (2-tailed)					
	N	104				
% of respondents who think that the government is to "a large extent" or "entirely" run by a few big interests	Pearson Corr.	0.647**	1			
	Sig. (2-tailed)	0				
	N	98	98			

% of respondents that have paid a bribe at least once	Pearson Corr.	0.145	0.348**	1		
	Sig. (2-tailed)	0.141	0			
	N	104	98	105		
% of respondents who consider public officials/ civil servants as "very corrupt" or "extremely corrupt"	Pearson Corr.	0.471**	0.547**	0.472**	1	
	Sig. (2-tailed)	0	0	0		
	N	101	96	101	101	
Perception of corruption of public officials/civil servants (weighted average)	Pearson Corr.	0.505**	0.561**	0.372**	0.970**	1
	Sig. (2-tailed)	0	0	0	0	
	N	103	97	104	101	104

** Correlation is significant at the 0.01 level (2-tailed).
Source: Transparency International (2013)

Table 1.2 *Satisfaction with public service by bribe*

Sector/Service		% of respondents not satisfied with service	% of respondents satisfied with service	% of respondents with contact
Education	Paid bribe	32	49	38
	Did not pay bribe	12	66	
Health	Paid bribe	39	42	82
	Did not pay bribe	18	67	
Police	Paid bribe	52	30	22
	Did not pay bribe	16	64	

Source: ANTICORRP European Quality of Government Index 2013 (see Appendix 3)

do not bribe significantly more (or less) in GCB 2013, although education and national income explain why more or less bribery is to be found in a given country, for instance. Employees in the private sector are less associated with bribery, while the self-employed are significantly more associated with it, since they are the ones who must negotiate more bureaucratic hurdles – Tunisia's Bouazizi a perfect example (for a model explaining bribery, see Appendix 1).This confirms that bribery develops as a way to counterbalance other types of favoritism (for example, where the individual or company who is not part of some network of privilege has to buy their way in), with favoritism far more widespread than bribery and no correlation between them (Mungiu-Pippidi 2014). Any individual might offer a bribe in a context where rules of the game are so shaped. Furthermore, of the majority of GCB 2013 respondents who thought their public service very or entirely corrupt, 71 percent considered personal connections matter a lot to get things done.

Finally, a fourth consistent category of evidence shows that people with some experience of bribery are the least satisfied with the public service they receive. Greasing the wheels of bureaucracy is seen as a supplementary tax that people who do not enjoy connections have to pay to get a similar service to those who do (see Table 1.2).

Data from the European Quality of Government Index (EQI) 2013 conducted in all EU member states and some accession-aspiring

Table 1.3 *Incidence of bribery and perception of equality in healthcare service provision*

	Equal Treatment		Unequal Treatment	
Region	% of citizens who agree that everyone is treated equally in the public healthcare system	% of bribe payers who perceive equal treatment	% of citizens who think they are treated unequally in the public healthcare system	% of bribe payers who perceive unequal treatment
Northern Europe	64	2	36	98
Mediterranean Europe	58	7	42	93
New EU Members	47	13	53	87
Non EU	53	10	47	90

Source: ANTICORRP European Quality of Government Index 2013

countries reveals that only 36 percent in the Northern European core group and 42 percent in Mediterranean countries perceive favoritism in their national health systems, versus 53 percent in the new EU member countries, where a majority of citizens claim they are discriminated against when dealing with various public services. The social, income, ethnic, or educational status does not explain this large perception of unfair treatment, which is grounded in the individual experience of respondents.

Around 90 percent on average of the minority reporting some experience of bribery accuse public services of favoritism (for example in healthcare services, see Table 1.3). It is impossible to understand the perception gap in public sector governance unless bribery, favoritism, and performance are indeed accounted for together.

The discussion of whether people are victims or perpetrators seems thus in many ways to miss the main point, which is that there is a comprehensive logic to governance where causes and effects become hard to distinguish, and a vicious circle of rationalizing need and justification is born, which is hard to break. It is difficult to decide in such a context whether the Tunisian street vendor was a tax evader and a smuggler and the policewoman accosting him was doing her duty, or if the situation was the other way around, with the street vendor the victim and the policewoman the exploiter.

Surveys and slogans nevertheless convey a clear picture of what people understand by a noncorrupt regime: one respecting a social contract based on reciprocal accountability and integrity, where the government does not collect taxes from the many to redistribute them as privileges to the few, where the state is autonomous from any particular interest group and able to seek the best solutions, maximizing social welfare through a process of consultation and transparency. Any self-interested deviation from the entailed integrity, impartiality, and fairness of the *process* of governing is seen as corrupt, as is any *outcome* resulting in an uneven or partial allocation of public benefits, benefiting the granter of favors or his associates.

How the anticorruption community understands corruption

Two quite different corruption control paradigms feature most frequently in the international community, both quite different from the popular perceptions described above. At one end of the spectrum we find the "eradication of corruption," at the other "integrity building" or "good governance." Eradication is a term borrowed from hygiene. It supposes that some invader (bacteria, insect, animal) creates a disorder in an organic mechanism which would not be there in the absence of the pathogen. Therefore, eradication of the pathogenic agent guarantees the restoration of the "good" equilibrium. For instance, the Oxford English Dictionary defines corruption as the "perversion or destruction of integrity in the discharge of public duties by bribery and favor," implying that somehow an existing public integrity was perverted or destroyed ("Corruption" 1989).

The second paradigm is somewhat subtler, as it admits that good governance cannot be "restored," but needs more complex "building." But it also stops short of understanding the nature of institutional arrangements in place and fails to see that a broad societal equilibrium can very well exist in the absence of good governance. As St. Augustine considered that Evil consisted merely of the absence of Good, the paradigm of integrity building presumes that building good governance is like building a barn: it just needs a plan and some builders. The concept that some people with considerable power may oppose the construction of the barn as they benefit from its absence is seldom discussed. All we need is to find an entry point, then societies are changed by reforms, and governments follow the plan. Both paradigms thus fail to grant corruption its central role in a societal social order as a specific mechanism of allocating pooled resources relative to power status. If corruption could be solved only by judges and policemen who are, together with legislators, perceived as highly corrupt according to the Global Corruption Barometer and thus seen as part of the problem and not of the solution, we should not have the present anticorruption grass-roots rebellions demanding radical overhauls of the entire establishment.

"Good governance" is definitely an unpopular academic concept, due to its vagueness and normative implications, although the policy world cannot dispense with it due to its less political and more technocratic character vis-à-vis "corruption." Its definitions from the United Nations Development Program (UNDP) and the World Bank read like whole shopping lists, mixing the features of process with the outcomes of governance (UNDP 1997; World Bank 1994). Academic definitions of corruption have long relied on legal and formal criteria, which obviously fall short of present popular perceptions, staying at the individual and organizational level, with much less discussion at the level of whole countries and political regimes. The classic scholarly definition of corruption as "behavior which deviates from the formal duties of a public role because of private-regarding (personal, close family, private clique) pecuniary or status gains; or violates rules against the exercise of certain types of private-regarding influence" (Nye 1967: 417) clarified an essential element: the blurring of the private–public border. However, the double reference to the "formal duties" and "rules" failed to take account of a frequently occurring situation whereby laws and policies themselves are corrupt and seek to create legal privileges for those connected with the source of authority granting the privilege. Kaufmann and Vicente (2011) introduced this useful distinction between legal and illegal forms of corruption.

Nye's formula was simplified in most current literature as "the abuse of public office for private gain" (Kaufmann 1997; Rose-Ackerman 1999; Tanzi and Davoodi 1997), with variants such as "abuse of power" or "abuse of entrusted authority." The underlying presumption remains that public and private should have clear borders and that crossing them is corrupt. Both public and private spheres are involved in a corrupt act. Fraudulent behavior between two private parties is less often called corrupt, as the term "fraud" covers most situations, and equating corruption with every dishonest form of behavior would only render the concept useless. There can be instances of corruption even among private parties, as the new public management approach outsources quasi-monopolistic government services to private parties, which thus come to dispose of public authority and enjoy public trust (You 2006). As Arnold Heidenheimer (1989) explained, corruption can be defined in relation to public office, as Nye does, but also in relation to public interest or trust. Many scholars and organizations have thus come to use the expression "abuse of public authority" instead of "office," as a private party might perform duties involving public trust (e.g., referees in a soccer game), with resultant harm to public interest if that trust is breeched. This extension is by no means a fundamentally different definition of corruption.

Corruption is furthermore defined as *deviation from the norm* (Scott 1972) because it presumes that authority or office exists not in order to promote private gain (for self or others), but to promote the public interest, fairly and quite impartially. But is that the case? The notion of public interest is culturally relative and has evolved considerably across history. What we consider "corruption" today is quite different from a definition taken from, say, the Chinese Empire or a European absolutist kingdom. This modern definition assumes that we have knowledge of the real norm governing a given society, not just the formal one, and that the governance norm is public integrity. This definition relies, in other words, on a presumption of modernity in all states and their correspondent societies, measuring themselves by the modern Western benchmark.

But is the presumption well-founded? A whole literature grappling with understanding how the state works outside the developed world reveals that such a presumption is frequently misplaced (Evans 1989; Macfarlane 1978; Migdal 1988). Even in Europe, let alone the rest of the world, only in the modern state is public office no longer considered a source of exploitable income; spoliation has been the norm for many centuries (Weber 1968) and it is debatable if it can be seen as "deviation" from some universal rule of impersonal government. In *The Gift*, French sociologist Marcel Mauss argues that the act of giving gifts creates a social bond with an obligation on the part of the recipient to reciprocate since "the objects are never completely separated from the men who exchange them" (1990: 31); in the absence of reciprocation, a loss of "status" and "honor" would occur. Roland Mousnier, a French historian, has further argued that until the eighteenth century, honor, status, and social prestige were far more important than wealth in certain European societies such as France and Spain. Societies of "estates" or "orders," as he defines them (insightfully including the USSR and fascist Italy among them), are split vertically by social ranks rather than horizontally by class; relationships between different estates operate through networks of patronage (Mousnier 1969). In their by now classic book, sociologists Eisenstadt and Roniger (1984) also described nonmodern patron–client relations that shape many contemporary societies in different cultures (Catholic, Buddhist, and Islamist) and decisively determine both interpersonal exchanges as well as the type of connection between people and their government. Neither historical sociology nor anthropology have ever made the claim that the kind of impersonal and objective bureaucratic relations that Max Weber described as informing modern states is some sort of final unavoidable stage in a long chain of evolution (Weber 1968: 959). It is of course remarkable that UNCAC demands them, but they are most definitely not guaranteed.

Presuming modernity also means that the default texture of governance is supposed to have the state on one side and individuals on the other. Even today, however, whole societies exist that rely on collectivistic rather than individualistic arrangements and where people interact with the state as groups, not individuals. Many societies are organized as groups of "clients" with varying degrees of influence and competing or overlapping interests. Multiethnic societies tend to use ethnicity as the chief marker, but also clan, religion, city of birth, political party, club, family, school alumni networks, etc. have all been reported to provide personal ties that inform exchanges and transactions between an individual and the state, crossing the private–public boundary permanently. Connections of every kind are used to personalize transactions with the state, and a multitude of particular transactions takes place daily – some illegal, others not. We should have to apply an extraordinarily large scope of conflict of interest definitions to render them all illegal. Therefore, we choose the easy way by criminalizing only particular exchanges, which include physical gifts (bribes) and which often occur in the absence of a bond or connection of some other nature but with the goal of establishing one. But consider a government captured by an ethnic group or a clan that distributes benefits mostly to its own members and forces others to engage in bribery to get some share of those benefits. What is the deviation there and what should be criminalized?

Max Weber originally described patrimonialism as a form of political domination trespassing the private–public border (Weber 1968). Patrimonialism occurs when the state is "appropriated" by a ruler who has near total discretion in the exercise of power at the expense of traditional limitations on authority. Power seems to be the main determinant configuring how social exchanges are organized and resources are distributed across various cultures (Eisenstadt and Roniger 1984). Such exchanges range from ethical universalism, where equal treatment applies to everyone regardless of the group to which one belongs (Parsons 1997: 80–82) to particularism where individuals are treated differently according to particular ties or criteria. An application of this dichotomy in the sphere of state-subject relations (regardless if on the side of the state we find a tyrant, a politician, or a bureaucrat) allows for the understanding of the evolution of a notion such as corruption control and its deep state-society foundation. The problem that development agents must solve is how to change from a governance regime based on particularism to one based on ethical universalism, which is a collective action problem (You 2006).

Weber went rather deep in his depiction of how power inequality shapes governance. For instance, he described premodern "status societies," dominated by certain groups and governed by convention (what we would call today informal institutions) rather than law (Weber 1968: 177–80). Such societies are not primarily structured by capitalist relations – that is, by the acquisition of wealth through market means – but rather by status. The source of status can vary across societies and time, but the undeniable primary source is power. Individuals with a similar level of power and access are joined in status-based groups of estates and also in the form of castes, orders, or networks. Authority and the allocation of public goods cannot help but be particular in such contexts: particularism is the rule of the game in such societies, and the standards for the way a person should be treated depend on the "estate" to which the person belongs. These are the societies of "estates," where access is determined by belonging to a certain group and the personal connections entailed by this affiliation (Mousnier 1969). Surveys on corruption and rule of law suggest that such societies are not historical relics. For instance, why do respondents of a survey in five Balkan countries, after stating strongly that certain people are above the law, rate politicians and policemen most highly in using the law to their advantage (Mungiu-Pippidi 2006a)?

Weber contrasted patrimonialism with the impersonal and functional relationships of the modern state based on abstract, impersonal, written rules (Weber 1968: 959). Modern societies have a different social organization. Individualism and universalism, not collectivism and particularism, are the main norms both in interpersonal relations and the relationship between the state and individual. Ethical universalism is the state's *modus operandi*: government is impartial and, when implementing laws and policies, treats citizens as mere individuals, "not taking anything into consideration about the citizen/case that is not beforehand stipulated in the policy or the law" (Rothstein and Teorell 2008: 170). Citizenship in a modern sense and market relations are possible only because of this impersonality and impartiality (the supply and demand mechanism, not kinship, determines price).

The international anticorruption community thus faces a daunting problem – changing basic governance – without a clear understanding of the dimension and nature of the problem. The attempt to agree on a universal definition of "corruption," as well as explaining variation across countries, is further complicated by the lack of communication across several of the disciplines dealing with the topic (see Table 1.4), all of which have made significant contributions without managing to provide a unitary theory explaining how corruption develops and is controlled. However, incorrectly defining the goal of a public policy is the chief danger. If indeed the norm is ethical universalism and corruption is a deviation (context A), it makes sense to build in a strategy for adequate control of corruption as something norm infringing (which indeed describes most of the current anticorruption industry's arsenal), based on suppression of corruption. If ethical universalism is not present and nonuniversal transactions of government are the most numerous (context B), the right strategy should be conceived instead along the lines of norm building, with suppression only complementing political reforms.

Table 1.4 *Level of observation and empirical analyses of corruption across disciplines*

Discipline	Level of definition and study	Preferred method of inquiry
Criminology	Individual or group	Court case analysis, social network analysis
Development/ institutional quality	National	Statistical Big N
Equilibrium theory	Individual	Game theory, experimental
Organization	Group and organization	Experimental
Economic policy	National or sector	Statistical Big N
Sociology	Mix of individual/national	Public opinion survey analysis

Some scholars work hard to find differences between various manifestations of particularism, for instance clientelism and corruption, in the observance of legal norms (Della Porta and Vannucci 1999: 273; Johnston 2005). Other scholars have struggled with depictions of various corruption categories (grand, petty, administrative, political, etc.). But at the end of the day, a reasonable definition of corruption at the societal level should allow us to structure more than just descriptive types of corruption, which could be endless. If particularism is the rule of the game, we are likely to find a cluster of corrupt practices: vertically structured favoritism (clientelism, patronage), horizontally structured favoritism (negative social capital networks, "old boy networks"), kinship-motivated particularism (nepotism, ethnic favoritism), but also embezzlement, bribery, and extortion. The predominance of particularism in a democracy also implies that political parties and candidates will get favors from private parties to aid their rise to power and will reciprocate once in control of public resources – and this will be a systemic and salient feature of the political system. But since the government side (returning of favors as preferential social allocation) is the one determining the private side (investing in political parties and politicians in the hope of some returns other than programmatic), what is the use of describing two types of corruption here, political and procurement-related? It is far more useful to have a holistic understanding of why preferential social allocation is possible and even becomes the rule of the game. In traditional societies, such preferential returns followed kinship lines – in modern times, the political party is the channel for private interests. But groups taking preferential advantage of public resources will always exist if control of corruption has not been achieved, and therefore the types of corruption can be innumerable. Johnston (2006) attempted the best descriptive systematization to date by country, whereby he combined particularism with power pluralism and accountability to identify four clusters: countries where profiteers of public resources are organized as cooperative elite cartels; competitive oligarchs and clans; official "moguls"; and democratic politicians who have far fewer means for rent seeking (influencing markets). Before any further attempts at classification, the essential diagnostic element to consider is whether or not the dominant social allocation mode is ethical universalism.

Concepts and plan of this book

The choice of a definition of corruption has thus important implications, both for the generalizing conclusions of a study (see Table 1.4) and in real life. Most of the modern anticorruption industry operates on the national level, but defines corruption at the micro level as *deviation from a norm of integrity* (ignoring whether it is the norm or the exception in the given context), while nonetheless aiming to change whole macro-governance contexts (making "Ruritania" less corrupt). This is the source of very serious problems, because context B (particular transactions are the majority) differs essentially from context A (universal transactions are the majority), and so will the behaviors and opinions of people living in such contexts. Social conformity, which to a great extent explains social behavior and generally favors the status quo (Asch 1955), will operate in favor of particularism in context B and in favor of universalism in context A. Evolving from B to A becomes a major development issue that can hardly be answered by repressing deviation, as in the legal definition, simply because appropriate behavior is different in different institutional contexts and in conformity with different social identities (March 1994); norms may be conflicting or split between formal and informal norms, and few people will ostensibly behave differently from how their peers would in a similar situation.

The story of this evolution from one governance context to another, as well as the understanding of the mechanisms underpinning each of them, is the central theme of this book. How is control of corruption achieved and can this evolution be expedited by policy intervention and more generally by human agency? The control of corruption is a given society's capacity to constrain the use of public authority to generate private rents detrimental to overall social welfare. This is what is assessed by survey respondents when they answer how corrupt their country is, as well as by risk experts asked to give an overall rating to a country. Any social group of people living together for any length of time, from a hiking expedition to a nation sharing territory and language, faces the problem of having to share resources to produce collective good. How a human community can achieve the management of common (i.e., pooled) resources based on fairness and integrity is a major problem as old as the social organization of mankind. Believing integrity and fairness in the management and distribution of public resources to be a default "state of nature" for social arrangement cannot be correct, as most of human history contradicts such an interpretation. Appropriation of joint resources by one group or individual for private use (rent seeking) is extremely common, and the development of a system to defend those resources from spoilage by violence, theft, or corruption is the product of a long historical evolution (Fukuyama 2011; Mungiu-Pippidi 2006b; North *et al.* 2009).

While the social representation of integrity in governance may vary across cultures and over time, there is no culture or political regime without some claim to integrity and fairness in government, however defined. Variation across cultures has been further reduced with the attempt of many countries to emulate some version of Western modernization, culminating in the adoption of UNCAC. But how do we get there, and what lessons can we learn from countries that have succeeded thus far?

If corruption control is the ability to constrain particularism and defend the state from being an instrument serving particular private interests rather than the public one, governance can be defined as the set of formal and informal rules determining who gets what (or how public goods are distributed) in a given polity. Governance orders, the stable configurations of such rules of the game, can be placed on a continuum with open access and ethical universalistic exchanges at one end and closed access and particularistic exchanges at the other (see Eisenstadt and Roniger 1984; Mungiu-Pippidi 2006b; North *et al.* 2009). They reflect fundamental patterns of social organization and power distribution in a society (Hofstede 2011; Lipset and Lenz 2000), so after reaching equilibrium they tend to remain stable and prove hard to undermine by elections or even changes of political regime. Such equilibria are described in different streams of academic literature as either "rule of law," "control of corruption," or "quality of democracy."

Corruption is studied therefore not at the individual level in this book – as undue profit from abuse of public authority – but at the societal level, as an intrinsic part of a certain governance context, a social allocation mode. A governance order is the salient and stable set of institutions (rules of the game or institutional context) determining who gets what. This definition of corruption thus includes other forms of favoritism beyond those motivated by bribes, reflecting both the current global perception of corruption as it is reflected in surveys – where large majorities across countries claim that they live under corrupt governments although only a minority have experienced bribery in any form – and in the broad approach of the UNCAC, whose ratifying states pledge themselves to governance excluding any favoritism.

Explaining control of corruption in complex modern societies is necessarily an inter-disciplinary effort, and indeed at least two interconnected concepts stretch across otherwise highly disparate theoretical and evidential bodies. The first is that individual rational choices, whether by leaders, bureaucrats, or citizens, are bound by cognitive and affective factors (Simon 1997). The second is that self-regulation of morality is not entirely an intrapsychic matter, because people are not fully autonomous moral agents impervious to the social realities surrounding them, but are bound by social contexts where social representations of moral concepts such as right and wrong are developed and sustained by social norms and everyday behavior (Bandura 2002; Moscovici 2001). Social cognitive theory and bounded rationality theory thus concur that *individual moral behavior is the product of the reciprocal interaction of personal traits and social influences* so that individual autonomous choice is actually grounded in social context (Anand *et al.* 2004; Bandura 2002). This traditional sociological approach, which began with Durkheim, can be encountered in relation to governance in classic historical sociology (Eisenstadt and

Roniger 1984; Weber 1968) and more recently in social psychology (Bandura 2002).

The fact that individual behavior depends crucially on the number of other individuals engaged in similar transactions also seems at last to have gained a certain amount of traction with economists (Acemoglu 1995; Andvig and Moene 1990; Murphy *et al.* 1991; Sah 2007). There is growing acknowledgment among institutionalist economists that societies develop "reward structures" that determine the allocation of talent between productive and unproductive activities (such as rent seeking). The existence of rent seeking creates a negative externality on productive agents and shapes expectations so that influence peddling rather than merit or handiwork will be the major reward factor, which may lead to society being trapped in a "steady state equilibrium of rent seeking" (Acemoglu 1995). As Max Weber remarked, the market operates by universalism, such that an allocation system on the basis of particularism is therefore subversive to capitalism (1968: 177–80).

To say that individual choice is bounded institutionally is not to claim that the individual has no choice and his behavior is determined entirely externally, nor that it is subject to norms and not to reason (Elster 1989). People reportedly prefer the distributive norms that favor them (Deutsch 1985: Ch. 11; Messick and Sentis 1983). Models of corruption at the individual level do exist, but they explain little, as the main dependent variable – tolerance of corruption, from the World Values Survey (see Appendix 3) – is skewed, with far too many respondents reporting that bribery is unacceptable under any circumstance, even in very corrupt countries (Dong *et al.* 2012; Gatti *et al.* 2003). Dedicated surveys such as the GCB include better-phrased questions on corruption, but on the other hand miss the kind of questions on individual values that would offer a model with good explanatory power at the individual level. Combining the two, however, we find evidence supporting a model of mixed choice, where individuals who have more dealings with authority are more often engaged in corrupt acts if they are in a corrupt environment (for instance, the self-employed or men), but we find also that those who have superior education are less tolerant of corruption and would perhaps be more willing to engage in changing the rules of the game (see Figure 1.1). Furthermore, the mere recognition of norms ("appropriateness") is itself filtered through personal and group behavior to reduce cognitive dissonance. In the EQI 2013 survey, for instance, individuals who

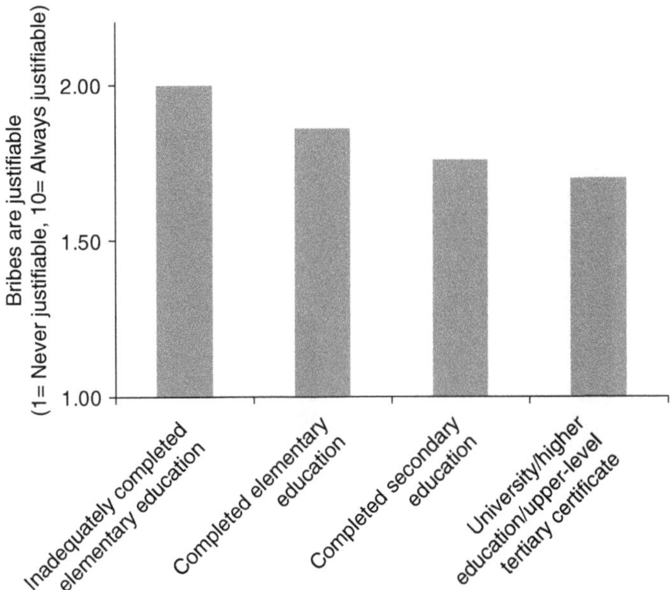

Figure 1.1 Individual tolerance of corruption by education level
Source: ANTICORRP European Quality of Government Index 2013

confess some experience of bribery also believe that the practice is largely shared across society, while those who have no such experience tend to think differently (see Figure 1.2). Moral justification of behavior is grounded in its context, and hardly anyone dares to justify an act other than by invoking conformity, the fact that "everybody else" behaves similarly.

This World Values Survey finding corroborates older data based on Hofstede's cultural indicators, for instance the connection between corruption and performance orientation practice or power distance. High levels of performance orientation practices are associated with lower levels of corruption, indicating that achievement-oriented cultural practices and performance excellence cannot coexist with systemic corruption. Moreover, measuring the inequality and importance of power status shows that societies with higher power distance are also more corrupt (Hofstede 2011; Husted 1999).

Just as individual behavior has to be placed in a certain governance context, the state too must be understood in the context of a given

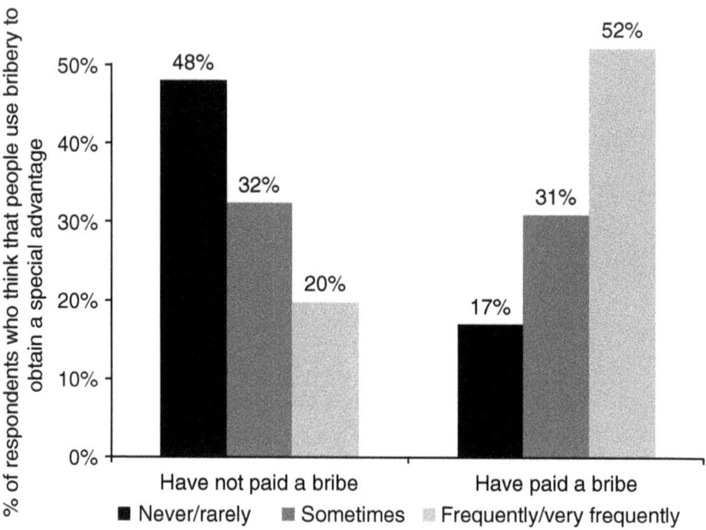

Figure 1.2 Context attributions by bribe payers
Source: ANTICORRP European Quality of Government Index 2013

society. Social allocation reflects the power distance in a society and the dominant exchange mode, based on either performance (market) or rent seeking (violence, corruption). Particularism is the wider governance regime indicating the dominant norm and behavior. In a society ruled by particularism, favoritism would be the main social allocation mode, with widespread use of connections of any kind, exchange of favors, and, in their absence, monetary inducements. Particularism in a society operates mostly to the advantage of those with more power resources, but no simple elite-theory type explains it. The weaker have their defenses, resorting to patronage, cheating, bribery, tax evasion, and a variety of other practices to reduce inequality (Scott 1972) once they perceive that the social contract imposed on them is unfair. Elites in societies with a great deal of particularism enjoy a culture of impunity (famously extended to things such as UN diplomats not paying parking fines in New York, as reported in Fisman and Miguel 2007), a culture mirrored by the self-indulgence of the rest of the population who see the behavior of elites as the best excuse for their own behavior. By and large, vertical and horizontal exchange networks intersect to create the systemic nature of the problem (Johnston 2005), which remains the particular, nonuniversal character of allocations, resulting in injustice and discrimination (Della Porta and Vannucci 1999).

Corruption in society is therefore not conceptualized in this book as an aggregate of individual corruption. The non-corrupt countries at the top of Transparency International's Corruption Perception Index (CPI) do not differ from countries on the bottom simply by the *number* of individuals engaged in corrupt acts, but by their institutions: in other words, by the rules of the game influenced by power distribution and the shaping of the allocation of public resources. The countries at the top of the Control of Corruption scale managed to institutionalize open and nondiscriminative access at some point in their past, and so their institutions differ substantially from the ones at the bottom (Asmerom and Reis 1996; North *et al.* 2009). Many countries in the middle struggle between two worlds, for in them both universalistic and particularistic practices coexist, more or less competitively (Van de Walle 2001). But regardless of how wide the variation might be, some sort of invisible threshold exists between a society where ethical universalism is the norm and one where the norm is particularism – and one can predict fairly well what treatment and what share of public resources to expect from the state if one knows where one stands in the status ranks.

An anthropologist might call such institutional arrangements *culture*. However, the most frequent question on corruption – whether or not it is "cultural" – depends greatly on how we define culture. If culture is defined as the rules of the game in a society, corruption is definitely a "cultural" phenomenon. Would it then not be a mystery why people complain about it so much when they have in fact lived with it for so long? More interesting still, why do immigrants find it so easy to abide by new rules in noncorrupt countries, seemingly the most attractive countries in the world as far as immigration is concerned? But if we give culture a deeper, more primordial meaning, it becomes even more difficult to claim that corruption is a cultural phenomenon. Individuals may value gifts and tradition more in some cultures and some cultures may be more collectivistic than others, but no culture on record values dishonesty and unfairness. Nobody wants to be discriminated against, which is what corruption invariably does.

Conceptualizing public corruption holistically in a broader governance context thus has important policy consequences. Particularism is not a social "malady," as corruption is usually described, but rather a default, natural state, and therefore arises frequently. Social psychology provides considerable evidence that the nature of man is sectarian, and that social identity results from biased intergroup comparison and self-enhancing behavior (Sherif and Hovland 1961; Tajfel 2004). Humans naturally favor their own family, clan, race, or ethnic group – what Edward C. Banfield (1958) called "amoral familism." Treating the rest of the world fairly seems to be a matter of extensive social learning and sufficient resources. Societies which have traveled furthest from that natural state of affairs and have produced a state which treats everyone equally and fairly are exceptions and products of a long historical evolution. Such evolution should not be taken for granted; indeed, as James Q. Wilson (1993) argues, universalism and individualism, which spread in the West after the Enlightenment to become generally agreed norms, are neither natural nor necessarily and invariably good principles. To understand individual behavioral choice, an understanding of governance context is therefore indispensable, and anticorruption strategies created in disregard to this are predetermined to fail (Huther and Shah 2000).

Having clarified how individual and collective behavior interact where control of corruption is concerned and thus having laid out the theoretical and empirical foundations for an institutional approach to corruption, this study will proceed to investigate how societies reach the point when ethical universalism becomes the main norm and particularism the exception in regard to how public affairs are run and public resources allocated. It will review what lessons we have learned from historical and contemporary experience of developing corruption control, to help policymakers and civil societies steer and expedite this process.

This book is therefore not directly engaged in explaining development and prosperity, although the nexus between control of corruption and development will be referred to frequently. Recent attention to corruption and institutions more generally is due to the presumed relationship with growth. This association, however, has also proved controversial, and there are important examples of good economic performance in a context of poor quality of governance in contemporary countries, ranging from China to Brazil. The classic modernization and political development theory argued by Lipset, Huntington, and Nye that only when societies become wealthier do people become more autonomous and more capable of demanding fair and accountable government; economic growth can advance and is even helped in the meanwhile by a certain degree of corruption. But short-term growth and development are two very different things: many development economists have come to argue presently that there are so few cases of long-term development precisely because government favoritism toward private actors and irrational (particular) allocation of public resources hinder development, which results in a vicious cycle of captive states and poor societies. The precise mechanism is not clear, because many institutional explanations of development from the current literature are attributed *ex post facto* and are based on a restricted sample of countries. This book builds on the premise pioneered by Johnston (2005) that patterns of wealth and power distribution across societies are associated with specific governance contexts or "syndromes" of corruption.

Corruption has long been marginalized in the grand development theories, and it has only recently started to be more prominent as the "extractive/inclusive" distinction in Acemoglu and Robinson (2012), the "limited/open" access distinction in North, Wallis, and Weingast (2009), the "governance" dimension in Norris (2012), and the rule of law in Fukuyama (2011). All these remarkable books, even without sometimes naming corruption explicitly, treat governance as an explanatory variable of prosperity. But since they all conclude that governance matters greatly, surely governance and changes in governance deserve to be explained by themselves, and that is what this book attempts.

More specifically, this book takes a broad development perspective by addressing three main questions:

1. *The development question*: What was the historical path to this equilibrium we call "control of corruption" in the few cases (states) where this was reached?
2. *The comparative question*: What factors determine and sustain corruption control in contemporary societies?
3. *The policy question*: Are there any policies that can prompt such evolutions, and who are the best actors to implement them?

This book seeks to answer the first question by an analysis of both contemporary and historical case studies of societies that have achieved control of corruption (Chapters 3 and 4); the second by a review of previous econometric work and the author's own contribution, both quantitative and qualitative (Chapter 4); and the third by a combination of econometrics with policy analysis, examining both domestic collective action capacity and international impact (Chapters 5 and 6). The quantitative work draws on a database of 189 cases of countries for which good governance tools and policies such as anticorruption agencies, ombudsmen, adoption of transparency legislation and UNCAC were documented, combined with national economic, social, and survey data (see Appendix 2 and Appendix 3).

Some field research at national and sector level in Eastern Europe, Latin America, and East Asia is used to advance new types of corruption indicators: Chapter 7 on the impact of international anticorruption and Chapter 8 on anticorruption strategies draw on policy analysis tools. Chapter 2 will introduce the evidence and arguments by clarifying the basic issues of how we diagnose governance orders, measure change, classify countries, and trace their progress.

2 *Diagnosis and measurement*

Operationalizing governance contexts

The issue of corruption measurement is as contentious as – and related to – the issue of defining corruption. How can an insidious phenomenon, where academics only agree that the boundaries inherent to any definition are culturally and historically specific, be measured in a valid, precise, and reliable way so to allow comparisons across space and time, leading to the elaboration of a comprehensive theory? While pressure from the international development community led to the creation of a first generation of indices such as Transparency International's Corruption Perceptions Index, the gains in terms of measurement are weighed down by limitations, in particular the bias toward the international business community, leading to a reductionist view of corruption mostly as bribery (Johnston 2000). Since this first generation, other measures more inclusive of other aspects of corruption, including favoritism, have been developed, but the major challenges of indicators to be comparable across countries and sensitive to change and policy intervention persist.

Many critics of the first-generation governance indicators argue that the absence of a good theory is what renders governance so hard to measure (Rothstein and Teorell 2012). But if the theory fails, it might be because terms such as governance, good governance, and quality of government are by nature too broad and ambitious, and those who interpret them more narrowly can measure them only at the risk of measuring something different than others understand. My particular aim is to measure the construct of "control of corruption" as described in Chapter 1. Is it not measurable if we focus simply on the continuum between ethical universalism and particularism and ascertain the transactional norm in a given country? Would this also not result in a taxonomy of governance less normative and confusing than discussions of "good governance," which can be used to justify both authoritarian and democratically elected governments? Some authors express skepticism over measurements of government based on procedures versus outcomes, agreeing that "procedures, however defined, may not actually correlate with the positive outcomes expected from governments" (Fukuyama 2013; Rotberg 2014). I would argue, however, that social allocation is far more than just a procedure, and if we can establish what the rules of the game are in such transactions, we can fairly predict other features of governance as well (such as rule of law and state capacity), as proven by a vast literature on governance from Bretton Woods institutions. A good example is the association between tax collection and control of corruption quoted in the previous chapter (Mungiu-Pippidi 2013a).

Quite a few recent contributions seem to converge on the centrality of control of corruption so defined for prosperity. The ideal Weberian governance types have evolved with authors North, Wallis, and Weingast (2009) into "limited access orders" – which they claim have dominated the last 10,000 years of history and which solve the problem of containing violence by political manipulation of the economic system to generate rents by limiting entry – and "open access orders" developed over the past 500 years. The latter manage to sustain social order through political and economic competition, rather than through rent creation. Acemoglu and Robinson (2012) make a similar point when they argue that bad institutions are the product of political systems creating private gains for elites in developing countries, even if by doing so they impoverish broader society. In fact, their theory nearly states that the type of exchange (here, corruption) explains development in full. But as they take such a multifaceted approach to their good, "inclusive" economic and political institutions – in contrast to what they call bad, "extractive" or "absolutist" institutions – it would be difficult to reduce their dimensions to some unified measurable concept, as some of their critics have argued (Fukuyama 2012).

An attempt to integrate these taxonomies resting on Weberian foundations and focusing on the notion of control of corruption is shown in Table 2.1. It combines the concepts of open access and power pluralism to create two governance order types dividing the continuum: open access orders and limited access orders, with the latter divided into three sub-types or -contexts: patrimonial (traditional or neo-), competitive particularism, and borderline. The first type of governance – open access orders – corresponds to Robert Dahl's

Table 2.1 ***Governance regimes and their main features***

	Limited access order			Open access order
	Patrimonialism	Competitive particularism	Borderline	Universalism
Power distribution	Hierarchical with monopoly of central power	Stratified with power disputed competitively	Competitive with less stratification	Citizenship
State autonomy	State captured by ruler	State captured in turn by winners of elections	Archipelago of autonomy and captured (islands)	State autonomous from private interest (legal lobbying, etc.)
Public resource allocation	Particular and predictable (extractive)	Particular but unpredictable (extractive)	Particular and universal (norm competition)	Ethical universalism (inclusive)
Separation private/public	No	No	Poor	Sharp
Relation between formal/informal institutions	Informal institutions substitutive of formal ones	Informal institutions substitutive of formal ones	Competitive and substitutive informal institutions	Informal institutions only complementary to formal ones
Mentality	Collectivistic	Collectivistic	Mixed	Individualistic
Government accountability	No	Only when no longer in power	Occasional	Permanent
Rule of law	No; sometimes "thin"	No	Elites only	General; "thick"

polyarchy or Karl Popper's open society. This type of regime is individualistic, with political equality, high personal autonomy, and high civic participation. The state is autonomous from private interest, and allocation and policy formulation are achieved on the basis of ethical universalism and transparency. There is very little contradiction between formal and informal institutions, and corruption, when it occurs, is indeed a deviation from the norm of ethical universalism and public impartiality. Open access orders have been promoted for several decades: first, selectively, by colonial powers when attempting to incorporate Western institutions into some of their former colonies (Acemoglu, Johnson and Robinson 2001); and second, in the post-1989 wave of democracy promotion, including the last fifteen years of good governance reforms. Currently there is an unprecedentedly large number of countries aspiring to be perceived positively: Transparency International's annual Corruption Perception Index has spurred competition among states wishing to prove that they are doing better than their neighbors. The real numbers remain controversial. According to North, Wallis, and Weingast (2009), open access orders have consolidated in about twenty countries that are both economically and politically developed. A governance order based on ethical universalism remains an ideal rather than an empirical fact: in global surveys, only very few respondents – generally from Scandinavian countries and a handful of others – see their own societies and states as operating on the basis of such norms.

Limited access orders are a different story. Most of the world is familiar with their pathology: the differences seem to present themselves in size rather than in kind. As they cover so many political regimes and development stages (unlike open access countries, which are all highly developed), some distinctions need to apply. It is perhaps useful to start with the ones about means. Prior to corruption, violence is the default mode by which a few grab the results of joint effort and appropriate public goods (North *et al.* 2009). To achieve the autonomy of the state toward private interest – meaning private actors' capacity to uphold some form of common interest and defend it from rulers and other powerful groups in society who consider themselves more entitled than others – a preliminary step must be fulfilled: the achievement of social control (Migdal 1988). This corresponds roughly to some thin form of rule of law. Nevertheless, the state can still be entirely appropriated by one powerful group or another, resulting in an uneven allocation of public goods. The development of corruption control, however, comes only after social control is achieved and violence is preserved within certain boundaries (Collier 2011).

The next important distinctions within limited access order governance contexts are between traditional and modern on the one side and between pluralism versus power monopoly on the other. In Weber's patrimonialism, authority rests on the personal and bureaucratic power exercised by a royal household, whose power is formally arbitrary and under the direct control of the ruler. Domination is secured by means of a political apparatus staffed by slaves, mercenaries, conscripts, or some other group (not a traditional land-owning aristocracy) that has no independent power base (Weber 1968). By controlling the instruments of power in this way, the patrimonial ruler can extend personal grace and favors at the expense of traditional limitations on the exercise of authority. In his 1973 book, *Traditional Patrimonialism and Modern Neopatrimonialism*, Eisenstadt used the derived term "neopatrimonialism" to describe a mixed system in which elements of patrimonial and rational-bureaucratic rule coexist and are sometimes interwoven. This regime imitates formal institutions of modernity from the West, with most informal institutions remaining patrimonial in nature.

In answer to critiques of the concept's looseness (Erdmann and Engel 2007), the neopatrimonialism concept should be restricted to mean only the nontraditional governance order based on a power monopoly (of a ruler, tribe, or party) treating the state as its "own" patrimony. Many new democracies no longer have such monopolist rulers, but rather competing political factions (parties) instead. However, they do have nonuniversal allocation systems similar to patrimonial regimes, including patronage, nepotism, and favors (O'Donnell 1996: 40). In many new democracies where free elections are held regularly, informal particularistic structures thus exist alongside, and tend to undermine, formal universalistic institutions (O'Donnell 1996: 41). We therefore need to add another specific governance context, "competitive particularism." Unlike patrimonialism and its modern variant neopatrimonialism, which are authoritarian or semiauthoritarian regimes, competitive particularism is characterized by the coexistence of rulers spoiling the state despite some form of institutionalized pluralism, such as regular elections.

Competitive particularism is thus a governance order that replaces violent power grabbing with elections (sometimes free, though not fair, since the results are also influenced by corruption). This ideal type can be seen as a step forward from patrimonialism, where power is a monopoly. Social allocation, however, remains particular and unfair in this governance context; rent seeking is common behavior; the rule of law is poor as those in power are above the law; and the state is perceived as an instrument of spoliation of the many and enrichment of the few, which greatly subverts its legitimacy and capacity. A similar concept – described as "competitive corruption" – was used in connection with postwar Italy (Golden and Chang 2001). I argue that both public opinion and policy evidence show we are looking at more than a chance country configuration, but rather an ideal type fairly widespread in new democracies, which can be described. People in such a regime do not expect to be treated fairly by the state, but they do expect those of the same status to be treated similarly. The social struggle, therefore, is to belong to the privileged group rather than to challenge the rules of the game. A culture of privilege reigns in closed access societies, making unequal treatment the accepted norm. This is close to the world based on "amoral familism" described by Banfield (1958).

The third subtype of the limited access order is the "borderline" category. This is not a governance order in full, but a transitional regime with fuzzy borders, corresponding to the "doorstep" category of North, Wallis, and Weingast (2009). In other words, this type captures those societies that have fulfilled some basic and necessary conditions of progress toward an open access order, in which the two normative orders (old and new) coexist confrontationally without one managing to become dominant.

The ideal-types of governance orders in Table 2.1 embody important differences that cut across state and society. Power distribution is uneven, from the classic configuration of one group (family/person) as the main holder of power and owner of the state with chief control over rents allocation (as in patrimonialism), to a larger strata (political elites) holding the same privilege (and disputing it across status groups) in competitive particularism, and finally to the equal power regime with open access in social pluralism.

Political pluralism does not necessarily bring about better governance in severely unequal societies, where informal client–patron relations structure politics in a vertical and particularistic manner despite formal horizontal institutions. Voters in such regimes act as clients "selling" their voice for favors; occasionally, unaffiliated voters manage to elect an uncorrupted president, but that leader then develops a new clientele, as there are insufficient constraints and no horizontal accountability between elections. (O'Donnell 1996). Under patrimonialism, the rule of law can evolve to "thin" at best (applied predictably, even if not "just" in its essence); under competitive particularism it will always be interpreted in favor of the group in power (hence, the danger of unleashing anticorruption campaigns that can be used against political opponents). Power holders are accountable in competitive particularism only when they fall from power; only in open access order regimes are rulers not above the law and answerable to prosecution at any time. Today we find that many democracies remain in the realm of competitive particularism, with a few southeast Asian and more Eastern European cases evolving to borderline situations. The borders between categories cannot always be well defined, and the exact moment in time when the threshold has been passed from one category to another might prove difficult to identify.

Diagnosing governance contexts

These governance context ideal-types differ across their defining aspects, some of which are more like features (relations between formal or informal institutions, autonomy of the state toward private interest, separation of public/private spheres, patterns of allocation of public resources), and others more like probable causes (power resources distribution). Do we have adequate instruments to diagnose and identify the governance contexts described here as ideal-types? Such a qualitative assessment is possible: angry Brazilian protesters at the 2014 FIFA World Cup have their own indicators by which they judge poor governance. A systematic assessment would first establish the outcome of interest – that is, whether a society manages to control corruption. What is the norm in allocating public resources? Are *all* public resource allocations distributed in a particular manner by default? Is this due to the real scarcity of public resources (underfunded medical systems, for example), or to other factors? Does the ruling party/clan distribute mostly to itself (associated local governments or regions, favorite companies)? How much of the total spending budget is rents? Does this change from one year (or government) to the next? These indicators can be completed with indicators on other features of control of corruption, such as public–private separation (for instance, nepotism or use of administrative resources for private interest), autonomy of the state toward private interest (for instance, degree of politicization of civil service, revolving door practices, or share of the market for businesses with political connections), and so forth. Such indicators would allow a placement of the country on a continuum between ethical universalism and full particularism. This variation explains the wide divergence of models arising from the literature, all of which simply describe very different points on the continuum. For instance, the state capture model described by Hellman, Jones, and Kaufmann (2003) and measured by World Bank firms' surveys presumes that firms themselves are the captors of bureaucrats (through bribes) – in other words, that there is a separation between the two. The Italian model, as described by Della Porta (1996), has no separation between the politician and the businessman, similar to the post-Soviet model that saw little separation between bureaucrat and businessman: old apparatchiks running the industry became its first capitalists – professional collectors of rents meant not only to enrich them personally, but to support the whole political regime, as we see in the entourage of Vladimir Putin (Sharafutdinova 2010). In the Della Porta model, the "business politicians" are part of a flexible interest group, an informal network that deploys people where they are most needed and does not make separations between sectors. One can be a minister today, tomorrow sit in the constitutional court, and meanwhile hold board membership of a public corporation while a private investor. It is rather difficult to calculate undue profit in such circumstances, as the profit goes to more than a single person, and consists not only in wealth, but also in influence. The main benefit of group membership is in securing privileged access to markets as well as public funds. In the Hellman–Kaufmann model, a strategy against bribery makes sense; in the Della Porta model, it risks punishing only those excluded from the preferential allocation cartel trying to enter the market on a more equal footing.

But can we collect numerical data on governance more systematically, allowing us to classify countries on the particularism–universalism distribution continuum? If the majority of state transactions are of the particular or the universal kind, we need a benchmark such as that enshrined in Swedish law, namely that the state should treat citizens as mere individuals, "not taking anything into consideration about the citizen/case that is not beforehand stipulated in the policy or the law" (Rothstein and Teorell 2008: 170). There is a rich literature on that sometimes thin border between a programmatic allocation (welfare payment) and a clientelistic one (also called pork barrel, in other words, government spending with economic or service benefits concentrated in a particular area or group, but costs spread among all taxpayers (Shepsle and Weingast 1981)), but with few exceptions the difference is not so hard to grasp or actually identify in law. Programmatic allocations are universal (apply equally to anyone in the same category, such as people with disabilities), formed in consultation with and with the approval of voters, and transparently publicly budgeted. Clientelistic allocations are nonuniversal (only voters from constituencies that voted for the bill's sponsor will get emergency flood assistance, for instance), opaque (often hidden as maintenance works, budget amendments added by MPs, and so forth), and irrational – they tend to push spending beyond planned limits or buy luxury goods in a community where basic needs go unmet, hence the correlation between budget deficits and corruption. Most countries have designed some sort of criteria for allocating money, apart from the legal process that itself provides a benchmark (were all procedures respected), so anywhere that it is possible to document the entire universe of transactions, this benchmark could be used to separate them into either universalistic or particularistic camps. The areas where such an instrument should be applied are many: allocation of public jobs, procurement; public service delivery; even allocation of subnational transfers (i.e., regions with particular ties to the central government receive disproportionately more funds). A few examples will better illustrate how we can document, measure, and trace such particularism.

The first example on public jobs comes from Brazil, a democracy which has been struggling with particularism for a while – in fact, Brazil is the country that popularized the term "particularism" through the work of political scientist Guillermo O'Donnell. Despite important progress in the field of transparency, public jobs continue to be seen as spoils in Brazil. Despite legislation promoting merit-based hiring and career advancement, the number of jobs filled independently of modern bureaucratic rules remains high. In 2008, the year when the Supreme Court prohibited nepotism in the executive, legislative, and judicial

Table 2.2 *Allocation of disaster fund per ruling party mayors in Romania over three electoral cycles*

	2004	2008	2010
	(Social Democrats)	(Liberals)	(Democrat Liberals)
% share of funds for main government party	49	45	62
% share of vote in local elections of government party	35.5	16.2	28.8
Clientelism score	1.4	2.8	2.2

Source: Romanian Academic Society
Clientelism index is the ratio between rows 1 and 2, so between proportion of government mayors' support from total votes cast in local elections and proportion of natural reserve funds allocated to them.

branches of government, the governor of the state of Maranhão nominated twenty-three relatives, including his wife, for "trust positions" within his government. By 2010, 203 cases of nepotism were investigated in the judiciary by the National Council of Justice, and 21,847 persons were officially listed in Brazil under the heading of functions of confidence and gratification (DAS 1 to 6 – Diretoria e Assessoramento Superior) in the direct administration, autarchies, and foundations of the Federal Executive Government (Brazilian Ministry of Planning, Budget, and Management 2010), with salaries ranging from 3,000 to 6,000 euros per month. The president/minister has the prerogative to appoint and remove individuals in these positions at any time, a freedom regularly used for political bargaining (Mungiu-Pippidi *et al.* 2011). The figure is many times higher than any federal government in the developed world, such as the USA or Germany, and it multiplies at lower tiers of government by similar arrangement. It can be traced in time to allow governance monitoring.

The second example involves the Romanian natural disaster fund. Table 2.2 is based on an investigation technique called data mining which looks for irregularities in spending patterns. In this case the distribution of the extra-budgetary natural disaster fund in the country is monitored during three electoral cycles. The benchmark here is simple: allocation of these funds, decided discretionarily by the government without parliamentary approval due to their emergency intervention character, should follow natural disaster patterns and no other. Table 2.2 shows, however, how a regular pattern of distributing emergency funds on political grounds (mayors of the leading party get the lion's share, regardless of who gets flooded) has persisted through three different governments (2004, 2008, 2010). The disproportionality between the ruling party's share of votes and the share of money received has grown consistently through those three electoral cycles, despite Romania having joined the EU in the interceding period, pledging good governance. From these favored local government allocations, public funds flow further downhill toward politically networked companies, which collect nearly every public contract (in which politicians sometimes have direct stakes or from which they have otherwise received electoral campaign contributions). Data mining allows the discovery of nonrandom patterns, and in this case it is crystal clear that funding distribution does not coincide with the random occurrence of natural disasters, but rather follows a clear and regular pattern related to the party in government.

Another example can be seen in Figure 2.1, where data mining of Hungarian procurement (from an online database including every allocation over 10 million euros for the period of one decade) highlights a nonrandom pattern which can only be explained by government favoritism. The graph shows how one group of dominant companies previously capturing most government contracts in the area of public infrastructure is replaced by a new group following elections and a change in the ruling government coalition (Fazekas *et al.* 2013).

All these examples have two things in common: they are based on a whole universe of transactions (no sampling) for one public agency or sector; and they trace irregularities from an expected pattern of social allocation through data mining. Such data allows the calculation of agency or sector capture by certain companies, capture risk, and even corruption costs by comparison across agencies. The availability of ever more data on government transactions through online services and other forms of e-government will make such methods increasingly accessible and reduce the labor intensity of data collection. However, such data is specific, objective, and concrete, allowing both the monitoring of change and increased sensitivity to an eventual policy intervention (reform). Data mining provides a rich source of information

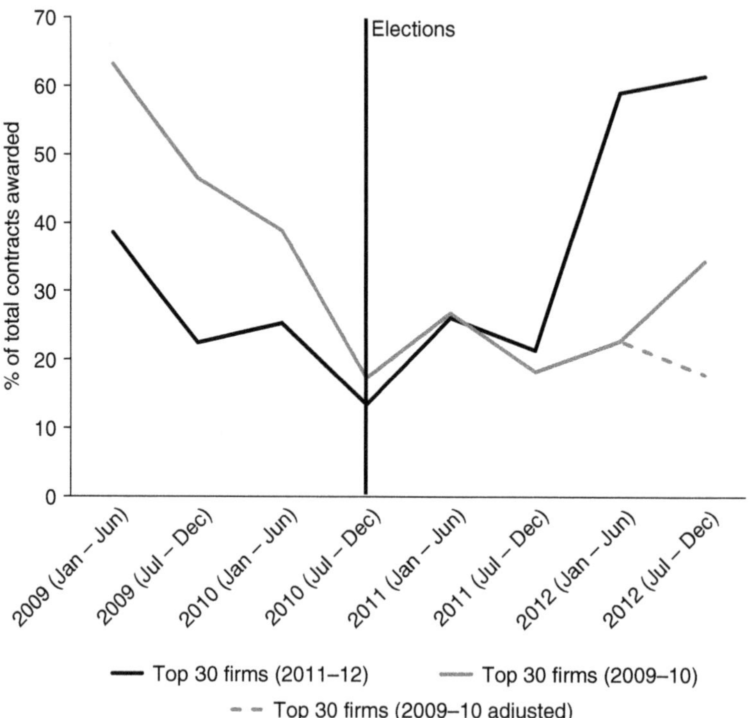

Figure 2.1 Change of fortune for top public contract winning companies after election, Hungary
Source: Fazekas *et al.* 2013

for governments and watchdogs alike who seek to monitor a government's progress.

Comparisons across countries with this sort of data are difficult, but not impossible. According to a Romanian watchdog organization, one-third of Romania's candidates for parliament in 2012 enjoyed government contracts for their private companies when their party was in power, while in Hungary such contracts can be traced to about 18 percent of all elected public officials.[1] Were greater effort made to extend the database on the Romanian side to all public officials, a complete comparison would be possible (Mungiu-Pippidi 2013b). "Politically connected" government contracts make up about a third

[1] Romanian data: Verifică integritatea canditatului tău (http://verificaintegritatea.romaniacurata.ro); Hungarian data: interview with Mihály Fazekas, Corruption Research Center, Corvinus University of Budapest.

of Hungary's EU funding allocations (Fazekas *et al.* 2013); if the same methodology were applied in Italy, a comparison between these two countries could be drawn.

Moreover, any form of audit would be ideal in understanding the norm in a given sector (corruption or integrity, discretion or non-discretion), tracing evolution, and assessing policy intervention (before-and-after designs). Even if all countries could agree on one sector to serve as comparison (for instance, public spending on infrastructure, which is notoriously vulnerable to corruption), that would still not allow safe generalization to other vulnerable sectors, such as education or planning permits for construction. Audit data and these kinds of indicator are more difficult to use for generalization and comparison across countries. For practical use, such strategies would be best, however. Once researchers establish that an allocation is not random, investigators can take over and collect evidence about the connection between an award granting authority and its beneficiaries. It would be cheaper and socially preferable to prevent corruption with this sort of monitoring than to punish (and measure) it after it occurs. But such measurements are still in their infancy, although there is great hope invested in the search for objective measurements of governance to replace perceptions of corruption.

While surveys of users of public services (as in Chapter 1, where respondents offered assessments of favoritism in public services) are based on respondents' direct experiences and measure only frequency and type of corruption, systematic audits bring more objective evidence to the fore, but in the end they too confirm that taxpayers who use certain public services, companies who apply for public contracts, and risk experts in banks who are aware of the rules of the game consider indicators like the ones in this chapter when offering their subjective assessment. Consumer or expert surveys are an easy way to check regularly on the impartiality of public services even when data (for instance, on procurement) is more difficult to access. We cannot know, however, how sensitive to change such opinions are, as people's experiences are anything but systematic. To monitor the progress of reform efforts, then, data mining offers an indispensable complement to any kind of consumer feedback survey.

The monitoring of distributional outcomes – in other words, how many transactions are particular versus random or are completed according to legal benchmarks – is useful also because it is not ambiguous like equally objective repression data, which cannot separate control of corruption from corruption itself. For instance, if Germany has opened more cases on the basis of the OECD anti-bribery convention than other EU countries, does that mean that German business people more commonly offer bribes when doing business abroad, or that Germany has been more active in enforcing the convention as compared to other countries? The same applies to the number of convictions. Notoriously corrupt countries have convicted very few people for corruption, as law enforcement itself is inefficient and perhaps corrupt.

Cross-country comparisons

Objective data is ideal for tracing the impact of reforms in one country, but how can one compare across space and over time? The first generation of corruption indicators had to draw on subjective data for this, and not much methodological progress has been made since. Business people, public officials, experts, and ordinary citizens were interviewed about their individual experiences of governance and their perceptions of corruption. Although all this kind of data can be seen as "subjective," the knowledge and sincerity of those interviewed varies greatly across individuals and categories. For public officials and business people, reporting corruption frequently amounts to tattling on themselves, so more reluctance is to be expected. Such surveys have high non-response rates and tend to correlate poorly with expert assessments and general surveys (Donchev and Ujhelyi 2008; Knack 2006; Olken 2008). Citizens are more outspoken and can be relied upon as far as public services are concerned, but they have less direct experience in certain areas such as grand corruption. Experts presumably use indicators like the ones shown in the previous section to rate a country, but as expert ratings tend to be notoriously opaque, we do not really know what indicators were considered.

Can surveys be used to measure trends? Although samples differ from year to year and we do not have a panel sample in an international survey on governance, survey results can be used to assess changes in governance. The problem is rather logistical, since surveys are expensive, carried out irregularly, with different providers of funding and variations in the wording of questionnaires, making it difficult to compare across years. The Global Corruption Barometer

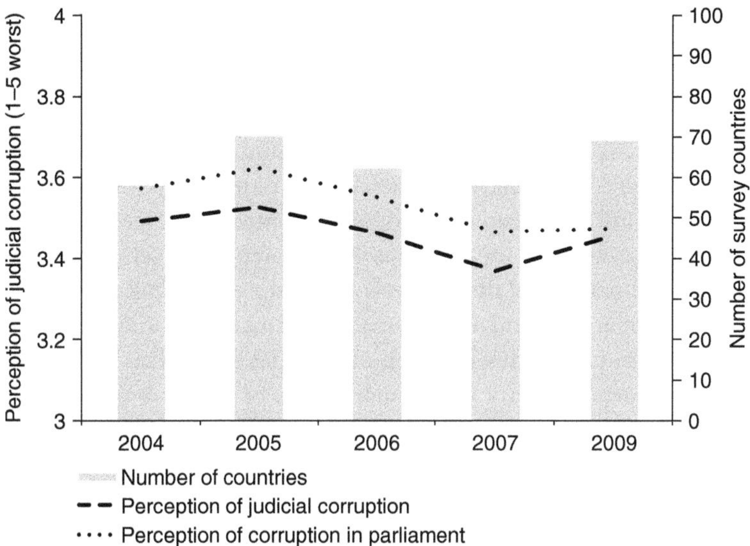

Figure 2.2 Perceptions of corruption in the judiciary and parliament (2004–2009)
Source: Transparency International (2013)

of Transparency International, for instance, has experimented so frequently over the years with new wording, has high non-response rates to many of its questions, and had such frequent changes in country coverage that it cannot offer the basis for a sound time series. A limited time series can be found in Figure 2.2, showing perceptions of corruption in the judiciary and legislative branches based on the Global Corruption Barometer, one of the few surveys with unchanged questions across the years, even as the number of countries surveyed has varied. Most of the public, however, does not have direct experience with either MPs or courts, and the remarkable consistency across these two very different areas (average assessments for the judiciary and parliament are very close) argues rather for the fact that people have a unitary diagnosis of their country's governance, which spills over into all areas where their direct experience is limited.

Can surveys be used to make a comparison across countries? We have no universal tool to measure corruption, and citizens of some countries might prove more critical or tolerant than others. Such sources of bias can be and are studied in experiments. The Eurobarometer

374 survey (European Commission 2012) asked nationals in EU member countries if their country was more or less corrupt than other EU countries. Sociologically, the question itself is mistakenly formulated, as respondents cannot know enough about other countries: the survey did not even ask if they were familiar with another EU country or had even visited one. Amazingly, the average rate of non-response was only 15 percent, and the three most corrupt countries (Greece, Romania, and Bulgaria) as well as the three least corrupt by self-perception (Sweden, Denmark, and the Netherlands) came up in similar sequence in both comparison and in national assessment. By and large, the ranking derived from this question comparing themselves with other countries returned remarkably similar results to the other questions in which they were asked to report on corruption in their own national or local authorities. Some countries might be more self-righteous and others more self-deprecating, but the bias is smaller than we would expect: people are not easily duped, and their opinions about corruption do not seem to be non-attitudes (i.e., random answers), but rather quite deeply felt. They also have a normative benchmark against which they compare, even if their knowledge of other countries is only hearsay. Furthermore, when we examine expert sources' ratings of a given country (such sources are frequently foreigners, for example risk assessors in the finance industry) with what citizens think about their own country, we also find a strong correlation (see Table 2.3). Citizens' corruption perceptions are nearly identical to ratings of corruption and quality of government made by banking experts. There seems to be something like a national context of control of corruption that people perceive, which is far less specific than the objective assessments per sector, but also quite consistent across years and variations in experience.

If sources are so consistent, then they can be aggregated into one corruption rating per country. That is what two of the most widely used measures of corruption do, either in the form of simpler averages, such as the Corruption Perception Index from Transparency International, or as more refined, unobserved components extracted by the World Bank Institute's experts (Control of Corruption, Rule of Law), which allow us to observe the differences between sources. While those indicators have been severely criticized for their lack of validity, reliability, and theoretical basis (Andrews 2008; Thomas 2009), the fact remains, as argued by Kaufmann *et al.* (1999) and Knack (2006), that as most

Table 2.3 *Correlations between different corruption indicators*

Variables	Control of corruption estimate	Perception of corruption among polit-ical parties	Perception of corruption among public officials	Quality of government index	Corruption perception index	Diversion of public funds	Source
Control of corruption Estimate	Pearson Corr.	1					World Bank's Worldwide Governance Indicators (2010)
	Sig. (2-tailed)						
	N	196					
Perception of corruption among political parties	Pearson Corr.	–0.0467	1				Global Corruption Barometer (2010–11)
	Sig. (2-tailed)	0.6497					
	N	97	97				
Perception of corruption among public officials	Pearson Corr.	–0.4455**	0.6041**	1			Global Corruption Barometer (2010–11)
	Sig. (2-tailed)	0	0				
	N	97	97	97			
Quality of government index	Pearson Corr.	0.8685**	–0.1323	–0.5234**	1		The PRS Group's International Country Risk Guide (2010)
	Sig. (2-tailed)	0	0.2332	0			
	N	139	83	83	139		

Table 2.3 (*cont.*)

Variables	Control of corruption estimate	Perception of corruption among political parties	Perception of corruption among public officials	Quality of government index	Corruption perception index		Diversion of public funds	Source
Corruption perception index	Pearson Corr.	0.9910**	–0.0894	–0.4893**	0.8672**	1		Transparency International (2010)
	Sig. (2-tailed)	0	0.4188	0	0			
	N	101	84	84	92	101		
Diversion of public funds	Pearson Corr.	0.8475**	–0.2523*	–0.5868**	0.7873**	0.9433**	1	World Economic Forum's Global Competitiveness Report (2010)
	Sig. (2-tailed)	0	0.0214	0	0	0		
	N	140	83	83	119	88	140	

** Correlation is significant at the 0.01 level (2-tailed).
* Correlation is significant at the 0.05 level (2-tailed).

sources are highly correlated, my exact definition of corruption – the (in)capacity of a society to control particularism – can indeed be thus measured. Of course, all perception data retains a degree of imprecision, but the consistency across sources shows that we manage to get close to the informal reality we are trying to assess.

That consistency seems to be not only across sources, such as the Global Corruption Barometer (a general survey) and the Global Competitiveness Report (an expert survey), as shown in Table 2.3, but also across governance areas. The Worldwide Governance Indicators' measurements on rule of law, corruption, regulatory quality and voice, and accountability have a correlation of 0.90 or higher between them. Governance seems to be extremely consistent across areas and across the perceptions of those experiencing it – a latent variable encompassing all the above; thus, if we know the state of a country's regulatory quality, corruption levels, or rule of law, we can closely estimate the other two, regulatory voice and accountability. This is evidence in favor of treating corruption within the framework of governance orders rather than as an isolated phenomenon – a theoretical position that has already been developed in this book as well as in my previous work (Mungiu-Pippidi 2006b; 2010; 2013b).

Nevertheless, the challenge of acquiring data that allows comparison of corruption across countries and across time remains daunting even if we trust perception data. The CPI from Transparency International, first released in 1995, was the first attempt to measure and compare corruption on a global scale. This index has been widely credited with placing the issue of corruption on the global policy agenda and raising international awareness of the phenomenon. Nonetheless, changes in methodology and the panel of countries made year-by-year comparisons on the basis of CPI unsound until a late methodology change in 2010 (Galtung 2006; Transparency International 2012). The corruption index developed by Daniel Kaufmann for the World Bank Institute remains the only aggregate computed on a yearly basis that can be used from 1998 onward for a significant number of countries. This indicator is available for almost 200 countries and is computed on the basis of data from about forty sources produced by more than thirty different organizations. From those sources, the definition of corruption ranges from the frequency of additional payments to get things done, to the effects of corruption on the business environment, to measuring grand corruption in the political arena or in the tendency of elites to engage in state capture (Kaufmann *et al.* 2005). To combine the various corruption indicators into a single index, an unobserved component is extracted. The estimate of corruption is therefore given by the weighted average of (rescaled) scores for each of the component indicators; the model also allows for computing the variance of a disturbance term, a measurement of how informative the index is. The variance of this conditional distribution provides an estimate of the precision of the corruption indicator for each country (labeled as a "confidence error"). As sources are close but not always particularly close, observing changes across years is difficult, as few changes exceed a confidence error set at 5 percent. Nevertheless, this aggregate index is the most "objective" indicator that can be used to compare across countries and years, because it includes most other sources of data, and is therefore widely used in this book, though for robustness, disaggregated indicators are also used in parallel.

Finally, we can find out information about corruption indirectly by surveying countries' institutional arrangements, such as procurement practices and budget transparency (Kaufmann *et al.* 2005). Such a survey measures not actual corruption, but rather the risk of corruption occurring. Some agencies make such surveys more or less regularly, although the country coverage is limited to certain developing countries and is not regularly updated. Examples include Global Integrity or the National Integrity System of Transparency International. The problem with such a review of tools is that no estimates exist on whether any of them really affect corruption, although, as later chapters will show, such tests can be applied. Many countries have adopted constitutional courts, ombudsmen, or anticorruption agencies – over a hundred of them – but that does not in the least mean that judicial review or control of corruption does not vary wildly across them. However, risk assessment can be refined if such tests are done and a country is evaluated only on those institutional arrangements which prove to have high significance across countries, as in a model developed for the EU (Mungiu-Pippidi 2013a).The controversial point remains that significance tests are carried out by associating a piece of legislation with the perception indicators relevant to it, since there is nothing else enabling us to make comparisons across countries.

Table 2.4 provides a short review of the potential of every method for making comparisons across countries and time. No single method is ideal, but for the purposes of a big N and a longer time series, subjective

Table 2.4 *Indicators for measuring corruption by data collection type*

Type of indicator	Comparison across countries	Comparison across time or before/after intervention	Observations
Perception of corruption: experts, general population, firms	Yes	Yes, but very precise	Highly relevant, but also subjective
Experience of corruption: experts, general population, firms, government agencies, state units	Yes	Yes; some limitations apply related to openness in confessing socially undesirable behavior	Both relevant and objective, problem of low response (underreporting) must be overcome
Institutional control of corruption features	Yes	Limited; we have evidence that poor correlation exists between institutional equipment for controlling corruption and control of corruption itself	Highly objective, but risks being irrelevant
Audits and data mining	No	Yes, if repeated	Should be organized on specific problems/countries

data must be used. The longest time series is the International Country Risk Guide expert rating of corruption compiled by The PRS Group, Inc. (PRS), which dates from 1984, but has undergone several changes in methodology. The safest in terms of the number of sources and transparency of statistics is the World Bank's Control of Corruption (CoC). Of course, any corruption research should triangulate using all the methods described above and try to bring them together to validate results. Such is also the design of this book – whenever possible blending qualitative and numerical indicators based on directly verifiable facts (historical and contemporary) with survey and expert data and relating one to the other through inferential statistics and policy analysis.

Counting governance orders

Objective indicators are helpful in diagnosing a country. But classifying all countries in the world into governance orders on the basis of such indicators requires a data collection effort that is only in its infancy. With every reservation, we must resort to subjective data. The World Bank CoC is the best and most transparent indicator, inclusive of most sources. The CoC 2012 score (-2.5 to 2.5) is recoded here as a 1 to 10 scale, with the current best performer, Denmark, plotted as ten. The upper third is considered best in control of corruption, with the Freedom House "freedom" indicator used to separate nonfree countries from the rest. This returns the following count (see Appendix 6):

- 47 **neopatrimonial** countries with poor control of corruption and an authoritarian regime (classified as nonfree);
- 35 **open access** countries, including the recent addition of 6 Caribbean islands. The last on the list is Portugal, with a score of 6.69;
- 109 free and partly free countries (of which 86 actually hold free elections) where **particularism** is the main rule in social allocation despite the existence of pluralism. There is wide variation in this category; the upper part of the control of corruption scale contains 22 countries (ranging from 6.47 (Israel) to 5.11 (Czech Republic)), which can be considered borderline cases where two norms (particularism and ethical universalism) coexist. At the same time, this category also includes 41 countries in the lower third of control of corruption (of which 6 are free and 36 partly free).

Singapore (partly free), United Arab Emirates, and Qatar (nonfree) are outliers in the top third of the control of corruption scale. Doubts can also be raised on Botswana as an open access achiever (its scores endorse it) and Cuba, Rwanda, or Bahrain as borderline cases. There is significant evidence that while bribery is under control in these countries, they cannot be qualified as open access or based on ethical universalism, a point we shall return to in Chapter 5. The achiever group remains larger than the estimations of North, Wallis, and Weingast (2009), though it is worth discussing whether so many small countries, from the Caribbean to Luxembourg, accused of being tax havens, really deserve such high rankings.

The exercise remains imperfect, but helpful to size and map good governance across the world. If we reduce the countries panel to just the ninety-eight where the GCB was measured and received sufficient responses, further interesting observations can be made. Competitive particularistic countries seem to display the worst of all worlds, with the highest scores of perceived corruption, perceived state capture, importance of connections to "get things done," and bribery experience. Unsurprisingly, the protests of 2013, a year rich in grass-roots anticorruption movements, are all found in this type of country: India, Egypt, Ukraine, Turkey, Brazil, and Bulgaria. Neopatrimonial countries look slightly better with less bribery, connections, and capture, but probably because their capture is institutionalized and the survey question on capture refers to "vested interests." If all thirty-five achievers are considered, the average figure of reported use of connections to get ahead in life is lower than in particularistic countries, but still very high compared to the Danish benchmark of ethical universalism. The continuum definitely does more justice to governance contexts than any categorization that leaves some cases on the borders, but the exercise allows a global mapping of governance, an easy and accurate understanding of a governance context's basic features just by its typological assignment, and the identification of countries where control of corruption works or has greatly improved, an invaluable source on lessons learned in the coming chapters.

Although we do not have a systematic measure of control of corruption before 1996, some historical indicators exist to inform us when countries have achieved control of corruption, or in other words, when corruption became the scandalous exception rather than the norm (given no perfect control of corruption). A wider historical view would thus divide the achievers of good governance into generations. The first generation, which we can call "historical achievers," is comprised of fourteen states, including atypical polities such as Luxembourg, Andorra, or Lichtenstein. This generation includes the Scandinavian countries, the creation of which was a result of diverse secessions, but which have forged their own distinct tools for good governance despite their common origins; Britain, the classic historical performer, and Canada, independent but part of the British Empire; the Benelux countries, which have shared the same political space for many years, although Belgium seems to have reached a lesser standard of governance later than the Netherlands; three historically German-speaking states – Austria, Prussia, and Bavaria – which were relatively free of corruption by 1900; France; and Switzerland (Neild 2002). Their achievement in good governance coincided with their modernity, leading to the belief reflected in UNCAC that the two can only go together, despite serious skepticism on that account voiced in the past (Huntington 1968; Nye 1967).

The second generation of "early" achievers seem to have gained reasonable control of corruption between the two World Wars. They are generally new states that seceded from a first-generation achiever, for the greatest part British Empire splinters populated mostly by populations of European descent (the United States, Ireland, Australia, New Zealand), which continued to follow in the traditions of British legal institutions mixed with their own democratic developments (Wallis *et al.* 2006). Also included here is Iceland, a splinter from Denmark.

Finally, contemporary "achievers" came close to the good governance benchmark after World War II, starting with two countries that evolved as Western protectorates following military occupation: Japan and West Germany. More recent achievers saw a new round of former British colonies, in particular Caribbean islands, a handful of Mediterranean and Eastern European countries, as well as some continental exceptions (Chile or Botswana). This suggests that historically, only a few countries have achieved the benchmark of "control of corruption" independently. There seem to be only a few streams and exceptions from broader continental contexts.

Trends in control of corruption

Objective indicators are useful when in doubt whether an individual country has progressed. But to understand if the whole world has progressed, we have no choice beyond the World Governance Indicators. Having an instrument (CoC) to assess trends, we can now return to the question of evolution: Has corruption decreased since the international campaign against it started, taking World Bank President's James Wolfensohn's 1996 anticorruption call as the conventional starting point? A considerable period of time seems to have elapsed since – but is such an interval actually sufficient for a country to modernize its governance? Countries placed presently in the superior third of the World Bank Control of Corruption ranking scale have reached their positions after a far longer interval, with very few exceptions.

Since the World Bank began monitoring the Worldwide Governance Indicators (WGIs) in 1996,[2] it seems that very few countries have managed to evolve in controlling corruption, despite the development of an international legal anticorruption framework and increased awareness of the systematic nature of corruption as a result of efforts by non-governmental organizations (NGOs) such as Transparency International. According to the control of corruption indicator, no region (continent) in the world has seen, on average, a statistically significant change in this period of time (see Figure 2.3). Surveys also fail to show much evolution – all changes between 2004 and 2009 in the GCB, for instance, are insignificant.

The best-performing group of countries at present as reflected by the CoC indicator is the first-generation European achievers and their former overseas colonies in North America and Oceania (see Figure 2.3).These countries' average control of corruption is separated by a gap of over 30 points on the 0–100 scale from the next region, Central and Eastern Europe (including the Baltic States and the Balkans). This region has evolved more than any other in the world since 1989 (up roughly 15 points on the scale), although that applies only to the successful Western section, since what is left of the former Soviet Union is actually ranked at the very bottom, below Sub-Saharan Africa and treated by the World Bank as a region apart. The rest of the world lags far behind the best-achieving area. A total of 151 out of 196 countries experienced no significant change in control of corruption in the same period. Only 21 countries have shown

[2] The World Bank Institute monitors six dimensions of governance for 215 countries, 1996–2013; seehttp://info.worldbank.org/governance/wgi/index.asp.

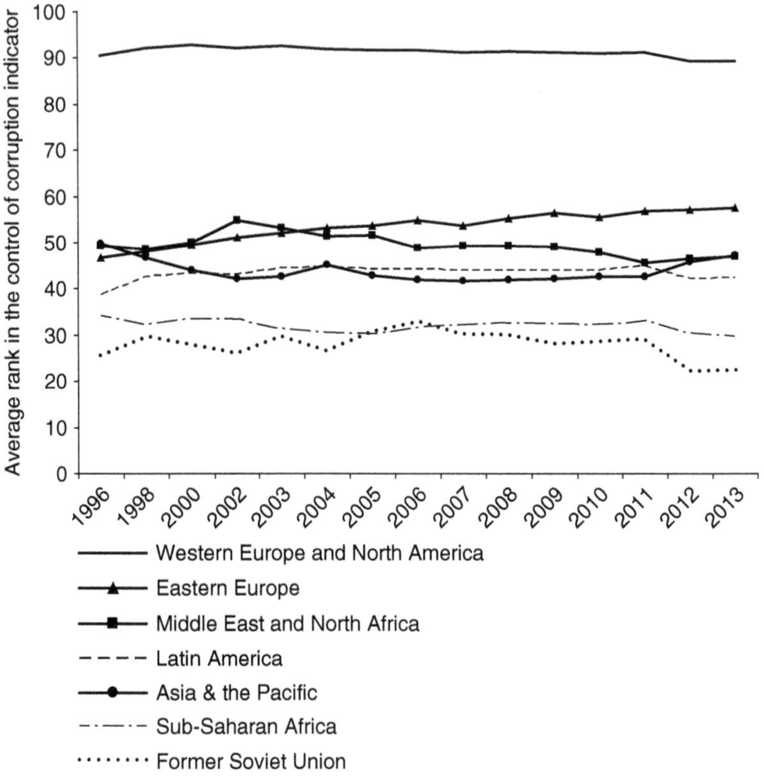

Figure 2.3 Evolution of the WGI control of corruption average by region (1996–2013)
Source: Worldwide Governance Indicators

a statistically significant improvement, while 27 countries have significantly regressed. On average, the regions with higher positive development were Central Europe (including the Balkans) and the Caribbean. On the other hand, the Middle East and North Africa, together with Asia and the Pacific, have on average worsened. Progress within the upper third of the ranking scale seems to have been made in atypical polities, such as the United Arab Emirates, Hong Kong, and Cape Verde, or progress remains controversial, as in Georgia, Rwanda, or Bulgaria. Estonia, Uruguay, and Botswana shine not only by their remarkable performances, but also by their singularity as uncontroversial achievers of good governance in this interval. Most other recent "achievers" are small islands. Some of the countries that have evolved within the previous decades have, in fact, regressed over the last fifteen years of global anticorruption efforts: Argentina and South Africa are notable examples. More evolution is to be observed in the lower part of the scale, but it is still too far from the upper third to offer any guarantees on the sustainability of their achievement.

As the global obsession with corruption is based mostly on the presumption that corruption is economically detrimental, it is worth studying these trends by reference to the income groups of individual countries. The upper-middle and high income categories have been joined by a considerable number of countries in the study interval 1996–2012: the number of nations has jumped from 27 to 52 in the upper-middle income category and from 40 to 56 in the high income group. The average for control of corruption has registered a decline in both categories, superior to the less marked decline of the other income groups (none progressed). That seems to indicate that newcomers in these two income groups are countries that do not present the same high governance standards observed in other rich countries, and are therefore in fact pulling the group average down (Mungiu-Pippidi 2013a). The additional implication is that these countries are actually becoming richer faster than they are improving their control of corruption, and that above a certain threshold (lower than the upper third) corruption stops being so detrimental to growth. But contexts with stronger control of corruption still seem to have delivered most growth. Except for the Middle East and North Africa, all regions of the world have increased their income level since 1996. However, Western Europe and North America, which also perform best in control of corruption, have managed to grow rapidly despite having an already high average income. Until 2008, the average income in those regions increased around 35 percent, more than in Asia, Latin America, the Middle East and North Africa, and the Caribbean in the same period (Mungiu-Pippidi 2013a).

As anticorruption protests on the streets seem to occur in democracies (Brazil, India, Bulgaria) but also in some non-democracies (Tunisia), progress should be checked across political regimes too. The Freedom in the World measurement from Freedom House ranks each of the countries and territories included in the index as free, partly free, and nonfree. A free country is one where there is open political competition, a climate of respect for civil liberties, significant independent civic life, and independent media. A partly free country is one in which there is limited respect for political rights and civil liberties. These states are described as frequently suffering from an environment of corruption, weak rule of law, ethnic and religious strife, and a political landscape in which a single party enjoys dominance despite a certain degree of pluralism. A nonfree country is one where basic political rights are absent and basic civil liberties are widely and systematically denied.

Between 1996 and 2011 there was a slight improvement in political rights and civil liberties, reflected in a reduction of autocratic regimes (from 53 to 47), an increase in the number of countries ranked as free (from 79 to 87), and the fact that 22 countries moved up in the Freedom House categories and only 12 moved down. The number of free countries increased by about 3 percent while the number of partly free countries remained stable at 31 percent. The slight positive development in democratization around the world has not so far been translated into a significant evolution in the control of corruption. Although countries ranked as free by Freedom House still have the highest CoC average, all political regime groups have lower scores on average in 2011 than they had 15 years before.

The fact that new democracies are really struggling to control corruption is shown when we average progress on corruption control by the autocratic/democratic dimension. A "liberal democracy" includes a substantial array of civil liberties and free elections, the definition of electoral democracies. Freedom in the World considers both civil liberties and political rights for its index, and all countries ranked as free qualify as both electoral and liberal democracies. By contrast, some partly free countries qualify as electoral, but not liberal, democracies, and the nonfree countries are basically autocratic regimes. Sixty-one percent of liberal democracies (50 of 82) rank in the highest tercile for control of corruption, against only 10 percent of autocracies (5 out of 50). Moreover, autocracies are more likely to be in the bottom tercile: 68 percent of autocracies (32 of 47) are in that category compared to only 6 percent of liberal democracies (5 of 82). However, two-thirds of the countries where corruption is a problem (89 of 131), i.e., those in the lowest and the middle terciles, are free or partly free, and most of them (59 of 89) qualify as electoral democracies. Democracies still outperform autocracies where evolution is concerned, but their record is mixed: 12 liberal democracies managed to score a positive evolution for control of corruption, while 10 regressed; the proportion is reversed as regards partly free countries (five progress cases to nine regress cases) and nonfree countries (4 to 8).

Regardless of political regime, 21 countries saw a significant positive development, whereas for 27 their CoC score deteriorated. Almost 60 percent of the countries that showed positive development (12 of 21) are considered free, and just under 20 percent (4 of 21) are nonfree. That also seems to suggest that civil liberties and political rights play an important role in the fight against corruption. However, those two factors by themselves do not seem to prevent countries from regressing: 10 free countries showed a statistically significant regression in their control of corruption (12 percent of the total of free countries), a proportion comparable to those of the partly free and nonfree countries that also regressed (15 and 17 percent, respectively). A review of continental evolutions does not return different results from this global view. Some of the "old achievers" (for instance, Spain) have regressed since the beginning of the economic crisis in Europe, but for the rest of the world, the main trend is stagnation.

Should the stagnation be blamed on the lack of sensitivity to change of first-generation corruption indicators (more change is visible if we lower the confidence error threshold)? Or rather should we accept that a governance context changes only incrementally, and control of corruption is tied into such contexts and thus very hard to change? The latter hypothesis seems more plausible if we check individual change stories by means of second-generation indicators. Romania and Bulgaria, for instance, have been implementing many anticorruption reforms and were subjected to the toughest anticorruption conditionality by the EU through the Cooperation and Verification Mechanism, which allows the sanctioning of a member country after accession if its targets are not met. Their scores in the CoC indicator show change, but mostly within the confidence error. But second-generation indicators point to a lack of fundamental change of both countries, confirming the ambiguity reflected in CoC (Dimulescu *et al.* 2013; Stoyanov *et al.* 2014). There seem to have been positive changes in Brazil and India, but people in the streets protest because they do not feel the impact of such changes.

The theoretical model of control of corruption presented in this chapter would indeed predict that change is difficult and is achieved over a long period of time. Governance contexts as the stable configurations of social allocation rules of the game may frequently transcend political regimes. As they reproduce fundamental patterns of social organization and power distribution in a society, they tend to be stable once reaching a certain equilibrium and prove hard to shake by elections or other changes of political regime. The model also implies that the only perceivable change in the control of corruption is from one context to another, from limited access order to open access order. People do perceive positive change in Uruguay, for instance, or Georgia, two of the handful of countries that have progressed in recent times. If rules of the game in social allocation do not change, other more limited developments (for instance, adoption of legislation or the sentencing of a notoriously corrupt person) are unlikely to be perceived as changes in the control of corruption.

But this does not imply that change is impossible. To investigate how corruption control has developed and been consolidated over time, three strategies are available. First is the big N strategy: we can compare states where control of corruption currently works against the rest; this strategy is hindered by data limitations, as we have only corruption perception indicators for so many countries and they only go back to the early 1980s (the International Country Risk Guide (ICRG)) and mid-1990s (CoC). Second, we can study the cases of "historical achievers" – the countries that first developed control of corruption and an open access order, creating the benchmark of good governance we use today. The problem is that conditions that prompted these historical evolutions have long since changed: it is more than one hundred years since a Western-type modernization process has been forced upon many societies, and only a few managed to evolve successfully, allegedly due to very different conditions than the ones informing British or Dutch modernization in Europe. Or third, we can examine the few cases that have managed a positive evolution in contemporary times. The disadvantage lies in their limited numbers, as well as the controversy still surrounding their achievement for some, if not all, of them. Starting with the development of historical benchmarks of control of corruption, the next three chapters will draw on all three strategies to understand how the control of corruption has evolved.

3 *The road to Denmark: historical paths to corruption control*

The norm of ethical universalism in governance

Why do some societies manage to control corruption so it manifests itself only occasionally as an exception, while other societies do not and remain systemically corrupt? And is the superior performance of this first group of countries a result of what they *do*, or of what they *are*? Most current anticorruption strategies presume the former, which is why institutions from developed and well-governed countries are currently being copied all around the world. At least on paper, there are few states left lacking a constitutional court, some form of checks and balances, or an ombudsman (47 ombudsmen in 1990, 100 in 2003, and 135 by 2008) (see also Table 4.2 in Chapter 4). Skeptics, on the other hand, endorse the latter view, believing in the cultural determinism of corruption and good governance. More recently, following the failure of the first generation of anticorruption reforms, a middle position has begun to emerge: the most relevant lessons lie not in what developed countries are currently doing to control corruption, but rather in what they have done in the past, when their societies more strongly resembled the conditions in today's developing world (Andrews 2008). However, as this subject area is largely unknown to governance scholars and practitioners alike, it is difficult even to estimate the potential value of such historical lessons. This chapter addresses this gap by asking not how corruption is eradicated today, but rather how societies have built systems over time to protect their common resources from being spoiled by individuals or groups. And it answers this question by looking at the oldest group of achievers: core European polities.

Thus far, Europeans have enjoyed the most success in building regimes based on ethical universalism, alongside a group of former colonies populated mostly by Europeans (e.g., the United States and Commonwealth countries) and a handful of other countries (Japan,

Chile, Singapore, a couple of tiny Asian monarchies) with designs that are mostly of European inspiration. European control of corruption can be regarded as almost the only historically successful process of state building in which a long transition to ethical universalism has resulted in an equilibrium where opportunities for corruption are largely checked by societal control of rulers and reasonable reciprocal control by the government. This evolution cannot easily be separated from the general European advancement to government accountability and rule of law. It is therefore of interest for the current community of anticorruption scholars and practitioners why, how, and when ethical universalism as a governance norm and good governance as its practical application managed to take root in European history. Furthermore, most states around the present world, both new and old, have thus come to subscribe to a norm based on classical European intellectual heritage: the *doctrine of ethical universalism in public life*. This evolution should not be taken for granted; indeed, as James Q. Wilson argues, universalism and individualism, which spread in the West after the Enlightenment to become generally held norms, are neither natural, nor necessarily and invariably good principles (Wilson 1993). The resulting ideology of equal treatment by the government of all its subjects nevertheless has a long Western tradition, running from the Stoics (doctrine of natural law) to Cicero (106 BC–43 BC), through medieval and Renaissance authors, to then become internalized in modern state-building doctrine in the work of Montesquieu and the American Federalists.

The legal philosophy of Cicero seems to have been the most influential early source (Carlyle and Carlyle 1903; Neumann 1986; Skinner 1989) – it can be traced directly through Aquinas and Florentine Renaissance authors to the desk of Thomas Jefferson, where a bust of Cicero still stands.

In the first Book of *De Re Publica*, Cicero argued for equal treatment of citizens:

> Since the law is the bond of civil society, and the justice of the law equal, by what rule can the association of citizens be held together, if the condition of the citizens be not equal? For if the fortunes of men cannot be reduced to this equality – if genius cannot be equally the property of all – rights, at least, should be equal among those who are citizens of the same republic. For what is a republic but an association of rights? (Cicero 1877: XXXII)

In *De Legibus* he further argued that both justice and law derive their origin from nature, while "wicked and unjust statutes" are "anything but 'laws,'" because "in the very definition of the term 'law' there inheres the idea and principle of choosing what is just and true" (Cicero 1928: *De Legibus*, bk. 2, sec. 11).

The ideas of Cicero had an impressive following in the Middle Ages, from Isidore of Seville (*c.* 560–636) who passed them to Aquinas (1225–74), then to Brunetto Latini (1210–94), who reformulated and transmitted the republican ethic to other thinkers (such as Dante), and also used it as the basis for his formal treatise on city-state government (Jones 1997: 461–62). Aquinas further developed the Ciceronian idea that if conflict arises between positive law (the law of the given community) and natural law (derived from God, therefore upholding the common good), passive resistance is not only a right, but a duty; the *lexnaturalis* is indispensable, and even God cannot dispense with it (Neumann 1986: 53). He explained the distinction between *lexnaturalis* and *lextyrannica* (Aquinas 2006: I–II. 92. 1–4), arguing that norms must fulfil three conditions to be considered laws: to serve the common good, to respect the principle of proportional equality when distributing burdens to subjects, and to be issued by the legislator only within the limits of their authority. Private interest, even that of the ruler, should never be promoted over the common interest. On the basis of Cicero and Isidore, Aquinas argued in the first article (Aquinas 2006: I–II, Q. 96, Art. 1) of *Summa*, "Whether Human Law Should Be Framed for the Community Rather Than for the Individual?" that "the end of law is the common good; because, as Isidore stated (Etym. v, 21), 'Law should be framed, not for any private benefit, but for the common good of all the citizens.' Hence, 'human laws should be proportionate to the common good,' and further, 'laws are enacted for no private profit, but for the common benefit of the citizens'" (Aquinas 2006: P(2a)–Q(90)–A(1, 2); see also Lindsay 1911). In *Defensor Pacis,* Marsilio of Padua (1275–*c.* 1342) further stipulated that though draft statutes are to be framed by the "wise" (*prudentes*) who, by virtue of their leisure and superior experience, are best qualified to propose just and useful laws, the wisdom of a minority does not entitle them to enact legislation on behalf of the majority. Rather, the whole citizen body (*legislator humanus*) should consent to draft statutes in order to make them mandatory laws for the community. Recognizable within Aquinas' authoritative views and Marsilio's influence are seeds of ideas of government accountability, "thick" rule of law, and public participation: the three key foundational concepts of what today is called "good governance." While these ideas (the thought, not the practice) were extremely widespread, particularly in Italy's communes, where they informed the special tracts of city government that erupted in the early thirteenth century and infused them with republican ideology, such arguments were also made on behalf of monarchs. John of Salisbury (*c.* 1120–80) argued in the *Policraticus*, Book Four, Chapters 1 and 2:

> Between a tyrant and a prince there is this single or chief difference, that the latter obeys the law and rules the people by its dictates, accounting himself as but their servant. It is by virtue of the law that he makes good his claim to the foremost and chief place in the management of the affairs of the commonwealth and in the bearing of its burdens; and his elevation over others consists in this, that whereas private men are held responsible only for their private affairs, on the prince fall the burdens of the whole community ... The prince accordingly is the minister of the common interest and the bond-servant of equity, and he bears the public person in the sense that he punishes the wrongs and injuries of all, and all crimes, with even-handed equity. (John of Salisbury 1927)

From the Renaissance to the Enlightenment, Cicero's work remained mandatory reading for elites and spread far beyond the circle of legal scholars. Montesquieu, allegedly cited more by the American founders than any other source apart from the Bible, praised Cicero for having made Greek ideas "available to all men, like reason itself" and wrote an introduction to Cicero's thought, *Discours sur Cicéron* (1709) (Fott 2002; Lutz 1984). The other source of the American founding fathers was, however, Machiavelli, who, unlike early Italian republicans, no longer held illusions about the citzenry and therefore was less normative in his approach. In Chapter XVII of his *Discussion on Livy*, Machiavelli soberly suggests that a corrupt people coming into their liberty can maintain their freedom only with the greatest difficulty. The foundation of control of corruption is in the mentality of the people: "Where the people is not corrupted, tumults and other troubles do no harm; but where corruption exists, well ordered laws are of no benefit" (Machiavelli 2009: 40). In Chapter XVIII, he associated freedom with virtuous behavior and answered in the negative the question "whether a free State can be maintained in a city that is corrupted, or, if there had not been one, to be able to establish one" (Machiavelli 2009: 41). Finally, Machiavelli openly discussed the possible inconsistency between legal mores and real mores, or between formal and informal institutions, when he stated, "For as good customs have need of laws for maintaining themselves, so the laws, to be observed, have need of good customs" (Machiavelli 2009: 49).

If the dividing line between ancient and modern political theory is somewhere between Aristotle and Cicero (Carlyle and Carlyle 1903: 8–9), two millennia had to pass until a Western tradition of upholding ethical universalism as a basic governance principle became universal doctrine. The foundations of the Western vision of "good governance" are Latin and pagan, but they were reinforced by mainstream Catholic doctrine in the twelfth century, long before the Renaissance and Reformation and their later rediscovery by the Enlightenment. Ethical universalism was therefore a strong component of European legal philosophy early on and was exported to British colonies; later, political and religious emancipation opened the road to broader interpretations of fair and virtuous governance.

Premodern arrangements

If ethical universalism can be followed from Antiquity to Modernity, the challenge of protecting public resources from spoiling by private interests is at least as old. However, there have been significant differences in this respect between countries ruled by one individual and their family as opposed to those with more inclusive forms of government. Under autocratic patrimonial regimes, the ruler is not accountable to either people or the law. In fact, the situation is reversed: the ruler is the principal who must monitor his unruly agents to ensure that he is not cheated. As discipline and personal loyalty almost always override the issue of integrity, there is little true anticorruption in such settings. When agents violate the leader's trust in relation to other issues, they are dramatically repudiated and condemned, often for corrupt practices they have indulged in for years (for example, the abuse of their privileged access to the ruler for more profit than that bestowed by patronage).

This depiction by a historian of a twelfth-century corruption scandal is paradigmatic:

> He has always been surrounded by temptation, as all suits and petitions to the Emperor came to him, plus he was also the intermediate of all princes and others who wanted favors of Federico. He was the chief controller of all administration, he left a huge fortune, and the Emperor was best placed to know if he could account for it ... In a time of such insecurity, such fraudulent behavior could in fact have disastrous consequences and was thus equated with treason. (Kantorowicz 1939: 259–60)

Autocratic anticorruption is always repressive and discriminatory. It manifests itself only occasionally and unpredictably, and then always with harsh violence. Corruption among the ruler's family is allowed; corruption of the patrimonial court is tolerated and could be used against any of its members when an occasion (of another nature) presents itself or when security is threatened by a corrupt act, as in the case of Pier Delle Vigne, the chancellor of Frederic II Hohenstaufen, cited above (Kantorowicz 1939, 259–60). Corruption and embezzlement are always invoked when a favorite falls from grace. The list is long, from Enguerrand of Marigny and Pier Delle Vigne in early medieval Europe to Antonio Perez, Rodrigo Calderon, and Nicolas Fouquet during the late absolute monarchies (Parker 1978). Anticorruption is thus an altar where sacrifices to absolute royalty and power discretion must sometimes be made, with the result of diffusing popular discontent away from the ruler toward some scapegoat person or category. Apart from the royal household, there cannot be any other "public" corruption, as nobody else shares in any public authority.

Patrimonial monarchs often passed exhaustive anticorruption regulations, which applied primarily to lower-level clerks. But because the rule of patrimonial monarchs is based on patronage and favor, the boundary between corruption and integrity is fuzzy. Patronage is an intrinsic part of feudal relations and medieval society and can play a positive role even in government: Elizabeth I rewarded her successful captains and ministers. Favoritism, on the other hand, is highly subversive as it is purely discretionary and not merit based. Bestowing favors on successful warriors is acceptable as it can be seen to be in the public interest, but bestowing favors on worthless favorites (for instance, for their charms, as the Stuarts did) on the basis of private sympathy was unpopular (Peck 1990).

The ancient democracies had already struggled with notions of justice, public interest, and fair government as a collective action problem: individuals shared significant tasks and pooled resources to be jointly managed. We cannot find this under feudalism, as the "state" was little more than a transterritorial and hierarchical connection between individuals, so this system was inferior to the Roman state in many respects. The result of such a network was not a "public" state the way we understand it today: public offices were completely patrimonial. In the same way that vassals equipped their own troops and came to fight for their overlord when summoned, judges and tax farmers (who collected taxes on behalf of government, giving the sovereign a quota and keeping the rest) were entrusted to fulfill such tasks as a feudal duty, using their own material and human resources. They were permitted to reimburse themselves from enemy plunder, fees from claimants, and other means; this in itself was not dishonest, as it was how the system worked. Thus, the "corruption" encountered in the Middle Ages and under patrimonial and feudal regimes has little in common with corruption in its modern form. It essentially consisted of different forms of dishonesty, primarily embezzlement. But since at that time no one even aspired to the norm of ethical universalism, one could hardly speak of corruption in a modern sense.

An entirely different situation could be found under the European communal system of government, which fought feudalism and escaped it to some extent, creating the governance tradition of European cities. Most prominent among this system is the story of the Italian republics, where government was not patrimonial and both public property and interest were clearly defined in reference to retrieved Roman standards. As a result of its still-existing or recovering ancient cities, Italy was one of the most urbanized parts of Europe at the beginning of the Middle Ages. City-states came to dominate the territories surrounding them, taking advantage of the competition between Pope and Emperor; the most successful became nearly colonial states, exploiting other cities in Italy or further afield. Between the eleventh and thirteenth centuries these cities turned into self-governing "communes" and managed to build elaborate constitutions, strong administrations, and effective bureaucracies in the midst of great adversity (Jones 1997). Traders and other business people needed governments to be able to effectively protect business and the prosperity of their cities against two foes: the armed noblemen who threatened to take government into their own patrimony, and the danger of particularism inherent to pluralism – in other words, the horizontal threat of corruption emanating from themselves and their peers.

Venetians emerged from Byzantine domination with a system largely free of patrimonialism: any attempts by the doges to capture the state ended dramatically, and it was traditional that every new office started with an audit of the preceding one. In Tuscany, the Florentines and the Sienese, by contrast, had to fight more against local noblemen. They were innovative in adopting an antimagnate regime which prohibited individuals and families with a long history of disproportionate power over common affairs from taking part in government. This approach prevented both the oligarchization and patrimonialization of the state. The people of Genoa, the third large, remarkably well-governed trade city, had to fight long and hard to protect themselves from nobles and monarchs. By and large, they succeeded in this for significant periods of time, which brought them both prosperity and good government. The Bolognese had a government dominated by notaries and lawyers, reflecting the importance assigned to controlling authorities' discretionary power.

Following these early successes, however, came some warnings that it was not only the disproportionate power of a ruler, but something more intrinsic to human nature that was a threat to good government: the new communal governments had to devise instruments to prevent their own peers from abusing joint resources. This experience is of particular interest as they developed full-fledged control of corruption systems based on collective action, not on the principal–agent model. The principal–agent model can hardly be said to work outside the patrimonial system, since there is no clear principal who defends the public patrimony (in a democracy, public interest cannot be said to reside with any one person with absolute certainty, and the alleged "principal" can himself be corrupt).

The key concept of their institutional design for anticorruption was the idea that corruption should be prevented rather than punished after the fact. A certain moral realism guided commune governance: it was taken as self-evident that government was generally used as a tool for self-enrichment and self-aggrandizement and that good institutions guarded against such corruption. Neither objectivity nor honesty are innate traits, so good behavior should not be taken for granted. If citizens are to be prevented from falling into the trap of favoring their own, institutions working against government particularism need to be built from the onset. In the Italian city-states, there was great fear of favoritism by families, clans, or various factions. For the top executive position at city level, many Italian city-states opted for what we would today call a city manager, a professional hired from among a pool of top bureaucrats. It was mandatory for this manager, or *podestà*, to come from a different city so that no local candidates could be favored. He brought his own staff with him, including law enforcers, clerks, and magistrates. He paid a security deposit at the beginning of his term and after his final management report was accepted, he received his money back along with his fee, less any fines incurred. He was usually appointed for a one-year term, serving as an executive with a local legislative body (e.g., a council, either elected or corporatist). *Podestà*, along with governors in Mediterranean colonies, were bound by strict conflict of interest regulations: neither they nor their staff were allowed to perform any activity other than service. Short mandates for elected or conscription-based public office (two months for the Council in Florence), rotation of positions held by family, recruitment by a lottery system or extremely complicated electoral systems, and appointments of outsiders all point to the Italians' understanding that conflicts of interest are ubiquitous and hurt government and business alike. These measures were aimed at building an objective government and preventing its capture by particular interests. Continuous controlling and auditing were regular features of government: in order to do it professionally, when the need arose, Bologna's top families created a fund from donations and outsourced auditing to an external auditor.[1] While one family might have to provide a tax collector, another was asked to provide an auditor. In Florence, citizens were obliged to serve periodically on committees responsible for auditing and checking the quality and value of public services.

Many services provided by the state to its citizens were funded by fees that passed directly from consumer to provider, without actually circulating in the treasury. This reduced opportunities for corruption. Tax collectors had short mandates and were strictly controlled by their peers: fines used to help enforcement also served as sources of public

[1] *Archivio di stato di Bologna, Tesoreria e contrallatore di tesoreria*, bb. 2 regg 107.

income. Short-term mandates in public office were designed to prevent the exercise of a duty from turning into the exploitation of a rent. All positions were based on very short mandates and were not immediately renewable. Governors of Genoese colonies were expected to leave by the same boat that brought their appointed successor. Notables acted as financial guarantors for lesser-known individuals.

The good governance designs of Italian communes were based on a political regime that can be called "republican" rather than democratic. The cities had a strong corporate character and a social organization based on guilds, neighborhoods, and families. Most bureaucratic positions were distributed according to a quota system organized by guild and clan (family), with the exception of the top executive position and the systems linked to it. This meant that many people participated in the governance of the city-state. Only clerks, however, were paid. When considered in combination with the military obligations of each clan, guild, or district, the system was very participatory and inclusive, especially given that these were relatively small communities with populations under 100,000 people (and sometimes only in the low thousands). Each family was thus socialized into public affairs and the business of government.

The first main feature of this governance system is therefore *participation in public affairs*. Compared to any other governance regime at the time, a variable but relatively high proportion of people in Italian city-states participated in decision making and government either directly or indirectly. In the thirteenth century, due to population growth, the main legislative body of many cities – the "great council" – grew impressively: in Padua 1,000 adults out of a population of 11,000 were members at one time, and in Bologna, the 50,000-person population was governed by a council which grew from 2,000 to 4,000 members (Jones 1997: 407). Frequent reselection made participation ever greater. This varied with time and place, however: some city-states had a more pronounced aristocratic character than others, some included only traders' guilds, others included some manufacturers, and so forth. The citizenry did not include everyone, but most people had someone represent them directly or indirectly, and various categories of the population rebelled at times to gain or improve representation.

The second feature of republicanism was the concept that *public office was not a privilege, but a civic duty*. People were drafted to serve on an equitable basis, mostly through co-optation rather than election (the latter existing only for certain top positions), and for limited periods of time. This republican principle of short-term, non-professional office holding seems to have worked reasonably well. It was not based on financial motives – most office holders were not paid – but on the shared need to protect common resources pooled for governing in the joint interest and achieving public objectives such as security. Brunetto Latini compared Italian governments favorably with France, arguing that election of magistrates and governors on the basis of merit by the citizen body was infinitely better than offering offices to the highest bidder, as was the practice of the French king (Jones 1997: 458).

The third feature of these republican regimes was *equality before the law*. Without being fully democratic, they were strongly bound by law, and the practice of government and economic activity were based on written contracts. There was concern that law be applied fairly and that individuals abide by it; creative designs were successfully applied to help commercial contract enforcement (Gonzales de Lara 2011). Efforts were made to ensure that the judge, like the *podestà*, was not bound by any conflict of interest.

Although colonial expansion is to some extent responsible for the economic success of Italian city-states, the government and the institutions developed during this period (e.g., contract and arbitrage courts, stock exchanges, public audits) were also crucial in ensuring an environment for trade to flourish (Greif 1998). Ideology and interest, Roman republican ideology (at the height of Florentine prosperity, Cicero was the author most revered by the top business people – his statue still looks down upon visitors to the Palazzo Pubblico in Siena) and the merchants' need for a government able to ensure freedom of trade and peace, had to come together for this institutional development. Between 1250 and 1350 there seemed to be more capital in Italy than in the rest of Europe, and Italian money funded crusades, princes' military conquests, and colonial expansion (Jones 1997: 197). Public budgets also increased constantly from the eleventh century onward, leading to the development of city governments. In 1162, 91 officials sufficed for Pisa, but by the late thirteenth century Bologna needed 1,800 (Jones 1997: 410).

By and large, a governance design based on civic duty, participation, cooperation, and direct and indirect elections – all in the framework of universally applied law – promoted the norm of ethical universalism. The practice was a different story: so many regulations were needed because there were constant attempts to profit or favor. Dante's *Inferno* has some notable corrupt characters that rose to eternal fame. Still, these designs worked to produce a reasonably effective, prosperous, and fair government. Of course, it was not a stable government, caught between a violent external environment and domestic struggles for class supremacy. Social tension was frequent, except perhaps in Venice: the much-praised government of the nine in Siena, an expression of what we could call today the middle class, ended when the noblemen and the lower classes united against it. But the only real failure of state building among city-states in the end is Genoa – there the commune ended after being appropriated by its lenders group, Casa di San Giorgio, who did not act in the public interest, but rather exploited public revenues for their own gain. Medieval republicanism is a permanent search for objective and impartial government more than its rule. The end of this regime was triggered by unfavorable external circumstances rather than some internal failure. For instance, Cosimo I de Medici, whose rule ended the extraordinary Florentine government experiment, was imposed by an international dictate over the head of the local community. Significantly, when he took over, he did so physically as well, moving into the quarters of the Signoria Palace where commune office holders resided for their two-month terms in office. He turned it into a permanent and hereditary residence, which from then on became both a personal and government seat. This is when the Signoria Palace was expensively decorated by Vasari and his colleagues, after being far more modest during republican times. Venice resisted the advance of the Ottoman Empire magnificently for centuries despite having a small population; only Napoleon managed to suppress this remarkable polity, trading it against another territory of interest to him at a peace conference. Their limited size, which helped these communities create good governance, ultimately led to their defeat by superior forces and a subsequent regression to patrimonialism. Local virtue alone cannot survive in a global order not based on virtue, unless it belongs to those having the largest battalions as well. And the drawing of associations between present success and virtuous circles in government – as, for instance, Acemoglu and Robinson

(2012) do in *Why Nations Fail* – risks missing all the virtuous circles that did not last until the present day and vanished for reasons unrelated to their virtue or prosperity.

Transitions from patrimonialism to modernity

Communes in Italy, the Low Countries, and France were merely enclaves in the context of feudal Europe where patrimonialism ruled and a true social contract based on a trust compact did not exist, only bonds between private parties based on personal loyalty in exchange for patronage: "corruption" scandals were mostly about cheating and dishonesty among private parties, as the public realm was still underdeveloped. The overarching word for infringement of public contracts of any kind was "fraud" (in Latin, *Fraus*), listed among bad governance practices (*malgoverno*) in the famous painted manifesto by Ambrogio Lorenzetti in the Palazzo Pubblico in Siena. The term "corruption" in both Latin and Tuscan at this time signified "decay" or "degradation."

The historical process of private–public separation was therefore lengthy, because the "public" part of the equation needed to be created from scratch. It was enacted first in the general law – even in feudal monarchies – and applied much later to other areas, such as finance and defense. The medieval kings of France financed wars from their own coffers or through loans from Italian financiers; the English kings ruined Florentine bankers with their defaults. Only when this central power lost control over tax farming and the sale of offices did something start to emerge resembling what we call corruption today. As long as the demand for offices surpassed the supply, conditions could be placed on bidders to fulfill certain competency criteria, and the funds they later collected could be regulated. When demand fell, however, criteria were relaxed and less competent or incompetent candidates began to fill these positions. They governed poorly and arbitrarily, resorting to extortion to cover their initial investments to purchase the office (Swart 1949: 92–94). It took nearly all of the Western European sovereigns using the sale of offices to finance wars time to realize that this was also a way to lose wars. In the eighteenth century, incompetent French and British officers who had bought their way into the army lost many battles in colonial territories before the practice of selling commissions was amended to involve consideration of competence. It took many private bankruptcies to promote the concept of public finance sheltered from a monarch's personal extravagance, just as it took heavy military defeat or the threat of defeat to bring about military reforms, such as merit-based promotions, in the Danish, Swedish, British, Hapsburg, and Prussian armies.

Initially, however, the sale of offices was a progressive act praised by Montesquieu, Burke, and Bentham – a way to open up offices previously held on the basis of privilege to new classes. This created an exit path from traditional feudal society into a new one where capital began to matter more than family. It was, in fact, a way to democratize access to power. The sale of offices and the financing of government through direct fees rather than taxes were stages in the development of the premodern state; it is questionable whether these could have been skipped altogether. Early modern society was very different from the feudal one, with a growing role for the state and a new ideology of government: Empress Maria Theresa and her son Joseph II had enlightened ideas, Edmund Burke advocated merit-based systems for the British abroad, the Federalists had read Montesquieu and Cicero, and so on. A great discrepancy existed, however, between new ideas and old realities: the first attempt by Louis XVI's minister Necker to render the budget transparent was greeted with public outrage, because the Court's expenses – part of public expenditure – seemed to the public both extravagant and exaggerated. By then the concept of public resources that needed to be managed in the common interest was already enshrined; this would have been inconceivable in medieval times. The French Revolution also introduced a clear separation between public and private. It took both a new ideology of public virtue that deemed patrimonialism obsolete and advocated for the enshrinement of ethical universalism as a norm, as well as an incontestable need to adjust the state to new challenges, to convert the European patrimonial monarchy. It seems in retrospect that the party of virtue would have remained marginal or in opposition if it had not become strikingly clear that the old system was leading to security disasters of enormous proportions in challenging new circumstances.

Denmark

The story of Denmark is most telling in this regard. Seeing that Pritchett and Woolcock (2004) considered "getting to Denmark" as the attainment of a perfect benchmark of good governance, it is highly relevant to understand how Denmark became Denmark. What might be regarded as a first set of control of corruption policies in Denmark was born with the creation of the absolute monarchy in the years following 1660. The king consolidated his position as the absolute monarch by centralizing power in Copenhagen and gradually replacing the traditional aristocracy in the crown administration (central and local) with new groups of bourgeois bureaucrats. Throughout the era of absolutism these civil servants were sworn in directly by the king, to whom they pledged loyalty and fidelity. As a general rule, non-noble civil servants did not have private fortunes and were reliant on the income from their public office, which led to a form of interdependence between the king and his civil servants (Frisk Jensen 2008). In 1736 the University of Copenhagen established a final examination in law, and over the course of the eighteenth century its graduates slowly took over bureaucratic positions, starting in the central administration in Copenhagen and gradually spreading to public offices at regional and local levels (Frisk Jensen 2008). In 1821 a law was passed making it mandatory for civil servants to have a law degree, thus formalizing a development that was already, to a large extent, a reality in public administration. Around the beginning of the nineteenth century, recruitment to the administration was fundamentally meritocratic (Feldbæk 2000: 318–26); only 10 percent of civil servants were nobles, primarily in the foreign service and diplomatic corps (Gøbel 2000: 103–07; Knudsen 2006: 66–71). The absolutist monarchy had succeeded in depriving the nobility of its political power, and later, inspired by the ideas of the Enlightenment, managed to build a fairly well-organized (by the standards of the time) bureaucratic state characterized by egalitarian norms.

This was done in a top-down manner in an effort to strengthen the state and make it able to cope with military challenges. *Defeat in war was the main incentive for good governance.* In 1658, as a result of military defeat, the Danish–Norwegian kingdom was forced to cede all the Scandinavian provinces east of the Oresund to Sweden, reducing the total area of the Danish–Norwegian kingdom by almost a third. This defeat also led to a political crisis in 1660 in which nobles were forced to transfer some of their power and privileges to the king, changing the form of government from an elective monarchy, dominated by the aristocracy, to an absolute monarchy. According to the New King's Law of 1665, the authority of the hereditary sovereign was unlimited. After a long period of peace and prosperity in the eighteenth century, Denmark became involved in the Napoleonic Wars. Denmark was an ally of France, so when France was defeated in 1814, Denmark was forced to cede Norway to Sweden. The cost of the war was immense; in 1813 the Danish state went bankrupt and the country was hit by a severe economic crisis. In the midst of a revolt in the duchies of Schleswig and Holstein, and shortly after the February Revolution in France in 1848, a public demonstration in Copenhagen demanded a liberal constitution. The Danish king responded by renouncing absolute rule, and by June 1849 Denmark had become a constitutional monarchy with a representative-elected government, separation of powers, and freedom of the press, religion, and association. The constitution also separated the private wealth of the monarch from the finances of the state (Frisk Jensen 2008). Control of corruption thus evolved through a succession of equilibria which took more than a century, as the modernization of the state by an enlightened despot was followed by a gradual transition to a more inclusive political society.

Great Britain

In Britain, the reform of sinecures and "old corruption" started in 1780, and the process of building a more impartial civil service was nearly complete by 1840. This was followed periodically by new waves of improvements (Cohen 1965). Electoral regulation reform also evolved starting in the early 1800s, culminating between 1868 and 1883. The main goal of these reforms was to prevent the vote from becoming a traded commodity, as it had been in the early years of British democracy. The integrity of the electoral process was ultimately delivered through a combination of a secret ballot extended beyond a privileged circle and very transparent and carefully audited election expenses, including spending ceilings. Unlike Denmark, where the monarch was the main principal of reforms, in Britain it was parliament and the local civil society that debated, investigated, and gradually adopted reforms to foster public integrity. An examination of records on electoral corruption in Britain in conjunction with reform proposals in parliament from 1868 to 1911 shows how the system shifted itself from generalized corruption to integrity and how central this debate was during the nineteenth century (Moore and Smith

2007; O'Leary 1962). Magistrates only accepted late and with great reluctance involvement in remediating electoral fraud claims, as they considered the issue to be far too political and a burden on the courts and their other primary duties. Thus, bilateral parliamentary committees investigated electoral fraud, and reforms were passed in agreement with parts of the opposition. State autonomy toward private interests was therefore reinforced instead of challenged during the process of political modernization, although both the extension of the franchise and the development of city governments brought about new opportunities for corruption.

France

There was also a Western revolutionary path, in which fairness of government was a central issue. The French Revolution was, to a large extent, an anti-favoritism revolution, directed more against *privilege* than against property as later Marxist revolutions were. The French Constitution of 1791 clearly stated that sovereignty "belongs to the nation. No segment of the people and no individual can appropriate it." Revolutionaries endorsed the principle of state impartiality in order to prevent a new capture by the absolute monarchy, yet the succession of regimes following the Revolution brought about anything but impartiality. In the ninetenth century administrative "cleansing" (*épuration*) initiated by the Revolution became the rule of the game in the relationship between political power and administration. Changes of regime in 1815, 1830, 1848, 1852, the great political turmoil of 1877–79, and 1883 were followed by a complete sweep of the previous administrations (Rosanvallon 1992: 77–79). Only a few technocrats emerged unscathed from these administrative overhauls. Appointing partisans to administrative positions assured that administrators would be loyal to the policies of leaders, whether elected or not. Civil servants did not swear an oath to the public interest, but to the party in power – a habit which persisted long into the twentieth century. While the nineteenth century saw a strong shift in public opinion against favoritism and particularism in general, the revolutionary path based on power and administrative overhauls did not prove conducive to the development of ethical universalism: patronage and political clientelism became resilient features. Rosanvallon (1990) cautiously saluted the arrival of the first impartial institutions beginning in the last quarter of the twentieth century. Politicization also became a motor of expansion for a public sector not driven by policy needs. The number of French civil servants has grown from 150,000 in 1815 to some three million today.

United States

The emergence of grass-roots political parties had a negative impact on the private–public separation in public affairs. In the era of small government in the United States, party machines provided services for the poor, the unemployed, and new immigrants. In such a way, party patronage allowed for the construction of mass-based parties; once responsibility for social services passed from parties to local governments, political participation declined steadily (Arnold 2003). The passage of the Pendleton Act of 1883, which introduced the merit-based system, was triggered by the assassination of President Garfield at the hands of one of his electoral campaign workers who was upset that he was not appointed ambassador as a reward for his service. The Act specified for the first time that "no person in the public service is … under any obligation to contribute to any political fund," and "no person in said service has any right to use his official authority or influence to coerce the political action of any person." The Act also gave presidents the authority to expand the number of positions covered by the merit system. Over the next two decades, presidents routinely expanded coverage, although under Lincoln nearly all positions were filled by political appointees. Had the law required from the beginning that *all* civil servants be tenured, it would have only provided incentives for infringements by the incoming party in power: this is the case in many countries today that have adopted instant "depoliticization." It took decades for the Americans to arrive at a merit-based, non-politicized civil service, although they did succeed in doing this before the French. Both the French and the American routes to universalism in governance, though fairly specific, were democratic from very early on, so they involved phases of intense politicization, public resources spoiling, and favoritism – challenges very similar to those facing today's middle-income developing countries. Why a few countries have managed to leave behind clientelism while many others have not is still a debated question (Piattoni 2001).

If modernization is the solution to favoritism in government, why is public corruption still so widespread today? And how do we explain the paradox of modernization actually *increasing corruption*, as Samuel Huntington (1968) noted, when we credit modernization with creating an impersonal Weberian bureaucracy and a state autonomous from private interest? There seem to be two main reasons. The first relates to political development: in the world at large it has been difficult to create a European-style situation in which the rule of law, autonomous bureaucracy, and political socialization of new groups are achieved *prior* to universal enfranchisement. Many countries today had free elections *before* achieving the rule of law and political accountability.

The second reason relates to the economy of public resources: compared to traditional communities, the modern state is entrusted with more management responsibilities and more public resources to achieve the nation's common goals. It may be freer of traditional privilege, more merit-oriented, and more objective, but it also has far more tasks to perform than people or traditional communities used to undertake before by themselves and far more resources as well. This creates numerous opportunities for those in power to use resources to favor particular interests – whether by legislation (Kaufmann and Vicente (2011) have written about "legal corruption") or administration (e.g., preferential allocation of transfers, subsidies, concessions, government contracts, etc.). There is no instrument or policy tool at the disposal of modern governments that cannot be used in a corrupt way, even without breaking formal legislation. The more instruments a government has and the more citizens entrust the government to manage their common welfare, the greater the harm that can be done if the state is captured by private interests. As criminologists say, opportunity is the initial reason for a crime to take place (Felson and Boba 2009).

The historical road to the contemporary state should not be seen as a linear progression toward less patrimonialism on the one hand and more democracy and accountability on the other. As welfare and development tasks shift from the community to government, there is an accompanying increase in corruption opportunities and a loss of traditional systems of self-control over common goods. This increase in opportunity subverts the control of society over its trustees and can result in defective state building. For instance, if new, nontraditional rulers prove unworthy of trust and divert resources entrusted to them for the common good, a regime based on competitive corruption results (Golden and Chang 2001) and people may respond by holding back the entrusted resources. The trust compact does not take hold and society retreats into informality, not paying taxes to predatory elites who collect from the many to redistribute to the few.

Historical origins of anticorruption "pillars"

In the influential Transparency International Sourcebook from 2000, "Confronting Corruption," Jeremy Pope developed the theory of "integrity pillars," key institutions within the state and society that should stand together to achieve control of corruption and whose absence or failure put it at risk (Pope 2000). The integrity pillars include: an elected legislature, an honest and strong executive, an independent and accountable judicial system, an independent auditor general (subordinate to the parliament), an ombudsman, a specialized and independent anticorruption agency, an honest and nonpoliticized civil service (bureaucracy), honest and efficient local government, independent and free media, a civil society able to promote public integrity, responsible and honest corporations, and an international framework for integrity. A list this wide ranging can only lead to equally broad anticorruption strategies, but because it does not suggest a dynamic of change – in other words, what puts what into motion – it is quite impossible to prioritize policies on its basis. Moreover, the clear specification of institutional design gives the illusion that adoption or establishment will lead automatically to control of corruption.

Although the performance of these institutions in contemporary times can be tested separately and will be undertaken in the next chapter, it is of great interest to understand their origins and the roles they played historically, as the institutions that are presently responsible for enforcing ethical universalism may not be the same ones as – or may only partially overlap with – those that originally helped this norm become enshrined. In other words, the explanation for the performance of historical achievers of control of corruption might not be found in their present constitutional and political frameworks, which may maintain rather than create control of corruption. A few historical examples might provide some answers to the question of the role played by some of the key "integrity pillars."

In the European communal government design, for instance, the role of the civil service or bureaucracy was far less important than in modern times, because government was based on conscripted citizens who filled offices as a civic duty (leading to incompetence in some famous Venetian battles); under absolute monarchies, bureaucracy was developed gradually to control aristocracies, so they played a strong role. In democratic contexts, such as France or the United States, bureaucracy was again not a factor in achieving control of corruption, but rather the result of arriving at this control by political means. Public jobs were much politicized and became a major resource for corruption; impartiality occurred extremely late. Even the British, who were the first to achieve a nonpoliticized bureaucracy, were still struggling with civil service reform in the years following World War II. The Chinese, who had been world leaders in promoting government by mandarins (bureaucrats during the imperial period), were unable to sustain it; by the early twentieth century they were thoroughly corrupt and a Civil Service Act copied from the British was adopted. The number of countries in the world where bureaucracies managed to achieve and preserve their autonomy against politically elected leaders are very few, and their strength came from other factors (the monarch, for instance, or their colonial source of authority versus locally elected politicians). In other words, where politicians and bureaucrats are by themselves at the advent of modernity, the spoiling system will prevail, and no autonomous bureaucracy able to develop and guard a state free of political capture will develop (Etzioni-Halevy 1989).

The development of an independent judiciary was a relatively recent occurrence in Western Europe. Britain was the leader, despite the fact that even today it retains a system of judicial appointments that can be seen as anachronistic. Two elements seem to have been necessary to bring about progress: the development of a legal elite with sufficient integrity, professionalism, and respect within society to be able to withstand political pressure; and the arrival at an equilibrium point where rulers had to surrender power over the judiciary (Neild 2002). Montesquieu's advocacy of a separation of powers found adherents from the American founding fathers to German liberals, but it was a challenge to implement. While the principle of equality before the law became an early part of the constitutional tradition in Denmark, Britain, the United States, and France, and a *Rechtsstaat* was a constant demand of liberals in nineteenth-century Germany, it was only in the twentieth century that judges managed to become truly independent. Moreover, issues of accountability and political partisanship have persisted until recently; in France and Italy, for example, a late battle between the executive and legislative powers after World War II has yet to end, and Germany needed a foreign military occupation to reinstate its *Rechtsstaat*. The independence of the judiciary is one of the most difficult of the control of corruption prerequisites to reach, because it requires a judicial elite (produced, starting in medieval times, by universities such as Oxford, Paris, or Bologna) on the one hand, and a situation of strong constraint upon rulers on the other. An independent judiciary did not lead to the historical development of control of corruption, but seems rather to have been *a result* of it, its development determined mostly by politics. As Stephen Holmes put it: "Law is a tool of power" (Holmes 2002). Bending power to allow independence of the law is necessarily a political act. Many, if not all, current rule of law programs fail because they lack – for obvious reasons – this political component and instead treat the development of rule of law as a problem of missing capacity and outdated legislation.

The office of an independent auditor subordinate to the (corporatist-based) legislature had strong roots in communal tradition, but was absent in modern monarchies. The auditor was the arm of the sovereign who checked on his subjects, not the arm of an elected legislature who checked on government. The office of the ombudsman can be traced back to an office created by Charles XII of Sweden in 1713 – although with intentions far removed from the nature of the institution in its later form. This office, denoted as the King's Chancellor of Justice, had the task of supervising officials in the exercise of their office while the King was in Turkish exile. But because the Chancellor had institutional loyalties, first and foremost to the king, the idea began to circulate that there was a need for an administrative post to supervise the government from a position of true independence (Bexelius 1967: 171). From these origins, the office of an independent ombudsman became anchored in the Swedish Constitution of 1809. It relies upon a reputation for impartiality and integrity, but formally has remarkably few powers: the ombudsman can make recommendations but cannot reverse decisions. He or she is to be granted unfettered access to all relevant documents, even if classified as secret; can initiate legal proceedings against officials who have erred in fulfilling their duties; and can petition the parliament to amend legislation.

Ultimately, the efficiency of this institution is dependent upon the existence of transparency, a concept whose origins lie in the same country and time period (Roberts 1986: 134; Samuelsson 1968: 120 ff.). The ombudsman and the principle of transparency were successful in Sweden because of demand from strong political challengers and public opinion sensitive to issues of corruption and abuse. In other words, there was a high demand for government accountability that reflected the existence of a powerful opposition challenging the existing equilibrium. Similar to judicial independence, these institutions were a *result* of specific historical Western transitions to control of corruption rather than their *cause*.

If this is the case with some of the main "integrity pillars" on the state side, let us consider briefly the "societal pillars": business, civil society, and the media. Here we find evidence for a more substantial historical role. In Sweden, Britain, and the United States, where freedom of the press was an early occurrence, anticorruption campaigns emerging from public opinion existed from fairly early on. These were not always perceived as such at the time, given that the media was wild as well as free, and a considerable amount of libel was also published. As a result of civil lawsuits, the media started to become more professional toward the end of the nineteenth century (although corrupt media has always continued to exist in parallel). Chapter 5 will return to an in-depth discussion of contemporary evidence of the importance of these institutions.

The role of business was similarly paradoxical. In Britain, starting from the time of the Scottish Enlightenment, it was manifestly the traders who constantly pushed for government impartiality toward private actors. This does not mean, however, that notorious companies such as East India were not doing exactly the contrary: extracting rents from the government and buying members of parliament – many of whose shareholders voted to use public funds to bail out the company from its difficulties. The situation was no different in the United States: while some corporations pushed for the government to step aside and let business develop without hindrance, many others developed due to privileged public–private partnerships. By and large, businesses promoted control of corruption mostly through their demands for fair, impersonal, and limited regulation, rather than by playing some direct role in anticorruption efforts. The heroes in the fight for ethical universalism were not, for the most part, businessmen; rather they were journalists, intellectuals serving as columnists and members of parliament, a handful of aristocrats, and many lawyers who, in the fight to redress particular injustices, actually promoted the greater cause of government fairness and impartiality. But the important lesson from this brief historical overview is that the adoption of institutions currently considered to be quintessential in the control of corruption followed changes in a power equilibrium – or threats to the existing one – that generated strong demands for better governance.

In lieu of a conclusion: three anticorruption orders

This chapter has described three different ways to control corruption, each from a specific society and its distribution of power. Under monarchical authoritarian regimes anticorruption is largely based on selective repression. Here, the breach of trust by "agents" is toward one "principal" (whose interest might be, but is not necessarily, equivalent to that of the "public"), repressed arbitrarily and violently. Anticorruption is used as a deterrent for other deviant individuals and as an instrument of political repression and loyalty enforcement. It seldom works, because under such regimes favor is officially allowed – it is granted discretionarily – creating thereby an incentive to keep on the right side of those in power, not of the law. This, of course, does not result in the rule of law per se. When Marshall Concini, the favorite of Queen Marie de Medicis of France, was assassinated, credit letters were found in his pockets, the value of which surpassed his official sources of income. The surplus was simply passed on to the assassins by King Louis XIII to reward them for removing his mother's favorite and thus consolidating his own power. There was no attempt to investigate Concini's extortions or to return the funds to their rightful source.[2]

Nevertheless, as European absolute monarchs needed to develop central, effective, rule-bound bureaucracies to confront challenges more effectively, they contributed to this one feature of modernity. The monarchies that survived the conversion to constitutional regimes seem to have enjoyed the most successful transitions from

[2] *Archivio di stato di Ferrara, Manoscritti, Corrispondenza Bentivoglio-D'Aragona.*

patrimonialism as well. It is not the same, however, if the authoritarian regime was not a traditional monarchy, but rather one where the autocrat is a self-appointed ruler. Such rulers need to build loyalty and find the resources to support them in power (and get rich) in the course of just one generation. Judging by World Bank good governance charts, enlightened despots still emerge with far greater frequency from traditional monarchies (Bhutan, United Arab Emirates, and Qatar are among the most successful recent evolutions to good governance) than from directly elected presidents (e.g., the Central Asian countries, Venezuela, Russia, and Colombia have all very poor ratings). A third of the world's best governed countries are traditional monarchies – mostly constitutional but not exclusively – and two-thirds of present monarchies rank in the top category of good governance. However, "Getting to Denmark" in the same way as Denmark got there – enlightened despotism followed by constitutionalism – is a minority option today, accessible perhaps only to a few Middle-Eastern, North-African and Asian monarchies. The rest of the world needs to struggle with a far greater collective problem than Denmark had to when building its control of corruption.

The next historical anticorruption arrangement, republicanism, has the elite as "principal." Under republican regimes, the breach of trust is already defined in relation to the public interest: emphasis is therefore on preventing particular interests from appropriating the state. All faction- and power-related privileges are repressed, and sophisticated community-based designs need to be created to prevent particular interests from taking more than their due. The collective action problem is successfully managed due to the limited size of the population and the corporate character of these societies, where everybody belongs clearly within some civil society grouping, ensuring the permanent surveillance of temporary governors. The elite is the trustee of public interest, but its interests in fact represent those of the broader society organized, in many respects, in support of them (Renouard 2009). The values that this elite builds upon, despite many Christian and humanistic touches, are in essence capitalistic values: the need to regulate human interaction through contracts and universal rules and to have a state able to enforce such contracts so as to allow for the pursuit of joint development.

Under the third scenario, representative democracy, where the size of both government and the citizenry increases exponentially, the solution chosen is the modern state (with the underlying presumption often unchecked that a modern society also exists). The state is entrusted to bureaucrats to manage in the public interest and to magistrates to repress deviance, but neither impersonal bureaucracy nor independent judiciary are easy to bring into being once political parties have power and create a *partitocrazia* (Sartori 1976), a highly politicized society ruled by political clientelism. Politicians seem the least suitable trustees for building control of corruption, as Renaissance anti-factionalist authors have always warned (Piattoni 2001). Parties are factions, and organized interests are supposed to be checked by one another and the state apparatus. At least, this is expected when modernization is accomplished.

It is also significant that good governance leaders mattered historically – be they medieval tradesmen, Renaissance lawyers, Scandinavian kings, American journalists, or British politicians. Human agency is then indispensable to progress in governance, and initial conditions, favorable or unfavorable, cannot fully account for a given state of governance. For instance, Denmark was a far less modern society than Britain at the end of the eighteenth century, and Finland was a rural society until very late – nevertheless both reached excellent control of corruption. But accepting that agency matters, how much does it matter? And what kind of agency is the right kind: enacting laws and ratifying treaties like UNCAC? Engaging in a revolutionary process? Liberalizing trade? Such questions require in-depth examination and testing, which is the focus of the next chapter.

4 *Structure and agency: determining control of corruption*

It is no easy task to find data and build explanatory models to disentangle a causal mechanism as complex as control of corruption, and the attempt must be approached with considerable caution. Still, the role of constitutional monarchy, island, human agency, or the state-society nexus can be statistically tested to complement our historical findings. The brief historical overview of how control of corruption came into being produced several findings that warrant further discussion, some of which can be tested. To further our understanding of how control of corruption actually functions or does not function, this chapter will resort to a large-N comparison method, wherein econometric methods will be used to test determinants of control of corruption across as many countries as possible (data allowing). Although an impressive amount of literature has already been produced to explain corruption by econometric means, discussing causality in governance is in general problematic due to the absence of time series data, dependent variables based on subjective data, reverse causality problems, and insufficient theorization (Fukuyama 2013; Rothstein and Teorell 2011; Seldadyo and De Haan 2006; Treisman 2007). The associations discussed in this chapter seek to expose in which contexts control of corruption is more likely to develop, addressing the reverse causality problem by reference to historical circumstances or policy context rather than statistical means. Where our theory and data sources are incomplete, application of advanced statistics alone is unlikely to produce more clarification, though theoretical statements of this work are clear and testable to a large extent. The most important problem remains the absence of a specific dependent variable to measure governance across countries, available for a longer interval of time and sensitive to change. In its absence, most causal models at the national level are based on expert scores, either one-source and nontransparent (like the most quoted work by Paulo Mauro (1995), based on Business Index, a risk score) or aggregated from various sources with different degrees of transparency (Corruption Perception Index, Control of Corruption). Another strategy explains corruption at the national level by creating a country average from individual survey responses, as shown in Chapter 1. Given the difficulty in producing robust and valid results, using only one dependent variable is likely insufficient. Testing has to draw on alternative sources of data, both popular perceptions (general population samples) and informed perceptions (businessmen and experts). The four main sources of data used in this chapter are thus the Global Corruption Barometer 2013 (111 countries), the Global Competitiveness Report (123 countries in the panel), the International Country Risk Guide (109–138), and the World Bank Worldwide Governance Indicator for Control of Corruption (CoC, 123–153 countries, subject to independent variables). Only results confirmed across all these datasets are considered robust and reported here. Bivariate tests are sometimes cited to explain a mechanism, but the tables included in this chapter only reproduce multivariate tests with all controls. Both cross-sectional and time series models are used; the former cannot be dispensed with as very little reliable data exists in time series. A description of all variables and scales used can be found in Appendix 2.

While many authors have tried to explain corruption, the vast literature on the subject can be divided into three strands. While other valid classifications exist (see, for instance, Lambsdorff 2008), I divide causality of good governance by its theory of change mechanism, be it assumed or nonassumed. Many governance scholars believe in a strong prevalence of structural factors, which explain why governance changes occur only incrementally and require important external shocks (financial crises, lost wars) for change to occur. A second group, which includes many practitioners in the anticorruption industry, believes in "institutional weapons," typically legal instruments that have performed in a few well-known cases – for instance the ombudsman in Sweden or the anticorruption agency in Hong Kong – and presume that such instruments act as brooms, sweeping out undesirable behavior. Finally, a third school exists that describes control of corruption as an equilibrium and sees the solution in a broader package of reforms, mostly economic.

In this chapter I shall first test structural factors or legacies – in other words, those factors that cannot be influenced by human agency at the beginning of a reform process. Two such factors were already advanced in the previous chapter: limited size and the presence of traditional monarchy. Many other factors come from modernization theory, which conceptualizes a political development process that is mostly society driven: certain conditions have to be fulfilled in a society for pluralism to advance (Lipset 1981), and in their absence rulers' predatory behavior remains unchecked (Moore 1966). Then I shall review the anticorruption instruments and formal institutional arrangements, used either in practice or discussed in corruption literature. Finally, all findings will be discussed in an attempt to draw them together in a theoretically meaningful model.

From structural factors to modernization models

Which structural factors seem to be more associated with control of corruption? Size (as in population) is not significantly associated with corruption today when all the states of the world are considered, although the previous chapter suggested that limited population might have played a historical role in enabling collective action. The majority of countries that have evolved to the upper scale of control of corruption in the last twenty years are, however, islands: two-thirds of island states are above the threshold of good governance, and half of the world's well-governed countries are islands. Most states that are not islands among the recent achievers tend to have small populations, such as Estonia or Uruguay.

Cultural homogeneity or cohesiveness is also reported to matter. For instance, ethnic or any form of sectarian fragmentation of a society creates more opportunities for corruption, since competition among particular groups and intragroup favoritism leads to systematic particularism and discrimination (Fearon and Laitin 1996). That finding was empirically confirmed (Mauro 1995) and still holds true with current data in bivariate regressions. In multivariate models with development controls, we find that metalinguistic and religious fragmentations are stronger determinants of corruption than ethnic fractionalization, but the mechanism remains the same. Fragmentation of a society into factions leads to competition to gain disproportionate benefits from the common state, thereby greatly favoring particularism based on ethnic, religious, or linguistic qualifications. The confusing use of the term "social capital" in the literature frequently blurs this result, which is nevertheless consistent with sociological theory. Trust can be based on either ethical universalism (i.e., we treat everyone the same and would trust and associate ourselves with anyone with similar ideas) or particularism (we associate with, cooperate with, and treat fairly only individuals with some particular tie to us, be it family, tribe, confession, network, and so on). Only the former should be called social capital, the second is closer to what Banfield (1958) called "amoral familism." The statistical associations are clear: where ethical universalism and universal trust are the guiding principle of human exchanges, we find control of corruption and development. Where trust is "high" only on particular grounds, we find systemic corruption and overall less benefit for society as a whole and thus less development. Both control of corruption and development seem to require the presence of ethical universalism and the objectivity it entails for a society to prosper.

The existence of natural and mineral resources have also been reported as being positively associated with corruption. Leite and Weidmann (1999) established a robust statistical relationship between countries' exports of oil and minerals relative to gross national product and the level of corruption for a sample of 72 countries. An abundance of natural resources earning substantial hard currency provides the opportunity for rent seeking. That finding is confirmed in cross-sectional analysis (for years 2008 and 2010) when regressing control on corruption on the indicator "Fuel exports as % of merchandise exports" (data available for 172 countries) and controlling for development. The effect of a "resource curse" over governance should be understood holistically as democracy, control of corruption, and political violence are all interconnected and affect each other (Karl 1999). Essentially, concentrated spoils are easier to grab than dissipated potential spoils (e.g., money collected from taxes), and thus, provide an irresistible incentive to competing spoilers. Botswana is notably the only case reported to have escaped it so far, though the degree of the "curse" varies greatly across countries. Timing matters, too; once a country – for instance, Norway – has reached historical control of corruption, the discovery of natural resources does not seem to affect governance negatively. Natural resources are, however, a major hindrance to the development of corruption control if discovered in the early stages of development, because they become a source of spoils and violent competition.

Finally, geography and living conditions have been favorite explanations for prosperity, although controversy exists regarding the evidence (Acemoglu and Robinson 2012). Where control of corruption is concerned, it would be easy to observe that, historically, northern countries seem to have performed better and it is they who spread their institutional standards throughout the rest of the world, as through the Commonwealth. The mechanism, however, is not altogether clear. We can presume either that the same geographical factors that favored prosperity and democracy in the north favored control of corruption also, or that the intermediation of one or the other of those two factors helped control corruption. That riddle is, however, something for historians, not econometrists! We know that in different historical periods, control of corruption was reached in other parts of the world – medieval Italy or Confucian Asia – but vanished due to the lack of sustainability of those regimes from causes unrelated to corruption. Recent achievers like Uruguay or Chile are clearly in the south.

Other "geographical" factors are combined with historical ones and do point to a certain geographical and historical path dependency. For instance, it is far more likely for a postcommunist Eastern European country to be corrupt when compared with the rest of the world (Sandholtz and Taagepera 2005). Clearly, proximity to the USSR increased a country's chance of being occupied by it at the end of World War II, and once occupied it was more likely to see the importation of the USSR's Communist institutions with their specific particularism. The cause of that was of course not simple geography but Communist social organization, which was far less modern than intended, creating in fact great power asymmetry, status groups, and the kind of economic shortages that make particularism thrive – all political regime factors. The same applies to postcolonial determinism. When testing on the CoC sample of 153 countries, a country is indeed more likely to have a lower control of corruption if it is a former colony; there is a geographical determinism in having been a colony. But the precise mechanism associating colonialism and corruption is still controversial or insufficiently studied (De Sardan 1999; McMullan 1961). Some studies, for example, reveal that British colonialism is actually associated with more control of corruption, not less (Treisman 2000). The discussion is far too simplistic, however, if reduced to econometric data. We know from the history of the British in India, for example, how complex the situation can be. It was the

British encounter with India that led to an explosion of corruption, involving the British Parliament at home as well as commercial and later colonial structures on the ground, but the Indian corruption scandal also awakened the need to build control of corruption on a universal scale. Comparing means of corruption control across all countries, the difference between former British, Dutch, and Spanish colonies is minimal. By and large, both in postcommunist Europe and in the former colonial world, there is enough variation in control of corruption to show that geographical-historical determinism, which is in fact a complex group of factors linked in very intricate mechanisms, can be overcome.

The next group of structural determinants is the one usually discussed in modernization theory. The classic modernization conditions that brought about political development in Europe and the United States were increased urbanization, the spread of literacy, diffusion of secular-rational norms, and an increase in individual autonomy and mobility (Lerner 1964; Lipset 1981). Modern societies are both urban and economically affluent, consisting of individuals who enjoy a significant degree of economic and political autonomy. Control of corruption is indeed significantly associated with most of these components of modernity. Low life expectancy, rural residence, and low average schooling (in descending order of explanatory power) all significantly increase the likelihood that a country will be corrupt (see Table 4.1). But since we already know that individual education does not discriminate between corrupt and noncorrupt behavior, the significance of education as a predictor of corruption must be elsewhere, in something that educated individuals as a group can perform, which would explain why countries with more educated people perform better. And this action aggregated in time seems to be the essential factor, otherwise when testing the impact of aggregate years of schooling in 1900 on control of corruption we should not find a staggering 70 percent explanatory power (Uslaner and Rothstein 2012), which indicates a long, complex determinism of the current governance regime. It also explains why governance evolution is so incremental and path dependent.

Table 4.1 shows that most components of modernity have an impact on control of corruption across all dependent variables: expert scores, public opinion surveys, and aggregate indexes. As proxies for material autonomy, I used internet and mobile phone subscriptions per

Table 4.1 ***Impact of modernization components on different corruption measurements***

VARIABLES	WGI Control of corruption	ICRG Risk of corruption	WEF diversion of public funds	GCB Perception of corruption of public officials
Adult literacy rate	0.03***	0.01***	0.01***	-0.00
	(0.006)	(0.003)	(0.004)	(0.004)
Constant	1.19***	1.70***	2.26***	3.66***
	(0.434)	(0.211)	(0.366)	(0.351)
Observations	142	109	106	79
R-squared	0.13	0.04	0.05	0.00
Adj. R-squared	0.13	0.03	0.04	-0.01
Rural population (% of total population)	-0.05***	-0.03***	-0.03***	0.00
	(0.007)	(0.004)	(0.005)	(0.003)
Constant	6.43***	3.65***	4.72***	3.25***
	(0.373)	(0.207)	(0.245)	(0.129)
Observations	188	137	132	102
R-squared	0.21	0.23	0.20	0.02
Adj. R-squared	0.20	0.23	0.20	0.01
Life expectancy at birth	0.15***	0.06***	0.07***	-0.02***
	(0.014)	(0.009)	(0.010)	(0.005)
Constant	-5.66***	-1.78***	-1.27*	4.52***
	(0.933)	(0.589)	(0.669)	(0.375)
Observations	181	138	133	103
R-squared	0.41	0.30	0.28	0.07
Adj. R-squared	0.40	0.30	0.27	0.06
HDI Education index	7.12***	3.14***	3.32***	-0.72**
	(0.634)	(0.387)	(0.498)	(0.281)
Constant	-0.09	0.62***	1.44***	3.89***
	(0.377)	(0.222)	(0.324)	(0.203)
Observations	186	136	133	102
R-squared	0.40	0.32	0.24	0.06
Adj. R-squared	0.40	0.32	0.23	0.06

Table 4.1 (*cont.*)

VARIABLES	WGI Control of corruption	ICRG Risk of corruption	WEF diversion of public funds	GCB Perception of corruption of public officials
Average years of schooling in 1900	0.95***	0.44***	0.45***	–0.12***
	(0.057)	(0.034)	(0.042)	(0.024)
Constant	2.82***	1.93***	2.70***	3.68***
	(0.228)	(0.133)	(0.167)	(0.089)
Observations	73	72	67	54
R–squared	0.70	0.61	0.56	0.30
Adj. R–squared	0.69	0.60	0.55	0.28
Mobile cellular subscriptions (per 100 people)	0.02***	0.01***	0.01***	–0.00
	(0.003)	(0.002)	(0.003)	(0.001)
Constant	2.34***	1.74***	2.38***	3.59***
	(0.268)	(0.173)	(0.256)	(0.154)
Observations	189	138	133	102
R–squared	0.21	0.13	0.15	0.02
Adj. R–squared	0.21	0.12	0.14	0.01
Internet users (per 100 people)	0.07***	0.03***	0.03***	–0.01***
	(0.003)	(0.003)	(0.003)	(0.002)
Constant	2.27***	1.66***	2.42***	3.68***
	(0.145)	(0.106)	(0.131)	(0.101)
Observations	181	133	133	100
R–squared	0.64	0.49	0.47	0.13
Adj. R–squared	0.64	0.48	0.47	0.12
Human Development Index	9.32***	3.90***	4.61***	–0.92***
	(0.685)	(0.449)	(0.552)	(0.305)
Constant	–1.67***	0.04	0.50	4.03***
	(0.432)	(0.281)	(0.373)	(0.220)
Observations	185	136	133	102
R–squared	0.51	0.38	0.35	0.08
Adj. R–squared	0.51	0.37	0.35	0.07

Robust standard errors in parentheses.
*** p<0.01, ** p<0.05, * p<0.10.

100,000 inhabitants, which proved to have great impact. The number of internet connections, which is strongly associated to control of corruption, is also a great proxy for modernization, as it captures both development (infrastructure) and education (computer literacy). As all modernity components are strongly correlated among themselves, to capture them together, one can use a composite index such as Human Development (HDI), which includes life expectancy, income, and years of schooling. By itself, HDI explains nearly half the variation in control of corruption across the 185 cases for which data is available – less than either internet connections or average years of schooling in 1900. In other words, if we know the degree of modernity of a society, we can predict to this extent how "corrupt" or free of corruption it will be. This reveals that limitations may exist for human agency in low development contexts, where a poor, dependent population is an easy victim for predators. The degree to which initial "structural" conditions are favorable to the development of good governance constitutes the "closeness of fit" of modernity as a predictor for control of corruption (Mungiu-Pippidi *et al.* 2011). Between half (HDI) and a quarter (average years of schooling in 1900 explains nearly three-quarters) of the variation is not, however, explained by path dependent factors, leaving some room for human agency (See Table 4.1).

The literature has made far less use of HDI (let alone the other modernization components) to test corruption, focusing mostly on income and its relation to control of corruption. Mostly equated with gross domestic product (GDP) per capita, income is indeed a significant predictor of corruption, but Kaufmann *et al.* (1999) and Hall and Jones (1999) question on good grounds the causal relationship between corruption and income. Two studies with panel data (Braun and Di Tella 2004; Frechette 2001) actually found that higher income increased corruption, especially when they imposed fixed effects. Such controversy shows not only the deficiency of quantitative approaches to complex problems, but also the need to find less controversial proxies – for instance, life expectancy or HDI – for development when explaining corruption. Similar controversy exists in relation to the impact of wage levels on corruption, with a number of scholars claiming that public sector wages matter (cf. Alt and Lassen 2003; Herzfeld and Weiss 2003; Rauch and Evans 2000; Van Rijckeghem and Weder 1997), while others doubt the significance of any relationship (Gurgur and Shah 2005; Treisman 2000). In fact, it makes little theoretical sense to test wages. In a poor society with very low wages in the public sector, corrupt behavior will always pay more. Underdeveloped countries cannot pay judges, customs officers, and members of parliament more than the amount they can make from corruption. Thus, the discussion of "incentivizing" people to be less corrupt should not refer to wages alone, for it makes no sense when an average bribe for a legislator or judge is far higher than the few dollars that might, exceptionally, be offered as a raise. Also, lack of income and its effect on corruption should be understood as a context, for it means that everybody – judges, clerks, lawyers, law enforcers, and witnesses – would all be "poor," with all the undesirable consequences and vulnerability to fraud and corruption that result from that. Poverty and great differences in income unbalance the so-called Schelling diagram, causing both corruption and assumptions about how corruptible people are given their material situation to lean toward the area where most people are engaged in corrupt transactions, whether that is belonging to patronage networks, exchanging favors, or taking bribes. This is exactly the development context the Human Development Index covers.

But the determinism of development is not absolute. Figure 4.1 shows the countries that overperform and underperform most in control of corruption given their levels of development. With the exception of Chile, Uruguay, and Costa Rica in Latin America and Estonia in Eastern Europe, all other countries in those two regions should be doing better in terms of control of corruption considering their developmental level. Turkmenistan, the country with the lowest HDI score (0.68) among the bottom five underperformers in Eastern Europe (Russia, Azerbaijan, Kazakhstan, and Ukraine being the rest), is closer to the levels of corruption registered in countries with significantly less development such as Myanmar (HDI = 0.48) and Afghanistan (HDI = 0.39). The model predicts that its level of development should place it closer to South Africa, a country that ranks in the 60th percentile for control of corruption. Russia is another peculiar case: with an HDI of 0.75, the model predicts a control of corruption score similar to that of Lithuania. Instead, Russia is closer to countries with an HDI of 0.5 such as Pakistan and Republic of the Congo. In the case of Latin America two of the five underperformers, Argentina and Mexico, have the second- and third-best HDI scores in the region, 0.79 and 0.77 respectively. In 2011 those two countries had a control of corruption

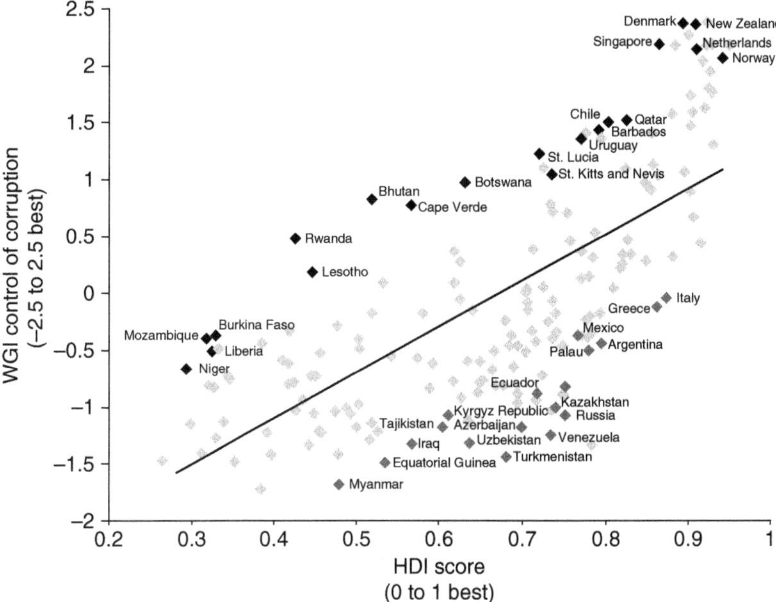

Figure 4.1 Predicted control of corruption scores based on the modernization model
Source: Worldwide Governance Indicators and United Nations statistics

score comparable to that of Burkina Faso, a country with an HDI of 0.33, although the model predicts a value closer to the control of corruption of South Korea. Figure 4.1 also shows that the model types of good governance (e.g., Denmark, Finland, New Zealand, or Sweden) are absolute overperformers. Despite their high HDI scores ranging from 0.88 in Finland to 0.91 in New Zealand, the linear regression predicts a control of corruption score equivalent to that of Estonia or Cyprus. These countries, however, are way above that score.

Such figures show that the modernity determinism of governance is far from absolute. Local history, notably human agency, matters greatly and can make the difference between an overperformer and underperformer. As Inglehart and Welzel (2009) argued, elites can perform better than population values (largely determined by the level of social and economic development) would predict. Development accounts for an important part of governance, but there is both a good governance dividend as well as a poor governance penalty that elites can incur. Overperformers such as the Scandinavian countries have managed better and responded more quickly throughout the global and EU economic crises due to superior governance capacity. In the lower part of the scale, really dramatic examples such as Syria, Congo, and the Central Asian states illustrate governance far below development level, stuck in a vicious circle of poor governance and underdevelopment.

Among indicators of a lack of modernity and predictors of corruption, informality deserves special attention. An informal economy is strongly associated with corruption and surfaces in models based on both national and individual data surveys (Johnson, Kaufmann and Shleifer 1997; Wallace and Haerpfer 2000). While nobody questions the correlation between corruption and an informal economy, the direction in which causality runs and its intricacies have long been controversial. Are the two phenomena complements (positively correlated) or substitutes (negatively correlated)? Is the Tunisian street vendor a victim, an accomplice, or a perpetrator? A context-sensitive answer was provided by Dreher and Schneider (Buehn and Schneider 2011; Dreher and Schneider 2010; Schneider 2007) who argue that shadow economies and corruption might be complements in developing (low income) countries, but substitutes (or unrelated) in developed (high income) countries. Highly developed countries are characterized by a low informal economy and low levels of corruption, whereas developing countries present a cluster of informal practices, particularism, and widespread tax evasion. Surveying change of these two variables over the last fifteen years for which data exists, some movement of the countries becomes noticeable on both variables within each equilibrium, but almost none between the two. The only countries that improved on informal economy (where there is far more considerable improvement than in controlling corruption, although also backslide) that also progressed significantly on controlling corruption are Estonia and Uruguay. A few other cases exist where positive evolution on corruption exists (e.g., Tanzania), but only within the lowest part of the scale, where no certainty exists they will ever reach the upper third.

The relation between informality and particularism therefore runs much deeper than the association made in developed economies between tax evasion and corruption, and it may well be that formalization policies (inspired by Uruguay or Estonia) are useful in building control of corruption as well. Successful modernization entails an important process of formalization, the integration of the many social contracts "out there" into one, "all-encompassing social contract" (De Soto 2002: 355). Societies become transparent, and thus modern, following a process of bargaining where individuals agree to pay taxes in exchange for access to certain public resources. That agreement does not exist in particularistic societies, as everyone is aware that allocation of public resources is not equal, which hinders the development of such societies. People hide from predatory elites to defend themselves; firms stay underground to "dodge the grabbing hand" (Friedman *et al.* 1999). In a neopatrimonial context, offering assistance to a regime to build tax-collecting agencies is often rather like helping predators extort more effectively from their victims (Von Soest 2007). This is why the few cases that progressed on corruption progressed also on informality, but not the other way around – progress on formalization is not a sufficient condition. The answer will be found in borderline countries such as Latvia, which registered progress on formalization but has yet to decisively enshrine ethical universalism, despite many years of effort.

The problem of reverse causality seems greater than ever in the relationship between informality and corruption as the influence is plainly reciprocal. However, history helps. Informality is a premodern legacy, associated with poverty and rural society. Public corruption is a later occurrence, coinciding with the growth of the state apparatus, the expansion of taxation and public services offered by the state. Informality does not recede gradually with development and can even grow due to poor economic policies and excessive red tape or restricted economic freedom once top-down modernization starts. Predatory behavior of rulers and bureaucrats only reinforces it. Control of corruption and the shadow economy are strongly associated in both cross-sectional and panel regression models, but their disentanglement remains a serious challenge: only a case study on historical state building similar to that by, for instance, Clifford Geertz (1963) on Indonesia can highlight the dynamic of this relationship. Informality feeds corruption and is reinforced by it. No sound anticorruption strategy would be able to dispense with some "formalization" strategy and vice versa.

Finally, political modernization has an equally complex relationship with the control of corruption. Modernization theory would predict that government accountability and control of corruption need autonomous citizens and a developed society able to demand their rights, and that is largely confirmed by the data. Democracy and control of corruption are positively associated (Treisman 2000), but mostly in older democracies, so the relationship does not seem linear: according to the World Bank's Database of Political Institutions, the older a democracy is and the older its main party the more likely we are to find that control of corruption will work (Beck *et al.* 2001). This indicates that experienced political elites are less predatory than new ones and have been socialized into more accountable behavior. The associations with personal autonomy (a score computed by Freedom House) or with the physical rights integrity index (Cingranelli and Richards 1999) are stronger. The personal autonomy index can by itself predict half of the variance in control of corruption; the physical rights index about a third. By contrast, the Legislative Index of Political Competitiveness (rating competitiveness of elections for 177 countries as part of the Database of Political Institutions) is a poor determinant. Property rights, either assessed by the Heritage Foundation or Economic Freedom of the World, are also strongly and positively associated with control of corruption. The association between the Freedom House-Polity 2 integrated democracy measure (pluralism on a scale from 1 to 10, where 10 is more plural) and WGI CoC is also significant, but not linear (Mungiu-Pippidi 2014). Moderate pluralism lowers control of corruption, although only by a small margin, and only countries with an advanced democracy (scores over 6) become increasingly associated with more control of corruption (Montinola and Jackman 2002; Sung 2004). In other words, what matters to a democracy in terms of control of corruption is not elections as one-time mechanisms for selecting between candidates, but rather the permanent capacity to ensure that whoever is elected respects individual rights, autonomy, and voice (Persson and Tabellini 2003: 173). In societies where particularism is the norm, political choice is actually reduced, and political parties do not differ greatly where decisions on social allocation are concerned. The parties are perceived as spoiling machines, as in the nineteenth-century model of James C. Scott, which explains why political parties lead in terms of perception, coming top in all corruption barometers (Scott 1969). Political parties seem a more highly evolved vehicle for organizing group benefit after family, clan, or tribe, but unlike those categories, they are a by-product of modernity and have learned to coexist fairly well with apparently modern organizations by informally draining them of their impersonal and objective character. The most widespread example is the politicization of public administration and the entire public sector (including hospitals and schools, where jobs are seen as party spoils). That explains the apparent paradox of democracies doing better at controlling corruption, although their main expressions, parties and legislatures are seen as the most corrupt – that is, as the most important contributors to the order of particularism.

Are all transitions from patrimonialism "unfinished modernizations," as not only Western scholars sometimes imply, but also reform-minded elites in those countries? Is every state "transitioning" toward a regime based on ethical universalism as part of some universal advance toward democracy, and is there certainty that they will all eventually reach it? In principle, countries that ratify the UNCAC effectively assume as much as a goal due to pressure from the international community, if not directly from donors. However, that does not mean that their governments and societies are in some state of transition to modernity, as understood as the massive norm change signaled by Samuel Huntington (1968). Rather, most of them are in a fairly stable equilibrium. They are not fair societies encompassing fully democratic political systems and mature markets, but neither are they undergoing a process of institutional change, nor have they significant groups pushing for change. Many developing countries have set up a superstructure of rational-legal administration, which nonetheless continues to rest on a deep foundation of patrimonial rule and particularistic behavior. The practice of modernization that is top-down driven thus creates a steady gap between an official norm and nominal goal on one side and the actual practices and rules of the game in a society. It is by no means certain that the gap can be filled by the simple passage of time if a certain type of agency does not occur.

Institutional determinants

While always assisting in some general modernization policies at the state level (e.g., civil service merit-based recruitment, administrative reforms, and support for a central auditing agency), the international anticorruption community has concentrated its efforts in past years on promoting specific international legislation against corruption and has pushed a few anticorruption tools for domestic implementation. An international normative anticorruption regime was gradually institutionalized with the adoption of the 1997 Organization for Economic Cooperation and Development (OECD) Anti-Bribery Convention. Several factors contributed, including norm entrepreneurs who raised awareness of the problem; strong advocacy from the United States, which was the first country to take action two decades earlier, thereby finding itself at a disadvantage in the global market once it had implemented the harshest regulations against overseas bribery; and the global explosion of democracy and information (McCoy and Heckel 2001). Over a span of less than fifteen years, policy and legal instruments were identified, agreed upon, and adopted en masse by numerous countries. Donors, consultants, and NGOs set out to implement the control of corruption agenda by selling a limited number of anticorruption instruments across the globe and by shaping the programs and budgets of development agencies accordingly. In the words of Peter Evans (2004: 30):

> Development theory has moved from a single-minded focus on capital accumulation toward a more complex understanding of the institutions that make development possible. Yet, instead of expanding the range of institutional strategies explored, the most prominent policy consequence of this institutional turn has been the rise of "institutional monocropping": the imposition of blueprints based on idealized versions of Anglo-American institutions, the applicability of which is presumed to transcend national circumstances and cultures.

The hope that the West's advanced institutions can be exported to the rest of the world in the same way that technologies can be transferred and put to use might seem patronizing today. However, it is worth recalling that this approach broadly worked in countries such as Japan, which embarked on its modernization path with a program similar to that of the West, determined in fact to beat the West at its own game. There was likewise a resurgence after 1990 of the belief – differently formulated than in earlier generations – that the "right" institutions can deliver development and that in their absence external aid does not work. That approach to institutional export is differently motivated, labeled, and marketed than was the case under colonialism, but its central belief – that societies can be modernized by outside intervention through institutional transplants to resemble the West more closely – remains in the end basically unchanged.

The contemporary approach seems no longer driven by imperialism, rather by convenience. Many donors are governments, so it is natural for them to advocate their own organizational style to the governments they assist or trade with in the hope that their assistance will generate better returns. Furthermore, good governance strategies based on knowledge transfers to other governments create a labor market for consultants from developed economies and can be easily packed into short-term programs. Anticorruption strategies anchored in domestic political dynamics are more politically sensitive, labor-intensive, and longer term, and therefore far less profitable for external consultants. An anticorruption industry quickly developed around this international anticorruption package and began to attract considerable funds while lobbying for more training and capacity building. But any assistance for progress has to have a theory of how progress is achieved. Although frequently this theory was implicit, its basis was the primacy of formal institutions. Given a "proper" formal institution, the informal one would catch up, and ethical universalism would come into being.

In his now classic book, *Comparative Constitutional Engineering*, Giovanni Sartori (1994) warned of the dangers of believing that formal institutions shape countries, showing that Latin American constitutions had not translated after many decades into anything comparable to democracy as known in the United States, their primary source of inspiration. Douglass North too was aware of local specificities, warning that "different institutional structures will yield different results" (Andrews 2008: 381). Furthermore, by copying the formal institutions of present-day Sweden or Denmark, "one-best-way" transfer models presume that the actual path those countries took to get where they are does not matter. "The good governance picture of effective government is not only of limited use in development policy ... It imposes an inappropriate model of government that 'kicks away the ladder' that today's effective governments climbed to reach their current states" (Andrews 2008: 402).

A few examples might help us understand better this "monocropping." The Council of Europe's Group of States against corruption (GRECO), a rotating peer review system, assesses individual European countries' anticorruption legislation and recommends that components of a universal repertoire of anticorruption measures be adopted everywhere, regardless of local circumstances. In 2004 it was Denmark's turn, which as discussed in Chapter 3 is generally considered to have one of the best quality governments in the world. GRECO (2009: 12) found Denmark's legislation imperfect on the grounds that it was a century old and was not used often enough for prosecutions (largely because it was an effective deterrent to corruption). Frequently the anticorruption industry seems to be driven by its own need to expand rather than by the needs of problem solving. Likewise, in spring 2012 the Australian government made the news for its refusal to implement UNCAC and adopt a single anticorruption agency as recommended by UN experts and a parliamentary committee, although the committee then stated that "there is very little evidence of serious or systemic corruption in the Australian public service" (Baker and McKenzie 2012). Australia's state anticorruption agencies (notably that of New South Wales) had been in the historical vanguard of successful control of corruption and the refusal of the Australian national government to change a system that worked well was perfectly justified – but it was badly received in the global trend of monocropping.

A reputable US-based NGO called Global Integrity (www.globalintegrity.org) – the work of which is funded by the World Bank and is an authoritative source of data for the US grant-giving Millennium Challenge Corporation – created an index that placed countries on a scale reflecting their institutional tools for fighting corruption. In 2011 they abandoned the index with little public explanation. The countries that had featured in the top five of the index in the previous two years were in fact extremely corrupt countries that had simply adopted more anticorruption instruments than anyone else – notably Bulgaria, Romania, and Macedonia, countries motivated by the need to show progress in their EU accession negotiations (Global Integrity 2010). Lambsdorff (2008) regressed the two measures of the Global Integrity Index, the legal framework and the actual practice, on Transparency International's Corruption Perceptions Index and the 2007 Global Competitiveness Report of the World Economic Forum (WEF) and found that only practice associates with better control of corruption. Too many laws can even make business people skeptical, as very often they are used as a cover for corrupt practices and are never really implemented. Global Integrity created a useful indicator called the "implementation gap" precisely from the difference between legal arrangements and practice, which in the cases of most institutionally "advanced" countries (where the international community's conditionality is stronger, like in the Balkans) can be higher than 50 percent, showing a major divergence between the "legal" country and the "real" country.

Assessments of the impact of this anticorruption repertoire on corruption levels around the world have not been very systematic. Some more work was done on the impact on economic prosperity of constitutions (Persson and Tabellini 2004), but the few existing assessments are all skeptical (Disch *et al.* 2009: 9):

> The literature can identify few success stories when it comes to the impact of donor-supported anticorruption efforts. Specialized anticorruption interventions have registered particularly little progress, although they represent the originally preferred approach because of the positive results attained by Hong Kong's Independent Commission Against Corruption (ICAC). That, however, hinged on strong political support, legal frameworks, and a court system that worked – the *will* and *capacity* to pursue corruption through *enforcement*. But it is the absence of exactly those factors that is seen as the key challenge in many countries.

As a partner in everyone's anticorruption efforts, one might have expected the World Bank to pursue a more systematic assessment effort, but a sobering evaluation by Huther and Shah in 2000 was not followed by much change in their operations. As an example, civil service interventions, such as training or public management toolkits, were found to be ineffective, but were continued despite no measurable positive effect. A 2011 World Bank evaluation was more general, but again pessimistic, declaring that since the World Bank supported only governments or other donors, its efforts could hardly be evaluated in isolation. Nevertheless, it did not identify any area of real impact, and the civil service was again singled out as an area with no potential for outside intervention (World Bank 2011).

Great hope among good governance consultants is invested in the reform of political institutions. The rationale for it, however, is unclear. In Italy, for instance, domestic agency has pushed for reforms of the electoral system several times in reference to corruption, but that did not prevent the country backsliding on CoC from 1996 (the first year of measurement) to the present despite *manipulite* and several electoral reforms. The mechanism of such persistence in reforming institutions with no proof of impact seems rather to be related to the external perception of such reforms. Passing a law or even amending a Constitution is simple and can be reported instantly as a successful reform, even if no real control of corruption follows. Persson and Tabellini (2004) have tested a good number of constitutional tools in a sample of ninety countries, finding only one robust effect, the magnitude of electoral districts (i.e., small districts are associated with more corruption), eventually combined with single seat constituencies, which they explain as a measure of open or closed entry into politics. Small districts are actually far easier to gain by patronage and clientelistic allocations, so they favor corruption, in comparison with larger ones that might require a more programmatic approach to electoral campaigning. In the larger country dataset, I was unable to find any significant relationship between electoral systems and control of corruption, testing different traits such as proportional versus majoritary systems, closed lists and the electoral thresholds. Reported results are mixed and controversial in the area of political reforms – particularly concerning federalism (Treisman (2000), for example, found it associated with corruption), decentralization, and electoral systems (Brown *et al.* 2005; Chang and Golden 2003; Kunicova and Rose-Ackerman 2005; Lederman *et al.* 2005; Park 2003). Generally, each of these papers covers only a limited number of countries and electoral situations, so the universality and robustness of their findings is uncertain. Another constitutional device without statistical evidence of its impact on control of corruption is the existence of constitutional courts.

One association that I did find in the dataset of 199 countries is that parliamentary systems are significantly associated with greater control of corruption with an average CoC score (recoded to a scale from 1 to 10 where 10 denotes the best performance) of 6.6 for parliamentary to 5.9 for other regimes. If the model is broken down by continent, Latin America in particular presents a robust relationship between presidentialism and corruption; however, the finding is not replicated in other regions. Persson and Tabellini (2003) too reported

Table 4.2 *The development of institutional interventions*

Year	UNCAC ratifications	Countries with FOIA	Countries with ACA	Countries with ombudsman
1990		15	12	47
2000		42 (27 new)	41 (29 new)	100 (53 new)
2008	145*	86 (44 new)**	98 (57 new)	135 (35 new)

*2003 to 2011 / **2010 data.
Hertie School of Governance database.

an association with presidentialism, although with some reservations. Keefer (2004) argues that what matters is a real effect of checks and balances, not how it is reached institutionally – just as long as one wielder of power manages to constrain the other. A measure in the Database of Political Institutions called Executive Constraints (scaled from one to seven) is indeed a very significant determinant of control of corruption – but rather than indicating a certain institutional tool, it indicates the outcome of a certain power balance at the top of a society, the extent of institutionalized constraints on the decision-making powers of chief executives. (Marshall and Jaggers 2002).

Assessments of the impact of various anticorruption interventions (ACIs) on corruption levels around the world have not been very systematic. To fill this gap, I focus on three distinct institutional efforts: the endorsement of freedom of information legislation/acts (FOIAs), the establishment of an anticorruption agency (ACA), and the creation of the office of ombudsman. While the adoption of UNCAC is relatively recent (2005), the other interventions have been around much longer – as such, their effect, or lack of it, has had more time to materialize. All of those tools have been promoted intensely by the international community, resulting in their importation by a large number of countries (see Table 4.2). FOIAs and ACAs have been adopted on a massive scale since 2000; an ombudsman was more popular as an accountability tool between 1990 and 2000, following democratic revolutions. The final result, however, is a virtual explosion of institutional imports all around the world.

Freedom of information is recommended by a growing body of treaties, agreements, and donor action plans. The FOIA clauses are included not only in anticorruption treaties, but also in agreements on environmental protection and natural resources management, as well as in a number of international human rights treaties and regional conventions (Banisar 2006: 8). UNCAC also recommends a variety of measures aimed at improving transparency as a means to fight corruption (Article 10 on "Public Reporting" and Article 13 on "Participation of Society"). Additionally, the Universal Declaration on Human Rights (Article 19) and the International Covenant on Civil and Political Rights both require that every person has the right to free expression and to seek and impart information. Among recently written constitutions from countries in transition (in Central and Eastern Europe as well as in Latin America), most include a provision on access to information (Mungiu-Pippidi *et al.* 2011). Additionally, a number of countries with older constitutions (e.g., Finland, Norway) have recently begun amending their constitutions to include a right of access to information (Banisar 2006: 17).

The establishment of a dedicated anticorruption body has been one of the main institutional recommendations in anticorruption conventions to date. The international community became the major proponent of ACAs, persistently recommending their creation as an important piece of a country's institutional architecture and its large-scale anticorruption strategy. ACAs were promoted by several conventions on the control of corruption – UNCAC, the African Union Convention, the Inter-American Convention, the Convention of the Council of Europe – as well as by the EU during its enlargement process.

While the UNCAC does not mention the ombudsman's office in the repertoire of anticorruption measures, this accountability tool is promoted by donors and by Transparency International as a measure to control corruption. The role of the ombudsman has mostly been related to making administrative law simpler for "aggrieved persons" wishing to challenge government actions in courts (Brown and Head 2004: 5). However, the ombudsman's mandate of protecting citizens from abuse directly addresses favoritism and lack of transparency. Even though nowadays "the mandate of the ombudsman generally goes beyond corruption cases and includes instances of maladministration attributable to incompetence, bias, error, or indifference that are not necessarily corrupt" (UNDP 2005: 14), cases exist where the ombudsman is given a mandate to investigate corruption complaints directly and takes on the role of an ACA (e.g., Philippines and Papua New Guinea). In any case, as guarantor of an accountable, impartial, and fair government, the ombudsman as an institution should contribute to better governance through improvement of government accountability (Mungiu-Pippidi *et al.* 2011).

All these tools have been promoted intensely by the international community since the 1990s, resulting in their implementation by a large number of countries. Thus their effect, or lack of it, has had enough time to materialize and can be tested empirically. Such tests can range from simple means of corruption or corruption change across the two categories of countries (those that adopted the institution and those that did not) to more complex means. To test the impact of the respective institutional intervention on control of corruption, I basically define an adoption of an intervention as a "treatment" that some countries implemented during the sample period while some countries did not, and estimate the average causal effect of this "treatment" on the evolution of control of corruption. That is, I exploit differences in control of corruption scores before and after the intervention within the group of "treated" countries as well as these differences across the "treated" and "non-treated" (i.e., control) groups. In particular, I estimate the following equation:

$$CoC_{it} = a_i + b_t + \beta ACI_{it} + \gamma' X_{it} + \varepsilon_{it} \quad (1)$$

where the subscript i refers to countries, while the subscript t refers to years. a_i and b_t denote country and year fixed effects, and ε_{it} is the usual unobservable error term. CoC_{it} stands for a country's control of corruption score in a given year from the WGI database, and ACI_{it} refers to one of the three anticorruption interventions (i.e., FOIA, ACA, and ombudsman). It is a dichotomous variable, which takes the value of 1 in the years after the adoption of the respective intervention and 0 otherwise, i.e., in the "treated" countries before the adoption and in the "control" countries during our entire observation time span, which covers the years 1996–2011. Hence, β is our main coefficient of interest.

Some anticorruption interventions are implemented at the end of the sample period. Taking into account that these policies require some time to have an effect, I consider only those interventions as "treatments" if I have observations for at least three years following implementation. For example, in Uruguay FOIA was adopted in 2009. Therefore, this country is considered in the sample as never having implemented FOIA, i.e., this country's *ACI* dummy takes the value of 0 during the entire observation period. By contrast, Peru adopted

FOIA in 2003. Therefore, this dummy takes the value of 1 from 2003 onwards for this country, and 0 from 1996 to 2002.

Finally, X_{it} is a set of time varying control variables. It includes the value of the natural logarithm of real GDP per capita to control for differences in the level of economic development between countries. To take into account the potential problem of reversed causality, I consider the one-period lagged values of this variable. In addition, I also control for the influence of press freedom, physical integrity rights (to capture the degree of political power discretion), revenues from natural resources, and executive constraints from the Polity IV database.

Certainly, evolution of control of corruption might be influenced by other processes, such as large-scale governmental reforms, which are not captured by X_{it} and might coincide with implementation of anticorruption instruments. Large political reforms are usually concentrated locally as well as at certain time points. I thus include in eq. (1) an interaction dummy between regional and year fixed effects in order to capture changes in control of corruption that might arise due to some time and regional specificities. Furthermore, effects of ACIs might be different across countries with respect to their initial level of corruption. Therefore, I also control for this type of country heterogeneity by interacting the first observation of *CoC* in the sample period with the corresponding *ACI* variable. Since the consequences of ACIs might also be different in developed relative to developing countries, I also report estimation results obtained from using a sample of only middle- and low-income countries.

The bivariate regressions show that neither of the tested anticorruption interventions has a positive significant effect on control of corruption. The presence of an anticorruption agency is even associated with a deterioration in the control of corruption (see Appendix 4). When controlling for additional factors that influence control of corruption, the partial effect of the respective intervention might turn out to be more promising. Yet Table 4.3 shows that the results are again sobering: Overall there are no significant differences in performance between countries that adopted FOIA and those that did not, nor between those having an ombudsman or an anticorruption agency and those that did not.

Of course, our context-sensitive theory of governance would not have expected much impact to start with. Is there an alternative explanation for why these popular interventions seem to work so

Table 4.3 *Impact of anticorruption interventions on control of corruption: multivariate regressions*

	All countries			Middle- and low-income countries		
Variables	1	2	3	4	5	6
FOIA	-0.029			-0.07		
	(-0.74)			(-1.38)		
FOIA x Initial CoC	-0.103***			-0.174***		
	(-2.67)			(-2.71)		
(ln)GDPPC (-1)	0.16	0.189	0.205*	0.299**	0.317***	0.306**
	(1.21)	(1.48)	(1.69)	(2.49)	(2.65)	(2.58)
Fuel Rents (% GDP)	-0.003	-0.003	-0.003	-0.002	-0.003	-0.003
	(-1.34)	(-1.47)	(-1.46)	(-0.99)	(-1.17)	(-1.13)
Executive Constraints (0–7 best)	0.025*	0.024*	0.023*	0.026**	0.024*	0.023*
	(1.94)	(1.87)	(1.76)	(2.09)	(1.94)	(1.8)
Freedom of the Press (1–100 best)	0.004**	0.004**	0.005**	0.003*	0.003*	0.004**
	(2.15)	(2.04)	(2.37)	(1.89)	(1.73)	(2.23)
Physical Integrity Index (0–8 best)	0.026***	0.026***	0.025***	0.024***	0.026***	0.024***
	(3.46)	(3.45)	(3.06)	(2.91)	(3.14)	(2.78)
ACA		-0.058			-0.068	
		(-1.57)			(-1.57)	
ACA x Initial CoC		-0.088**			-0.118***	
		(-2.48)			(-2.74)	
Ombudsman			-0.011			-0.079
			(-0.17)			(-1.06)

Table 4.3 (*cont.*)

	All countries			Middle- and low-income countries		
Variables	1	2	3	4	5	6
Ombudsman x Initial CoC			–0.107			–0.194**
			(–1.64)			(–2.51)
Constant	–2.530***	–2.389***	–0.354	–2.646**	–2.741***	–2.975***
	(–4.64)	(–4.61)	(–0.26)	(–2.31)	(–3.35)	(–3.02)
N	1916	1811	1795	1489	1404	1403
Countries	153	144	142	128	120	119
Adj. R-squared	0.96	0.96	0.96	0.9	0.9	0.9

Ordinary least-squares (OLS) regressions covering a sample period 1996–2011. The dependent variable is "control of corruption" from WGI. By country, clustered standard errors are used; t statistics in parentheses: *p<0.1, **p<0.05, ***p<0.01. All regressions include country and year dummies as well as year dummies interacted with regional dummies.

poorly? A part of the answer is, certainly, that these measures simply capture the presence of the respective ACI without taking into account country-specific peculiarities of these institutions. In particular, these estimations do not contain any information about the actual effectiveness and enforcement of the rules resulting from the existence of these institutions. Beyond comparison across countries, they could certainly be evaluated by means of second generation indicators. If we had full procurement data as in Hungary and diagnose what the norm of allocation is on a yearly basis, we could certainly evaluate interventions with a before-and-after approach. It is clear that in the case of Hong Kong the anticorruption agency worked. But there is no certainty even in countries where it is reputedly active. The European Commission in Brussels, for instance, has praised Romania's anticorruption agency since 2007, while a Eurobarometer survey in 2012 found two-thirds of Romanians believe corruption had actually worsened in that interval (Mungiu-Pippidi 2013b).

National circumstances shape, however, the effectiveness of similar institutions. For example, Doig *et al.* (2005) acknowledge that context is the essential element for the success of an anticorruption agency. Other works warn that ACAs can be effective tools only when they respond to national consensus and are supported by a broad domestic coalition (Heilbrunn 2004: 2) and they should not be created without a "systematic assessment of the local (political) context," for there is a risk that they could use their special powers to engage in a witch hunt against political opponents rather than genuinely pursue anticorruption goals (Meagher and Voland 2006: 5). The same logic certainly applies to the installation of an ombudsman. Implementation of FOIAs in turn is based on the view that the provision of greater transparency is an effective tool in the fight against corruption. Yet the evidence on the role of transparency in fighting corruption has been mixed so far (see, e.g., Bac 2001; Islam 2006; Kolstad and Wiig 2009). Moreover, there is some anecdotal evidence suggesting that a successful FOIA goes hand in hand with strong civil society and citizen activism. For example, Kocaoglu and Figari (2006) show that implementation of FOIA was poor in countries where the law was adopted as part of a top-down government reform plan (e.g., Albania), as an international initiative (e.g., Bosnia), or as a result of lobbying from civil society elites (e.g., Peru). By contrast, in counties where civil society coalitions pressed for access laws (e.g., Slovakia, Romania, and Bulgaria), the resulting legislation, even if far from perfect, was used as a weapon for disclosure by civil society, journalists, and members of the general public alike. Monitoring in Bulgaria and Romania already showed that by 2006 more than 50 percent of requests filed elicited the information sought (Kocaoglu and Figari 2006) and that NGOs were winning spectacular litigation cases against government in court, forcing disclosures that led directly to accusations of corruption (SAR 2011).

The lack of (especially time series) data that properly captures the strength of civil society makes it difficult to validate the above argument in a more systematic way.[1] Nevertheless, employing an indicator on social openness as a proxy for an active and open society, I also want to provide at least some systematic evidence of this relationship. In particular, I use the so-called KOF index on social globalization provided by Dreher (2006), which is based on objective data on personal contacts (telephone traffic, foreign population, international tourism, etc.) and information flows (internet users, trade in newspapers, etc.). A higher value of this index implies a larger degree of social openness. I interact this index with the dummy variable that captures the presence of FOIA in a country and include the resulting interaction term in eq. (1). For the sake of completeness, I repeat this exercise for the remaining anticorruption instruments. Table 4.4 presents the corresponding estimation results. Although the isolated effect of an FOIA is significantly negative, the influence of the corresponding interaction term is significantly positive, implying that the presence of an FOIA has a positive effect on control of corruption if it is implemented in a society with a higher degree of social openness. The effectiveness of two other ACIs is not affected by the inclusion of social openness and remains unchanged relative to the previous results.

In conclusion, this review of the impact of favored anticorruption interventions, tested alone or with development controls, suggests that a country does not progress simply because it imports an institutional tool – or, indeed, all of them – *when state and society actually operate largely by particularism*. These results do not mean that outliers do not exist, nor that such tools are ineffective everywhere and in every

[1] Using the number of civil society organizations, Mungiu-Pippidi *et al.* (2011) confirm the hypothesis that the interaction between transparency and activism from civil society exerts an effect on control of corruption in a cross-sectional empirical analysis.

Table 4.4 *Impact of anticorruption interventions on control of corruption: interaction with social openness*

	All countries			Middle- and low-income countries		
Variables	1	2	3	4	5	6
FOIA	−0.264**			−0.269**		
	(−2.29)			(−2.20)		
FOIA x initial CoC	−0.160***			−0.196***		
	(−3.41)			(−2.83)		
FOIA x social openness	0.005**			0.004*		
	(2.10)			(1.79)		
(ln)GDPPC (−1)	0.149	0.179	0.202*	0.271**	0.285**	0.273**
	(1.14)	(1.41)	(1.7)	(2.21)	(2.33)	(2.22)
Fuel rents (% GDP)	−0.002	−0.003	−0.003	−0.002	−0.002	−0.003
	(−1.26)	(−1.35)	(−1.38)	(−0.91)	(−1.05)	(−1.03)
Executive constraints (0–7 best)	0.025**	0.023*	0.022*	0.025**	0.023*	0.022*
	(2.03)	(1.82)	(1.73)	(2.1)	(1.85)	(1.75)
Freedom of the press (1–100 best)	0.004**	0.004**	0.005**	0.004*	0.003*	0.004**
	(2.11)	(2.07)	(2.41)	(1.95)	(1.82)	(2.27)
Physical integrity index (0–8 best)	0.028***	0.027***	0.025***	0.026***	0.027***	0.025***
	(3.71)	(3.59)	(3.11)	(3.14)	(3.29)	(2.86)
Social openness (1–100 most open)	0.004	0.006	0.004	0.007*	0.009**	0.008*
	(0.92)	(1.51)	(1.06)	(1.77)	(2.16)	(1.94)
ACA		−0.055			−0.071	
		(−1.46)			(−1.57)	

Table 4.4 (*cont.*)

	All countries			Middle- and low-income countries		
Variables	1	2	3	4	5	6
ACA x initial CoC		–0.083**			–0.115***	
		(–2.38)			(–2.67)	
ACA x social openness		–0.001			0	
		(–1.20)			(–0.07)	
Ombudsman			–0.014			–0.079
			(–0.21)			(–1.04)
Ombudsman x initial CoC			–0.1			–0.178**
			(–1.58)			(–2.24)
Ombudsman x social openness			–0.001			0
			(–1.58)			(0.29)
Constant	–0.247	–0.666	–2.582***	–2.968**	–3.500***	–3.418***
	(–0.18)	(–0.46)	(–5.27)	(–2.42)	(–3.09)	(–3.03)
N	1915	1810	1794	1488	1403	1402
Countries	153	144	142	128	120	119
Adj. R-squared	0.96	0.96	0.96	0.9	0.9	0.9

OLS regressions covering a sample period 1996–2011. The dependent variable is "control of corruption" from WGI. By country, clustered standard errors are used; t statistics in parentheses: * $p<0.1$, ** $p<0.05$, *** $p<0.01$. All regressions include country and year dummies as well as year dummies interacted with regional dummies.

context. But they do warn strongly against over-reliance on an institutional toolkit and a mechanism of change based solely on imports of formal institutions. It may be that an institution such as the ombudsman might have more impact if reformed along the lines of FOIA – that is, entrusting it to the "losers" of corrupt arrangements, making them the implementers and stakeholders rather than subordinating it to parliaments or governments, with the attendant risk of their being just as likely to be part of the problem. What is ultimately needed is not a nonexistent silver bullet, but rather *a better alignment of tools with contexts, in particular with already existing human agency in favor of change*. Few institutional weapons are effective as autopilots, for they need active agents to put them to use in order to achieve success.

Equilibrium models

Despite an exponential increase in work on corruption since the mid-1990s– only the last in a series of phases with the topic throughout the twentieth century, followed by as many episodes of fading from academic attention – the field remains divided between micro-theoretical models and macro-empirical models at the country level, with much confusion and no real communication between individual, organizational, and national level. This muddle is directly responsible for the poor performance of anticorruption, showing that a simple increase in funds and human resources resulting in a whole new assistance industry is insufficient in the absence of a unitary theory linking these levels and explaining why a certain governance context first comes into being and then eventually changes. Not only is the disconnect between these levels of analysis a serious impediment, but so too is the absence of time series data which would allow a theory of governance change to develop. There has simply not been enough change since 1984 when The PRS Group started measuring corruption risk to allow valid inference, and older expert scores are even less reliable (additionally, PRS had a methodology change, making even their time series corruption risk measure to some extent debatable). But change did take place in the twentieth century. Some first generation achievers of good governance continued to evolve during this interval, with, for example, the Americans and the British cleansing urban politics of corruption, the French gradually depoliticizing administration, and certain British colonies such as Australia and New Zealand laying the foundations of an accountable independent government. All those developments cannot be captured except by qualitative methods, as we have no quantifiable dependent variable. As to the sequence of modernization and good governance, grass-roots demand, and top-down reforms, of this we do have knowledge enough to inform a theory of change, if not to test it.

The most insightful research question was asked by Samuel Huntington (1968) when he wondered why the modernization process increases rather than decreases corruption. Indeed, if modernity is the quintessence of good governance with its build-up of a critical mass of enlightened citizens, accountable politicians, and trustworthy magistrates, why does the process of "getting there" itself look such a critical mess? Huntington suggested that the answer lies in the transition process between new norms and the old social order, with disputed access to resources for new groups never fully consented to by old elites, leading to the development of informal strategies of social mobility, or, in other words, corruption as a shortcut against old privilege. Public corruption emerges indeed from many development studies as a catchword for the lack of the institutionalization of a market economy and democracy in transition societies (Wallace and Haerpfer 2000). Modern rational-legal bureaucracy has the advantage of being less discriminatory than systems founded on personalized exchange relationships. In Weber's terms, it creates a better investment climate and thus encourages economic development (1976: Ch. 22, 30), which makes for the mantra of "modernization policy." Many developing and transitional countries have set up such rational-legal administration superstructures, but particularism continues to be the rule. Modern impersonality and objectivity, which lie at the basis of behavior in the public domain including market transactions, do not necessarily emerge in every case, which is why control of corruption has come to be seen by economists such as Acemoglu and Robinson (2012) as the major problem of development.

Modernization, as Huntington saw, does not bring about only increased constraints on the behavior of rulers with the *political* modernization process (reducing power distance in societies, excepting twentieth-century totalitarian systems), but also something else. The increased role for the state to fulfill all new functions called for the serious growth of public resources (and therefore potential spoils).

Historically the two processes seem to have developed in opposite directions (Mungiu-Pippidi 2014). As political discretion decreases and people become citizens in the modern sense, endowed with civil and political rights, potential spoils grow in time due to the state's scope growing (at least until the neoliberal austerity policies of the late twentieth century), as people begin to pay higher taxes than before to finance a state that takes an increasing number of tasks upon itself. In the middle and below the intersecting point we find the only equilibrium area where corruption is controlled, as the two factors balance one another. The increase in potential spoils is brought about by modernization in all its forms, including Communism: from communization (nationalization only brings more spoils to the class above the law capturing the state) to decommunization (noncompetitive privatization offers rulers great opportunities for spoiling). Furthermore, the reduction of power discretion is anything but guaranteed. Even in countries that hold elections, the accountability of rulers remains for many electoral cycles more of a desire than a reality.

In other words, conditions for control of corruption at the advent of modernity were not uniformly good. Only a handful of Protestant and to a lesser extent Catholic societies enjoyed widespread literacy at the advent of modernization to ensure some foundation for accountability.

Corruption at the individual level has been attributed, as have other criminal activities, to individuals' weighting of the expected costs and benefits of their actions in a given context and making their decisions on how to act "not because their basic motivation differs from other persons, but because their benefits and costs differ" (Becker 1968: 176). Following Becker, other macro- and micro-level studies of corruption have advanced the idea of control of corruption as a balance between resources and costs (Aidt 2003; Becker and Stigler 1974; Huther and Shah 2000; Klitgaard 1998; Nye 1967; Rose-Ackerman 1999). When costs are low and opportunities are high, it is rational for individuals to be corrupt; especially if those around them behave similarly. Most individuals just follow the existing rules of the game rather than dissenting (Della Porta and Vannucci 1999; Karklins 2005). But that structure of opportunities and penalties can eventually change, as winners and losers cannot go on eternally in a sustainable way. Even if that seems an insurmountable obstacle to change, dividing public resources always to the advantage of spoilers and managing to buy off eventual dissenters is sustainable only when unlimited resources exist (for instance, spoils from natural resources can be spread widely in exchange for political support through what are known as "clientelist" policies). It seems therefore that governance evolves only incrementally and can be described as a series of equilibria.

The understanding of corruption as an equilibrium was already pioneered by World Bank scholars, first by Robert Klitgaard (1988: 75), then later developed at the macro level by Huther and Shah (2000) as resources versus costs. Klitgaard, whose work is also associated with some successful anticorruption at the city level in Latin America, proposed this formula:

> Corruption = Monopoly + Discretion - Accountability
> (C=M+D-A)

Corruption emerges when someone has monopoly power over a good or service, has the discretion to decide who receives it and how much they receive, and is not accountable. The solution too seems to derive from there: by reducing or carefully regulating monopolies, curtailing official discretion, and enhancing transparency (Klitgaard 2000) – thereby increasing the probability of being caught. There is only one problem if this model is considered in a given governance context, which is that the principal who should enforce all this against the unruly agent is seldom there. A hero like Klitgaard's Filipino reformer Justice Efren Plana is not easy to find, and many of the policies he should enact would be above his hierarchical level, meaning he risks being replaced if his actions jeopardize the profits of the ruling party or dictator. Corrupt contexts often look like pyramids of extraction, with those on top extracting maximum rents. Huther and Shah (2000) tried to get around the problem by qualifying governance contexts as institutionally strong, medium, or weak. But creating thresholds between those categories is equally difficult.

The ideal model to explain control of corruption should be an equilibrium model without a principal–agent perspective. What we need to explain is corruption simply as a result of constraints imposed by society as a whole, which cannot prevent opportunities for undue profit being taken advantage of – either by the spoiling national leader or the tax-evading peddler. What such a model would measure is the collective capacity to enforce governance based on ethical universalism, any deviation from it creating social loss and discrimination. Empirical literature has, in fact, ample evidence to support such a model, although the idea of this holistic approach to a causal model was advanced only recently (Mungiu-Pippidi *et al.* 2011). Factors could be grouped as follows:

Under opportunities or *resources*:

- Discretionary power resources due not only to monopoly, but also to privileged access under power arrangements other than monopoly or oligopoly – for example, status groups (Weber 1968), negative social capital networks (Olson 1965), and social orders, cartels, etc. (North *et al.* 2009).
- Material resources, such as state assets and discretionary budget spending, foreign aid, natural resources (resource curse), public sector employment, preferential legislation to influence markets (Johnston 2006), and any other resources that can be turned into spoils or generate rents.

Under deterrents or *constraints*:

- Legal constraints, supposing an autonomous, accountable, and effective judiciary able to enforce legislation, as well as a body of effective and comprehensive laws, with control agencies able to monitor their implementation.
- Normative constraints, which imply that existing societal norms endorse ethical universalism and permanently as well as effectively monitor deviations from that norm (through public opinion, media, civil society, critical citizens/voters, etc.). For effective sanctions we need a population of autonomous and critical citizens capable of collective action, not a mass of citizens merely conforming to the corrupt rules of the game.

Control of corruption or its antithesis, particularism, could thus be summarized in the following formula:

Control of Corruption = Constraints (Legal + Normative) –
Opportunities (Power Discretion + Material Resources)

This equilibrium formula can be tested empirically and offers a more complex picture, not only of the individual causes of corruption (or even categories of factors), but also of their interaction, which allows for a better understanding of why certain policy combinations work and others do not. All elements of the formula can be affected by human agency. Resources, for example, are not an absolute given; they can be manipulated by policy. Administrative discretion, which is a major resource for corruption, can be increased by discretionary regulation and red tape and decreased by transparency; many anticorruption policies focus on that area.

Resources can include a variety of items: for example, natural resources in state property, foreign aid (Easterly and Levine 1997), discretionary expenditures, public jobs, public contracts, preferential bailouts, subsidies, loans from state banks or any form of monetary rents, preferential concessions and privatizations of state property, and market advantages in the form of preferential regulation. Opportunities are a mixture of resources and the discretion to allow them to be used for rent creation. In bivariate models economies based on fuel or aid are indeed associated with greater corruption, but in more complex models direct material resources lose their significance – they seem to be a "curse" only in very poor, dependent societies, which in itself is problematic and increases the responsibility of Western donors or companies acting in such environments. Government investment in capital formation is a stable finding on the small number of countries on which such data exists (Mungiu-Pippidi *et al.* 2014). Countries that spend more on "projects," either in the EU or in developing countries, tend to exert less control over corruption.

Some economists have argued that government intervention in the economy only creates resources for corruption. Vito Tanzi (1994), for example, suggests that government intervention in free markets creates rents and leads to a sharp rise in corruption payments. Several papers on trade agreements and aid present evidence that control of corruption is associated with more economic freedom, less regulation, and more competition (Ades and Di Tella 1999). Kaufmann (1997) tests the relationship between an indicator of regulatory discretion and corruption and finds a strong correlation in a small sample of developing countries. Power discretion is actually a robust determinant of corruption whatever the proxy used, but proxies such as economic freedom (i.e., indices of either the Fraser Institute or Heritage Foundation) and red tape (World Bank Ease of Doing Business) are especially robust.

Power discretion has already been tested in this book, finding that individual autonomy and physical and property rights are positively associated with control of corruption. Husted (1999) tested a more specific "power distance" measure – the extent to which less powerful members of society expect and accept unequal influence – and found it positively associated with corruption. That finding greatly supports the idea that social conformity allows power discretion in societies dominated by particularism, but such surveys exist for only a limited number of countries. The ideal proxy for power discretion would be a direct measure of power inequality or power status which would allow a direct test of Weber's theory. Survey questions do exist where people are asked if the "same people hold power and privilege regardless of changes in government" or if "people are equal before the law," which could provide useful proxies, but such questions are infrequently and unsystematically asked.

The association of control of corruption with economic freedom and low levels of red tape illustrates how power and material resources interact: for instance, rulers promoting regulations that only increase their discretionary power or create resources for their own further spoiling. Discretionary regulation offering opportunities for extortion can be promoted under any regime – by a group of parties just as well as by a dictator. Thus, proxies for political determinants become insignificant when tested simultaneously in the model. The equilibrium model should not, however, be understood in terms of separate variables or even groups of them, but as a complex mechanism in itself. More discretionary resources in the hands of a corrupt government only increases corruption, but once the equilibrium is reached where corruption is controlled, it is possible that if more spending were dedicated to welfare, social trust would be increased and play a very positive role (Rothstein and Uslaner 2005; Tanzi and Davoodi 1997). It is not the volume of government spending, but rather the discretion over spending that matters. Since all variables are interconnected and some basic modernization factors influence many of them, a path model would be needed to illustrate their relationships. Figure 4.2 suggests such a model.

Constraints, on the other hand, have to be seen as societal constraints to be truly independent of the core cause of particularism, which is inequality between power resources resulting in uneven access to public rents. In other words, the government should not be expected to constrain itself through an autonomous bureaucracy. The autonomous bureaucracy developed historically as an answer to a principal–agent problem, generally when absolutist monarchs needed to broaden their taxation base or improve their tax capacity: where its birth was

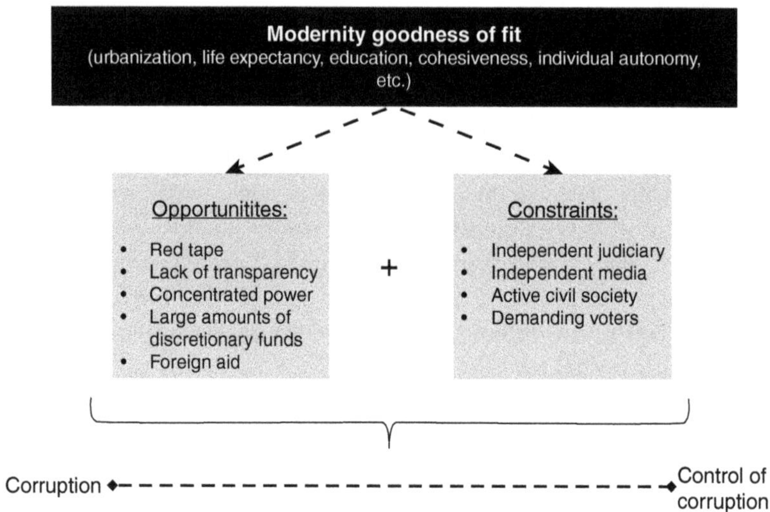

Figure 4.2 Theoretical path model of control of corruption

ulterior to democracy, as in the United States or France, the problem of bureaucratic corruption was more persistent (Heidenheimer 1996). The existence of an autonomous bureaucracy is so much part of the definition of control of corruption that it should be considered to be part of the dependent variable and not a truly independent factor if we are to avoid the vicious circle of "when the solution is the problem" described by development scholars (Pritchett and Woolcock 2004). In corrupt countries bureaucracies are entirely part of the problem through politicization, nepotism, or patronage. Could the same argument be made for the judiciary? Only to a limited extent; there exists the principle of separation of powers for judiciaries, presently enshrined in most constitutions, which does not exist for bureaucracies and which matters both in constitutional and practical terms (recruitment, dismissal). A bureaucracy, regardless of how it is organized, exists to implement a government's will, so in the end it is prevented from being truly "autonomous." The judiciary is there to control government, and few governments still have direct appointment powers. Of course, the government has other tools to prevent the judiciary from censoring it; nevertheless the distance is greater than in the case of bureaucracy, and factors besides the government also intervene in shaping an autonomous judiciary (Neild 2002).

A judiciary might be independent, but still corrupt: a good performance measure of the judiciary must look at its capacity to perform impartially and effectively, not just its independence (for instance, tenure). We find a strong association, as expected, between control of corruption and autonomy of the judiciary, an expert score compiled by the World Economic Forum (conceiving independence from private as well as political interests). That score is a highly significant and robust determinant of control of corruption, and the significance of the judiciary performance has been previously reported (Ades and Di Tella 1997; Ali and Isse 2003; Broadman and Recanatini 2000; Brunetti and Weder 2003; Damania *et al.* 2004; Herzfeld and Weiss 2003; Leite and Weidmann 1999; Messick 1999; Park 2003). However, due to the high degree of discretion involved in its activity, the judiciary remains in practice one of the most difficult areas for external donors to treat, so there is a great distance between its significance and some meaningful recommendations (Fukuyama 2004).

Any model explaining control of corruption – no matter how carefully built and tested – is bound to be reductionist. Figure 4.2 suggests that the broader development and stability context influences nearly all factors in the equilibrium equation (in other words, proposes a theoretical model like a two-story building) and can, in turn, be influenced by many of them in the long run. This model is a simplification: within the two stories a complicated path model is to be found, raising major issues of endogeneity for statistical tests. The "equilibrium" model thus builds on the modernization model, but takes a further step in tracing the intermediate variables by which modernization acts and allowing for all its factors to be influenced by policy. I exclude therefore purely historical determinist factors, such as former colony or Communist country status. Still, its empirical validation proves challenging. The complex associations of variables make it difficult to find clearly distinguishable indicators for each of them. As a result, serious colinearity problems may arise. In addition, the absence of time series data for appropriate indicators renders such an empirical path model hardly feasible. On the other hand, a simplified cross-sectional model may also raise potential endogeneity problems. Table 4.5 proposes, however, a parsimonious model that is robust across three different measures of corruption (CoC aggregate score, WEF business survey, GCB general population survey) and where no colinearity problem was found.

As proxies I used:

- for power discretion, the score of physical integrity rights;
- for administrative discretion, the ease of doing business (also, services offered as e-government and other transparency indicators, economic freedom, economic globalization index);
- for factionalism, ethnic fractionalization;
- for material resources, any indicator on the abundance of natural resources. Other indicators can be the amount of spending going into procurement (this data is difficult to find for many countries; for EU-28, where data is available, the respective variable is significantly associated with control of corruption) or amount of assistance funds as percentage of GDP;
- under legal constraints, the expert score produced by the WEF on judicial independence;
- under normative constraints, the determinants tested were press freedom, civil society (measured in simple numbers of civil society organizations (CSOs) per 100,000 inhabitants), internet access (signifying the presence of well-informed and therefore potentially critical citizens), and social globalization index.

The parsimonious cross sectional "equilibrium" model (see Table 4.5) proves to be robust across the three dependent variables and highly significant, and to have high explanatory power while controlling for development as well as regional differences.[2] Power discretion, both administrative and political, turns out to be significant, but material resources lose significance in more complex variants of the model. On the constraints side, civil society, press freedom, and the existence of enlightened citizens (newspaper readership, internet connections) positively influence control of corruption. In particular, press freedom and civil society have previously been reported to be significant by Brunetti and Weder (2003); Grimes (2008); and Mungiu-Pippidi (2010; 2012). Legal constraints (independence of the judiciary) are also highly significant.

[2] When using the GCB measure on corruption as a dependent variable, regional dummies are not included because of the limited sample size. Furthermore, models IV–VIII additionally control for the effect of the squared term of the freedom of the press score due to its nonlinear relationship with the respective corruption indicator.

Table 4.5 *Equilibrium cross-sectional models*

	WGI Control of Corruption			WEF Diversion of public funds (1–7 very uncommon)			% of GCB respondents who consider public officials corrupt	
Variables	Model I	Model II	Model III	Model IV	Model V	Model VI	Model VII	Model VIII
Physical integrity index (0–8 best)	0.095***	0.095***	0.099***	0.086***	0.086***	0.094***	0.259	0.263
	(4.6)	(4.59)	(4.46)	(3.1)	(3.04)	(2.95)	(0.22)	(0.22)
Judicial independence (1–7 best)	0.391***	0.389***	0.305***	0.718***	0.716***	0.668***	–4.130**	–4.114**
	(14.17)	(13.75)	(7.66)	(14.65)	(14.47)	(11.86)	(–2.05)	(–2.03)
Ease of doing business rank (1–183 worst)	–0.002***	–0.003***	–0.003***	–0.003**	–0.003**	–0.004**	0.095*	0.096*
	(–3.00)	(–2.87)	(–3.52)	(–2.02)	(–2.06)	(–2.25)	(1.68)	(1.68)
Ethnic fractionalization	–0.022	–0.048	–0.038	0.015	–0.03	0.046	12.82	13.15
	(–0.15)	(–0.28)	(–0.27)	(0.08)	(–0.15)	(0.22)	(1.65)	(1.45)
Freedom of the press (1–100 most free)	0.005**	0.005**	0.004*	–0.036***	–0.035***	–0.028**	1.135**	1.128**
	(2.07)	(2.14)	(1.69)	(–3.44)	(–3.44)	(–2.39)	(2.24)	(2.14)
Freedom of the press (squared)				0.0002**	0.0002**	0.0002	–0.011**	–0.010**

Table 4.5 (*cont.*)

	WGI Control of Corruption			WEF Diversion of public funds (1–7 very uncommon)			% of GCB respondents who consider public officials corrupt	
Variables	Model I	Model II	Model III	Model IV	Model V	Model VI	Model VII	Model VIII
				(2.12)	(2.09)	(1.4)	(−2.14)	(−2.06)
CSOs per capita	0.005**	0.005**	0.003	0.008**	0.008**	0.009***	−0.322**	−0.322**
	(2.58)	(2.54)	(1.64)	(2.56)	(2.52)	(2.82)	(−2.26)	(−2.24)
Internet access (per 100 people)	0.007***	0.008***	0.010***	0.005**	0.007*	0.006	0.117	0.107
	(4.14)	(3.49)	(3.8)	(2.12)	(1.91)	(1.66)	(0.99)	(0.7)
Natural resources dummy	−0.109	−0.1	−0.121	−0.159*	−0.144	−0.132	6.217*	6.078
	(−1.32)	(−1.18)	(−1.60)	(−1.67)	(−1.47)	(−1.30)	(1.72)	(1.63)
HDI		−0.192	0.448		−0.317	−0.601		2.386
		(−0.48)	(0.77)		(−0.57)	(−0.85)		(0.11)
Asia and the Pacific			−0.037			−0.232		
	(−0.19)				(−0.91)			
Eastern Europe and the Baltics			−0.486***			−0.516***		
			(−4.18)			(−2.73)		

Former Soviet Union			−0.294*			−0.148		
			(−1.74)			(−0.58)		
Latin America			0.0214			−0.343		
			(0.14)			(−1.50)		
The Caribbean			−0.684***			−0.728**		
			(−3.35)			(−2.51)		
Middle East and North Africa			−0.094			−0.11		
			(−0.64)			(−0.48)		
Sub–Saharan Africa			0.196			−0.373		
			(1)			(−1.30)		
Constant	−2.277***	−2.150***	−2.207***	1.516***	1.697***	2.119***	31.42*	30.1
	(−12.39)	(−6.12)	(−5.31)	(3.36)	(2.87)	(2.99)	(1.67)	(1.38)
Countries	123	123	123	123	123	123	85	85
Adj. R–squared	0.9	0.9	0.93	0.88	0.88	0.89	0.44	0.43

OLS regressions using data for 2010. GCB data is for 2012. Data on CSO numbers and ethnic fractionalization stems from 2008 and 2001, respectively. Robust standard errors are used; *t* statistics in parentheses: *p<0.10, **p<0.05, ***p<0.01.

Table 4.6 *Panel regressions*

	All countries				Middle– and low–income countries			
Variables	RE	RE	FE	FE	RE	RE	FE	FE
Physical integrity index (0–8 best)	0.056***	0.056***	0.053***	0.049***	0.048***	0.046***	0.050***	0.046***
	(5.03)	(4.8)	(4.46)	(3.85)	(4.24)	(3.7)	(3.88)	(3.17)
Freedom of the press (1–100 most free)	0.006***	0.008***	0.002	0.004	0.005***	0.007***	0.002	0.005**
	(3.69)	(4.03)	(1.22)	(1.47)	(2.95)	(3.33)	(1.27)	(1.98)
Social openness (1–100 most open)	0.019***	0.015***	0.009**	0.006	0.012***	0.011***	0.013***	0.012**
	(8.17)	(5.11)	(2.18)	(1.56)	(5.81)	(3.56)	(3.14)	(2.5)
Economic openness (1–100 most open)	0.006***	0.007***	0.006**	0.007***	0.005**	0.006**	0.005**	0.007**
	(3.29)	(3.23)	(2.61)	(2.67)	(2.58)	(2.54)	(2.15)	(2.09)
Natural resource rents (% GDP)	–0.073**	–0.068*	–0.083**	–0.089	–0.073**	–0.064*	–0.068	–0.058
	(–2.37)	(–1.79)	(–2.03)	(–1.59)	(–2.41)	(–1.81)	(–1.62)	(–1.04)
Rural population (% of total)		–0.005*		–0.002		0.001		0
		(–1.84)		(–0.28)		(0.44)		(0.02)

Tertiary school enrollment (% of total population)		0		−0.001		0		0.002
		(−0.13)		(−0.51)		(0.09)		(0.65)
Constant	−1.667***	−1.373***	−0.964***	−0.779	−1.377***	−1.541***	−1.331***	−1.525**
	(−12.19)	(−4.73)	(−4.37)	(−1.43)	(−10.25)	(−5.68)	(−6.53)	(−2.36)
Observations	724	525	724	525	559	384	559	384
Countries	148	137	148	137	121	111	121	111
R–squared (overall)	0.72	0.71	0.69	0.69	0.49	0.47	0.47	0.45
R–squared (within)	0.12	0.12	0.13	0.13	0.15	0.17	0.15	0.17

The dependent variable is "control of corruption" from WGI. The data sample consists of three-year averages covering 1996–2011. Clustered standard errors by country are used; *t* statistics in parentheses: * $p<0.1$, ** $p<0.05$, *** $p<0.01$. All regressions include period dummies.

As mentioned above, in order to test the model predictions with time series data, we have to use different indicators compared to those that have been used with cross-country analysis due to the lack of availability of certain variables. Therefore, the estimation models presented in Table 4.6 introduce two new indicators that have not been used in the previous analysis and are part of the KOF Index of Globalization, provided by Dreher (2006). One is a measure of the degree of economic globalization, capturing freedom of trade as well as financial openness. The idea behind the use of this indicator is that the less restricted the economic transactions of a country with the rest of the world are, the less room there is for administrative discretion and, more generally, red tape. The second indicator measures the degree of social openness that I have already used as a proxy for an active and open society in Table 4.4. The data covers the years 1996–2011 and a sample of 148 countries. I use three-year averages to account for the persistence of institutional indicators and apply two standard estimation methods for panel data analysis: a random effects model and a fixed effects model. The latter is used to additionally account for potential effects of country-specific unobserved time invariant factors such as political culture, tradition, etc. I include indicators for rural population and education to control for the effect of development, because HDI data is not available annually. Furthermore, since the results might be driven by the inclusion of developed countries, columns (5) to (8) repeat the estimations from the previous four models considering only middle- and low-income countries. Overall, the panel regression models explain more than 70 percent of the differences in the level of control of corruption in the total data sample, most of which, however, result from cross-country rather than time variation (which suggests that causes determining the evolution or change in control of corruption are different to causes explaining why it is sustained or why at a given moment in time certain countries enjoy it and others do not). The general findings are consistent with those obtained from the cross-sectional analysis. In particular, the results show that high power discretion and dependency on natural resource revenues tend to determine poor control of corruption. By contrast, more economic openness (allowing freer competition) and greater "normative constraints" (captured by the degree of social openness as well as press freedom) positively influence control of corruption.

The factors in this model can interact to create equilibria at various values, so only individual assessments can diagnose a specific country and find remedies; no universal silver bullet exists. Indeed, if the norm is not ethical universalism, then the specific term "anticorruption" might even be inappropriate in itself. What is needed is complex state building and deep democratization; empowering the losers under current institutions; the upsetting of the current equilibrium and the achievement of another, superior equilibrium. Cases such as Uruguay, Costa Rica, Estonia, and Georgia prove that this is possible.

A forecast based on this model would imply that change in governance order can occur only gradually and by a succession of radical actions and disequilibria until a new equilibrium is achieved with better control of corruption. That explains why so few success stories exist, and why they seem to result more from domestic agency and broad reforms than from typical anticorruption efforts focused on repressive agencies.

In conclusion, control of corruption in a society has to be understood as a complex balancing act rather than as a group of separate factors determining corruption. Therefore anticorruption efforts cannot be effective unless they are contextual – in other words, adjusted to the real equilibrium level (in which particular transactions are either the exception or the norm). If particular transactions are widespread, anticorruption efforts also need to be comprehensive to affect more than one element of the equilibrium and radical and strong enough to affect the balance and thus trigger disequilibrium. Finally, human agency matters. In a context where particularism is the rule of the game, anticorruption needs to involve both state (e.g., fiscal transparency) and society (watchdog NGOs) in order to influence both sides of the formula. It also needs to be grounded among those who oppose the institutional status quo (genuine "principals," who lose out under power inequality and corruption) and cannot be simply conceived as top-down "reforms" driven by nobody's interest in particular.

5 Understanding contemporary achievers

The search for control of corruption determinants across present countries and historical achievers has so far returned some pieces of a very complex puzzle to their rightful place. It is time now to pursue this investigation across the last set of cases in this book: contemporary achievers. To what extent do countries that have progressed since World War II seem to replicate the paths taken earlier by historical achievers? To what extent is the contemporary equilibrium described in the previous chapter discernible in and relevant to these new evolutions?

Examples of recent achievers are not only hard to find, but are rarely agreed upon. What may appear from the outside as a significant achievement for a country in controlling corruption is seldom perceived as such by the people living there. The sustainability of these achievements is also difficult to judge. How many years, electoral cycles, or favorable corruption ratings are needed before a country is considered to have passed the point of no return into sustainable control of corruption (assuming such a point exists – Italy is one example of back and forth movement)?

In the case of the oldest "contemporary achievers" such as Chile or Botswana, it has long been perceived that they are faring better than their neighbors. Even in these cases, however, more recent evolutions are not entirely positive. It is hard to suppress pessimism even in relation to the most successful examples of transitions to control of corruption, and locals always remind external researchers that definitions of "success" when it comes to corruption control are mostly based on the views of foreign experts with a pro-market and pro-business bias. It is difficult not to agree with them when considering Rwanda, which has risen in all World Bank charts to a level superior to Bulgaria and Romania, but whose last presidential elections returned the incumbent with 95 percent of the vote and whose government party owns companies bidding on public contracts (and winning many of them)

(Bozzini 2014). Or Qatar, an equally impressive fast riser in governance charts, engulfed in allegations of bribery to win a tender for the next FIFA World Cup and which has only recently separated the public budget from that of the royal family (Khatib 2014). The post-2000 editions of Transparency International's GCB also illustrate pessimistic and distrustful majorities in nearly all the world's new democracies. Only people in a handful of northern European countries strongly believe their governments have the will to and actually control corruption effectively.

Bearing in mind these widespread subjective reservations and the general absence of significant progress on control of corruption, evidence does exist, however, of some positive developments. The remainder of this chapter investigates the transition to control of corruption in such countries with the aim of identifying changes that explain each country's improvement. The time frame for this analysis corresponds to the most recent period of democratization in each country, although information about previous periods is sometimes provided.

The choice of this particular group of countries was driven by three criteria: first, the case had to be classified in the upper third of all countries on the World Bank CoC scale *or* a regional achiever doing significantly better than its region/continent or its modernity goodness of fit (see Chapter 4); second, the country had to be an electoral democracy; and third, the country had to have achieved its control of corruption in contemporary times, particularly during the last twenty years overlapping with the control of corruption agenda. The Worldwide Governance Indicators (WGI) Control of Corruption indicator was used as a reference for the first criterion, as it is the score that includes most available sources on all countries; the Freedom House Political Rights score was used as a reference for the second criterion; and International Country Risk Guide (ICRG) and Business Index scores (which have fewer cases, but longer time series) was used for the third. The choice to study only countries with some degree of pluralism leaving aside the handful of authoritarian achievers like Singapore, United Arab Emirates, or Qatar is justified by the following reasoning: countries where rulers are above the law do not qualify as ruled by ethical universalism even if they have managed to control bribery and build well-performing bureaucracies and business-friendly environments. Enlightened despots can exist and have existed: once in place, their choice of good governance reforms is clear if they want to emulate "the king of Denmark." Policy expertise cannot, however, influence the rare occurrence that *makes* a despot enlightened: the challenge remains in building control of corruption by democratic means, therefore by solving collective action dilemmas.

The group of "achievers" thus selected is highly varied, encompassing Estonia and Georgia in Eastern Europe, Chile and Uruguay in Latin America, Botswana in Africa, and South Korea and Taiwan in Southeast Asia. Despite regressing after the economic crisis of 2008–09, Slovenia is above the cut-off threshold in Eastern Europe. In Asia, Japan has the best and oldest control of corruption. Apart from these countries, this case selection leaves aside very few cases that have reached control of corruption through a democratic process over the past two decades (mostly small islands in the Caribbean and Africa, such as Barbados, Cape Verde and Mauritius, and tiny kingdoms in Asia like Bhutan). This group of achievers, however, includes two cases – South Korea and Georgia – that are both still below the designed cut-off for the first criteria described above (65th percentile in control of corruption), despite improvements in recent times. These countries qualify due to their superior performance in relation to their region as a whole, but should be considered borderline cases rather than achievers. The evolution of these eight countries over the period 1996 to 2011 is shown in Figure 5.1. Chile is on top with a score better than the United States, France, or Austria (ranked 1 in Latin America), followed by Uruguay (ranked 2), Estonia (ranked 1 in the Eastern European region), Botswana (1), Taiwan (2, after Japan), South Korea (3), Georgia (1 in the former Soviet Union), and Slovenia (ranked 2 in Eastern Europe, after having held first position originally).

How do these achiever cases compare with the rest of their continent, and what enabled them to outperform other countries? This analysis follows a three-step methodology. I first analyze how well these countries fit the modernization model and the model of regional (continental) corruption,[1] comparing the country's performance against the continent as a whole. I then examine briefly the dynamics of the

[1] The continental model of control of corruption is a variant of our equilibrium model (control of corruption as main dependent) using countries on only one continent. Although these models have smaller N, using the continent and not the entire world population has two advantages: it allows for new variables to be introduced (for example, data from the Afrobarometer or other regional surveys), and case selection provides another way of controlling for continental factors.

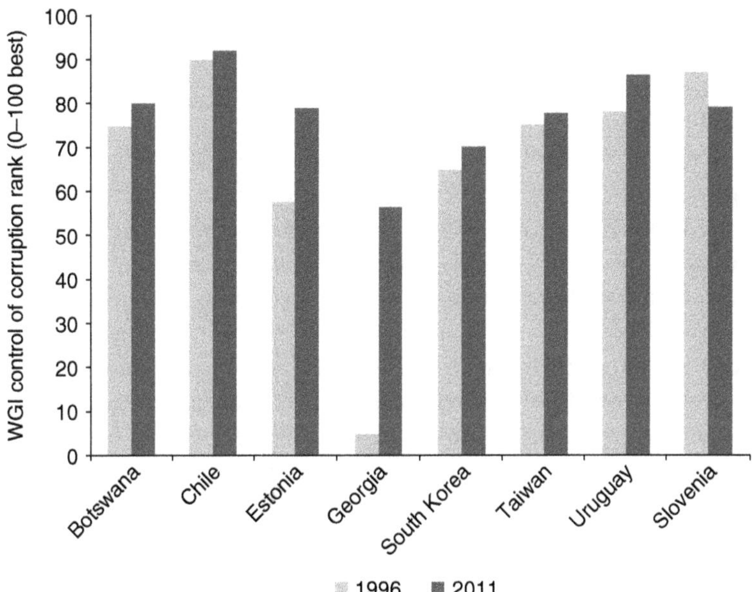

Figure 5.1 Selected achievers' evolution. *Control of corruption reflects perceptions of the extent to which public power is exercised for private gain, including both petty and grand forms of corruption as well as "capture" of the state by elites and private interests*
Source: World Bank. World Governance Indicators

change process (the political economy of change) in the country in order to understand the context, underlying agency, and drivers of change in the control of corruption. Finally, I analyze the formal institutional framework in general and anticorruption interventions in particular to check to what extent progress was due to special anticorruption interventions. In the end all cases are compared.

Chile and Uruguay

Latin America has two achievers (Chile and Uruguay) and a country nearing the threshold (Costa Rica), which also match the countries with the longest democratic tradition on the continent. Uruguay, together with Argentina, was among the wealthiest countries in the world around the First World War but stagnated for most of the remaining twentieth century, only later resuming growth to arrive at the second-best economic performance on the continent. Chile and Uruguay perform better on income compared to the rest of Latin

America (Chile with over $11,301 GDP per capita, PPP, and Uruguay with $9,087, compared to the Latin American average (excluding the Caribbean) of $6,465 by 2010), and on literacy, political rights, and ethnic homogeneity, which are all important factors for control of corruption. Chile does better than average and Uruguay worse on property rights and trade openness, and they are both unitary states, with federalism a significant determinant of corruption in the Latin American explanatory models of control of corruption.

Both countries have better control of corruption scores than their HDI would predict, while countries like Venezuela and Ecuador are exactly the opposite. In other words, there was no clear predetermination for the good governance of these two countries. Resources for corruption were unevenly spread: ethnic homogeneity was better than in other Latin American countries, but mineral resources existed and provided rents. Uruguay was the least rural of the Latin American countries and did not share in the land inequality pattern of its neighbors. Chile had land inequality that quite a few leaders had tried to tackle in the twentieth century, and its inequality measured by the Gini coefficient remains close to the continental average, while Uruguay is doing much better with less inequality. Both countries have high informal sectors.

Chile has experienced since its independence all three types of governance regime based on patrimonialism, competitive particularism, and ethical universalism. During the colonial period, state "ownership" was concentrated in the hands of a few, power distribution was unequal and access limited, and informal institutions and rules were dominant, often making the distinction between private and public blurred. Following independence in 1810 (with the last Spanish governor retiring due to a corruption scandal) and the development of pluralism, elite groups began to contest important positions in the government and amass state rents. The decision in favor of a unitary centralized state created fairly early an autonomous bureaucracy (the model was the French Napoleonic state) able to generate a separate power hub from the temporary holders of executive power, which remained also constrained by the legislative. The autonomy of the state from private interest, a major component of control of corruption, seems to have been achieved early. After the First World War in recession-stricken Latin America only Chileans adopted an extremely strong audit agency, despite common problems (lack of sound public finance) and similar foreign advice (from the American "money doctor," Princeton professor Edwin Kemmerer) across all countries.[2] There followed a Controller General (created in 1927, introduced in the constitution in 1943), a unique institution of its kind, and simultaneously an Accounts Court, auditor, supreme judicial reviewer (also on constitutional matters) of all government bills, and ombudsman reporting neither to parliament nor to government. Previously Chile had separate agencies to cover these functions. No president can change the head of the "*Controleria*," elected until the age of seventy-five and, remarkably, none has attempted this since its creation. The presidents do appoint the comptroller who is confirmed by the upper chamber. Only the dictator General Augusto Pinochet replaced a comptroller for refusing to countersign a bill for the organization of a plebiscite.

In close relation with a strong autonomous central bureaucracy, Chilean governance acquired early on remarkable checks and balances, even exaggerated ones. The presidents were already institutionally constrained in the nineteenth century: when a budget was voted down, a reformer president committed suicide for failing to impose his will on Congress. Extension of political rights did not challenge these early features. Presidents can only be elected for one mandate in succession. Congress refused to approve travel abroad in the twentieth century for President Frei Montalva (Valenzuela 1989). The judiciary, especially the higher courts, have lifetime tenure and thus acquired independence early on.

The autonomy of the bureaucracy and accountability of the president toward peers were nevertheless achieved in a highly unequal society where only a restricted elite enjoyed political access, not unlike eighteenth-century Britain. In the twentieth century the executive became more important and parties more clientelistic as political modernization progressed and political participation expanded. The distinction between private and public remained poor, and only reforms in the 1950s and 1960s eliminated most vote buying and pork-barrel allocations (Valenzuela 1977). Most features of premodern governance like particularism of social allocation were eliminated in the late 1950s and especially during the term of the Christian Democrat President Eduardo Frei Montalva (1964–70). Even at the time when favoritism was still reigning supreme, however, political leaders were

[2] Author's interview with Controller General head of staff, Santiago, May 8, 2014.

not in the game of personal enrichment. The last president to run Chile from the presidential palace rather than his own house was in power in the 1950s (the presidential palace also included presidential offices and the coin factory) and none has returned since (Gazmuri 1999). The last conservative president before the dictatorship, Jorge Alessandri, himself the son of a previous president, is still remembered for walking by himself from his office in La Moneda palace to his apartment: since then, Chilean presidents have only a summer residence provided by taxpayers.[3] The elite background of Chile's rulers and this valuing of austerity in public life seems to have played a role in creating a pattern of presidents behaving more as chief stakeholders among trustees than of spoilers of common assets.

By the 1950s, accountability in Chile was already institutionalized, with an independent judicial system, the strong oversight mechanism of the Controller General, and other autonomous agencies. Despite this, the clientelistic nature of politics was evident in persistent scandals related to campaign slush funds and pork-barrel legislation (Valenzuela 1977). To rein in particularistic allocation in a highly competitive Congress, one which had almost unlimited powers to legislate benefits for key constituencies (e.g., pension benefits) (Chumacero *et al.* 2007: 16), a constitutional reform was passed at the end of Frei Montalva's administration expanding the budgetary authority of the executive and effectively depriving Congress of the prerogative of legislating in the areas of social security, taxation, wages, and fiscal budget. Laws that targeted spending aimed at specific constituencies were also forbidden, thus consolidating the autonomy of the state toward private interest (Montecinos 2003). The need to rationalize expenses was, however, older, and the trend had begun already under Jorge Alessandri to replace clientelistic allocations with universalistic welfare: but only Frei Montalva gave free rein to the full ideology of ethical universalism (he was a Christian democrat intellectual, a reader of Jacques Maritain) (Gazmuri *et al.* 2000) and enjoyed enough of a majority ("partido unico") to be able to leave behind the old transactions to build a majority in the Congress and move ahead with reducing inequality and increasing rationalization of expenditure (Valenzuela 1977). He also promoted other reforms, including land reform and strong incentives to develop civil society (cooperatives and other associations,

[3] Author's interview with Alfredo Joignant, contemporary historian, Santiago.

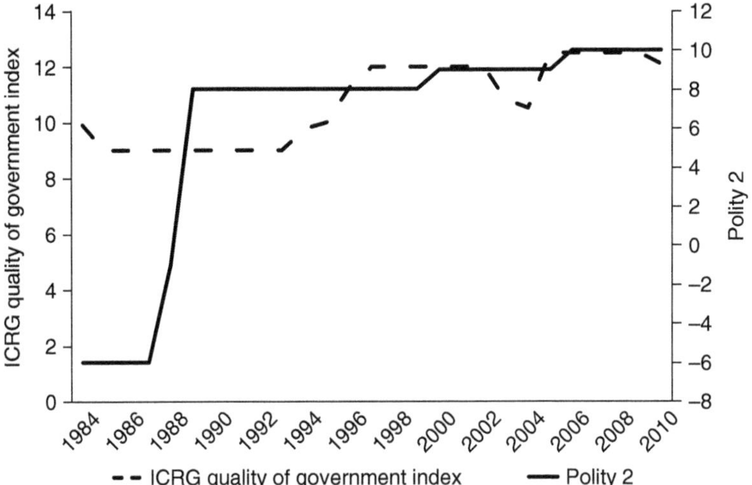

Figure 5.2 The Chilean path. Governance more stable than politics
Source: The PRS Group and Polity IV data

for instance) and community-level collective action. The growth of the state under Communist Salvador Allende and the unprecedented power discretion of some army circles under dictator Pinochet led to the multiplication of rent opportunities again, but Chile never returned to premodern practices on a large scale. In fact, the trend to eliminate the personalistic and particularistic intervention of the brokers in politics continued under Pinochet. Officers, the new power holders, tended to solve issues hierarchically; on the one hand, people did not have the courage to approach them with their problems as they had done with civilian mayors, and on the other, they themselves did not dare to intervene on small, private matters with their hierarchical superiors (Valenzuela 1977). Consequently particular allocations in local politics dried up, and the tendency to promote universalistic welfare allocation rather than concentrated, client-based territorial benefits was mostly preserved in the subsequent dictatorship of Pinochet and the democratization that followed (see Figure 5.2).

The 1980 constitution passed under Pinochet reaffirmed many of the budgetary rules that were already present in the legislation prior to the authoritarian period. For example, the president alone has the right to propose legislation related to wages, public employment, social security, and other entitlement programs.

Congress, therefore, has "limited opportunities and mechanisms to bargain with and extract concessions from the executive branch" (Montecinos 2003: 14). Unlike other authoritarian regimes in the region, the Pinochet regime promoted economic reforms based on decentralization and privatization, which further reduced opportunities for rent seeking. The main reforms that might have played a role in control of corruption came from neoclassical economics: property rights security; a subsidiary role of the state, which limited state interventions to cases of clear market failures (except for the preservation of the state ownership in the mining sector); freedom of choice, reflected in rationing procedures, price controls, and the elimination of trade permits and prohibitions; fiscal consolidation and orthodox management of monetary and foreign exchange policies; and trade and financial openness, which would provide both the impulse for growth that the limited size of the domestic economy could not provide as well as the creation of competition in the local economy. There was also a systematic reduction in public discretion and potential arbitrariness – impersonal rules were introduced whenever possible – and an institutionalization of the "rules of the game" in such a way that it would not be easy to change them, with the purpose of granting stability to those rules under different governments (Edwards and Lederman 1998).

After the redemocratization of 1990, politics were dominated by two large coalitions, one more defensive of the legacy of the authoritarian regime and the other against it. Pluralism was quickly installed, but governance did not change, and despite a slight backslide the country did not return to competitive particularism. Corruption and government favoritism in Chile remain the exceptions rather than the norm. New institutions introduced as an Office for Transparency and E-Government have helped foster a change of culture after dictatorship, though it remains exceptional to Chile that the previous lack of transparency did not seem to foster corruption.[4] As to the legislation passed after 1990, it may be that its greatest merit has been continuity rather than innovation, considering Chile's good governance roots.

Chile is an example of the gradual building of control of corruption. Each period of democratization left some positive heritage, as

[4] Author's interview, Office for Transparency, Santiago, May 7, 2014.

did authoritarianism. Chile's success seems to be related to the liberalization of the economy and the need for a sound financial system (after all, the Comptroller was created to save money and rationalize expenses more than to control corruption), the privatization of companies that offer public services, and the consolidation of markets – in other words, to the fact that resources for corruption gradually dried up. But Chile has natural resources that provided rent opportunities all along, so its achievement is all the more remarkable. Control of corruption to a great extent seems to have preceded the economic liberalization under Pinochet – it has been a declared concern of nearly each presidency and the crucial time seems to have been the 1960s. In addition, there are traces of earlier control of corruption reforms that managed to take root. Current proposals to "improve" on these institutional arrangements – for instance by making the Comptroller accountable to parliament or creating an anticorruption agency – should be regarded with caution. The strength of Chile's institutional arrangements lies in their originality and organic development.

Uruguay has a long tradition of liberal democracy going back to the beginning of the twentieth century, and in public opinion surveys citizens strongly endorse its political regime. Unlike Chile, where citizens tend to be more skeptical of the integrity of politicians and magistrates, public trust is very high in Uruguay.[5] Although this democratic tradition was interrupted by a military dictatorship between 1973 and 1985, the country has not only succeeded in democratizing peacefully, but also in bringing to justice those accountable for misdeeds during the authoritarian period. The integrity of the ruling elite, military and civilian, has a long tradition. Again, rulers seem to have been for most of the time major stakeholders in the country, not upstarts. The unanimous opinion is that people have never joined politics to become rich: there have always been better alternatives for that. However, business and politics are not clearly separated, and public integrity in Uruguay needs further explanation than the original integrity of its ruling elites, which runs through several generations of elite-born rulers (visible in the modest museum of previous presidencies in Montevideo) to the current president, Jose Mujica, a former urban

[5] Author's interview with Latinobarometer Director Marta Lagos, Santiago, May 3, 2014.

guerillero who rules from his private apartment and drives his old VW Beetle to the office.

Uruguay has a semipresidential system with two chambers, a functioning system of checks and balances, and it has many decades' experience of consociative institutions inspired by Switzerland, granting to the opposition seats in many executive positions, including the board of public companies (Altman 2008).[6] Government actions are subject to parliamentary and judicial review, the latter by the the administrative high court, members of which are usually career judges appointed by parliament and perceived as neutral. The judiciary is traditionally independent, free from unconstitutional influence, differentiated and professionalized, although it sometimes suffers from a lack of efficiency and expediency against organized crime. Uruguay has a long history of interest representation, organization, and pressure group formation, evidenced by the dense network of differentiated interest groups reflecting competing economic and social interests. Labor, both urban and rural, is well represented. Political parties have deep societal roots, having existed for more than 150 years, and have managed to integrate new parties successfully. Civil society has been an important contributor to democratization and has a long tradition in the mostly urban population, descended predominantly from European immigrants. Uruguay has a large well-educated elite in politics and public life and far less inequality than other Latin American countries.

During its last period of democratization Uruguay experienced a positive evolution of all four components of the equilibrium model: a reduction in power discretion and material resources and a strengthening of legal and normative constraints. As in Chile, however, we find that the recent transition to control of corruption is built on an older history and grounded deep in society. Even before the last democratic transition, for example, a strong civil society and media contributed to increased normative constraints – voters punished corrupt behavior, although patronage was widely accepted. Clientelistic social allocation is nevertheless conducive to deficits. For nearly fifty years after World War II Uruguay's growth was far inferior to the growth of public employment and state pensions (Buquet and Piñeiro 2014). This fed the political and social conflict of the 1960s, when the level of urban violence and contestation reached its peak, making political parties

[6] Author's interview with David Altman, Santiago, May 3, 2014.

realize that the traditional ways of gaining support should give way. A reduction in material resources began during the military regime, when important privatizations occurred, and continued throughout the 1990s and also the 2000s, following an economic crisis. Starting in the early 1970s, Uruguay's economy became more outward-oriented. But Uruguay is no triumph of the Washington consensus like Chile: quite the contrary, it retains a large public sector with high public employment. After the dictatorship, however, parties respected fiscal consolidation, clientelistic allocations dried up, and creative tailor-made policies reduced both the informal economy and tax evasion. The consolidation of an independent judiciary also took place early, not long after redemocratization, with an agreement to appoint Supreme Court judges with a two-thirds majority of parliament.

Between 1985 and 2004, the Uruguayan party system seemed to reach a new equilibrium, which decisively influenced control of corruption as it shifted the lines of political competition from a clientelistic logic to a programmatic logic (Buquet and Piñeiro 2014; Kitschelt *et al.* 2010). The military dictatorship itself was an attempt to prevent what had been perceived as a radical challenger party from shaking up traditional rules of the game. The later integration of this programmatic left-wing former guerilla party, Frente Amplio, into politics ultimately forced new rules of the game with traditional parties reconciled to the changes. The social and technological modernization during years of dictatorship had already considerably changed the old patronage society, and ethical universalism triumphed for practical as well as ideological reasons. There was political consensus that a return to previous rules of the game (which had played their part to stir radical contestation and then dictatorship) was no longer possible, and this consensus generated the new policies enshrining the end of particularism in a society where corruption had never been pervasive to start with, but where particularistic distribution of benefits and public services had been the norm.

The WGI CoC had already placed Uruguay in the "green area" in 1998. Later positive developments, such as the adoption of specific anticorruption legislation, appear to have reinforced the foundation that was already in place. The most successful policies were in the field of tax collection and reduction of the informal economy, showing that a main motivation beyond Uruguay's evolution was the need for fiscal consolidation. Tax simplification, smart incentives, and commissioning tax collection largely to the private sector led to the most spectacular growth of collection in the world after 2000.

Estonia

Estonia has been a regional leader in urbanization and literacy since the nineteenth century. But it is also overperforming in its excellent modernization goodness of fit. As a champion of liberal economic policies, civil society, and e-government, Estonia progressed considerably after 1989. Estonia's success in transforming into an open access order remains the most significant in postcommunist Europe, if not in the entire world. It is worth mentioning that Estonia has been mostly governed by center-right coalitions since the fall of communism and has excluded from the vote most of its Russian-speaking residents, resulting in an unusually homogenous and politically cohesive community of voters numbering under 900,000.

In less than twenty years Estonia has made rapid and notable progress from a totalitarian regime to a quality democracy. The principles of ethical universalism seem to have taken root in the country's governance, although the country is not free of corruption, and the public mentality still remains tributary to the Soviet era. For example, a 2004 survey carried out on behalf of the Ministry of Justice found that about one-half of respondents did not consider giving gifts to officials to be corruption; about the same proportion found that an official who orders computers from a firm where his son is a partner is not wrong in doing so. Respondents deemed misuse of official positions to be the most common form of corruption, and bribery the least common: 16 percent of the respondents overall acknowledged giving bribes, 24 percent of entrepreneurs claimed that they had been asked for a bribe for performance of a public service, and 27 percent of public sector employees claim to have been offered a bribe (Kasemets 2012).

The country has seen almost simultaneous improvement in all four dimensions of the equilibrium since restoration of independence with the collapse of the Soviet Union. During the first government of Mart Laar (1992–95), policies were implemented that reduced material resources and strengthened legal constraints. Estonia pioneered important liberal reforms such as the adoption of a flat tax, which later became very popular in Eastern Europe as an instrument to combat tax evasion and the informal economy, and embraced advanced e-government reforms inspired by neighboring Finland. But Estonia's key successful reform was anticommunism. In barely two years, from 1992 to 1994, Laar, a former anticommunist historian who declared that the only book on economics he had read before becoming prime minister at the age of thirty-two was *Free to Choose* by Milton Friedman, was the first in Europe to introduce the flat tax, privatize most national industry in open and transparent public tenders, abolish tariffs and subsidies, and achieve macro stabilization despite opposition and protests. Part of his abrupt break with the USSR was to restore the prewar currency and peg it to the stable Deutschmark. Laar often spoke about corruption and explained that these early reform choices prevented Estonia from sliding into the corrupt transition from "plan to clan" as many other postcommunist countries had done, evolving to crony capitalism rather than ethical universalism. As he put it "any reform which increases the competitiveness of the economy will reduce corrupt behavior" (2007).

As part of the same policy seeking deep and fast separation from the Soviet legacy Estonia adopted a radical policy toward the Soviet-era judiciary, opting to replace most of the inherited system and start afresh with newly trained magistrates (the cost: courts were practically closed for many months). Normative constraints are also high, with public opinion intolerant of bribery (though relatively tolerant toward other forms of particularism), an active civil society, and a free press that benefited from investment from its Scandinavian neighbors. Estonia's commitment to civil society development is also greater than its neighbors, with dedicated EU funds and a pact committing all parties to the rule of law (Kasemets and Lepp 2010).

Since February 2000, when the Estonian Parliament passed legislation guaranteeing the general population access to the internet, Estonia has become one of the most technologically connected populations in Europe; some have nicknamed the country "E-stonia." The country's high internet usage rates are due not only to the prevalence of household computers, but also to the availability of free internet access points countrywide. All schools in Estonia are connected to the internet, more than half of all households pay their bills electronically, and the state portal eesti.ee allows citizens to access official records and to log into various information systems (e.g., the e-Tax Board or the Land Registry) (Kasemets and Lepp 2010). In addition to high rates of internet usage, nearly 90 percent of the population have mobile telephone subscriptions and more than half have digital identity cards. Another cornerstone of the control of corruption is Estonia's system of public e-procurement (RISO 2012) and the more recent online public expense tracking system riigipilv.ee (*ERR News* 2012).

The cost of Estonia's neoliberal consensus was the exclusion of non-Estonian speakers from the vote – about one-third of Estonia's population are Russian speakers who settled in the country during the Soviet period. According to the World Values Survey 2000, this group shows greater support for collectivism and lower support for the market economy and democracy than the Estonian-speaking population and its by-passing by political decision probably helped Estonia's swift reform advance. Nationalism and liberalism therefore combine to explain Estonia's success. The country's achievement is not a minor one, considering that it inherited the same institutional problems as all other parts of the former Soviet Union, and that party competition presented the same incentives for political clientelism as in neighboring Latvia, which evolved into typical competitive particularism despite having the same existential threats from neighboring Russia. Slovenia, the other prominent Eastern European success story, began from a far stronger position (e.g., early economic integration with neighboring Austria, a small urbanized population, far higher income, and excellent modernization goodness of fit), but as it turned out in recent years its new capitalism is far more based on rents than previously acknowledged (*Al Jazeera* 2013; Cerni 2013).

Botswana

Botswana, like Uruguay, was already considered in the "green area" by the World Bank at its first assessment in 1998. Transparency International also has consistently rated Botswana as the least corrupt of all African countries included in its Corruption Perceptions Index. The country is frequently pointed to as a classic anticorruption success story, largely due to its anticorruption agency – although there have been recent suggestions that its role might be overrated (Acemoglu *et al.* 2003; Von Soest 2009). Nonetheless, Botswana's achievements are obvious considering that it started out as one of the poorest countries in the world when it gained independence from Britain in 1966 and is now overperforming its modernization goodness of fit. Since that time Botswana seems to have traveled a virtuous path in comparison with its neighbor, Zimbabwe, which has descended into social and economic collapse. Its structural determinants – geography, urbanization, and health – were no better than those of its neighbors.

But Botswana's achievement is quite different from the ethical universalism ideal and the resources/constraints model. For one thing, material resources for corruption are high, given the country's large potential rents. Diamond reserves are the most important resource in the country (successfully exploited through a monopoly jointly operated by the state-run Debswana and the private company De Beers), although cases of corruption in this sector are rare (Bertelsmann Stiftung 2009). Botswana's public sector is a heavy weight in the economy. Government consumption spending as a share of GDP has remained above 20 percent since 1980 and reached 24 percent in 2009 – the highest level among the six contemporary achievers examined here. Public sector employment accounts for around 45 percent of total employment. Since the early years following independence, recruitment into the public service has been mostly merit-based (Von Soest 2009), although some public positions have been subject to patronage (Johnston 2005).

Botswana's road to positive evolution was started by Seretse Khama, the country's first president, who pursued a tough stance against corruption (e.g., Adamolekun and Morgan 1999: 592) that quickly earned the country a reputation for "clean" management of public resources. Although its political system has limitations in terms of competition, among the cases studied here it is the country with the longest uninterrupted democratic regime. Throughout forty-five years of democracy, power concentration and material resources have remained high. Nevertheless, two positive aspects can be traced back to the foundation of the state: the establishment of an autonomous civil service, which has been protected from widespread politicization; and the development of an autonomous judiciary.

Policy formulation and public spending are, however, some of the most transparent aspects of Botswana's governance system. Budgeting, development planning, and prioritizing processes are extensively consultative, involving communities, local government structures, non-state actors, and political institutions. The social allocation process is targeted but universalistic, as there are specific programs for poorer sections of the population, such as inhabitants of remote areas, including indigenous San people. All allocations are included in a national development plan, which is openly debated long in advance, leaving little room for discretion.

Botswana's political system has a dominant role for the president (Von Soest 2009), who is constitutionally accountable to parliament and has the power to dismiss the legislature, but who cannot be impeached by it (Freedom House 2010). Botswana is also an exception among the countries examined in this chapter with regards to political competition: the same political party and political elite have been in power since independence. Although the country has a multiparty system, the Botswana Democratic Party (BDP) has remained largely unchallenged by the opposition and its presidents have enjoyed very long tenures (four presidents in forty-five years). Its current president, Ian Khama, is the first-born son of Sir Seretse Khama, who was the country's foremost independence leader and who served as president from 1966 to 1980, himself the male descendent of the traditional ruling family of the Bamangwato people and the great-great grandson of Kgosikgolo Sekgoma I, Chief of the Bamangwato (1815–85). While the good governance mantra advocates short, non-renewable mandates as a better model for control of corruption, Botswana has all the features of a paternalistic and enlightened constitutional monarchy, with political domination by one group rather than real competition, despite regularly held elections. Most senior political positions including the president, vice president, foreign minister, and speaker of parliament were held between 2008 and 2013 by former public servants. The cabinet is regularly filled with blood relations or village connections of the president and the diplomatic service is filled with former ministers (Sebudubudu 2014).

The public–private separation of Botswana's political and economic elite is incomplete, which in all likelihood allows certain particularistic practices to flourish. Members of the BDP government are often owners or directors of commercial companies and farming enterprises, and the BDP has consistently refused to pass legislation requiring MPs and cabinet ministers to declare their assets and economic interests. Recurrent reports have also criticized the relationship between the BDP and De Beers, including evidence that De Beers has financially supported the party, particularly during the presidency of Ketumile Masire (1980–98). Botswana is a rare case where ethnic particularism and elite capture are formally organized and coexist with the rule of law. The House of Chiefs (upper chamber), for instance, only has representatives of the country's eight main tribes.

The autonomy of the state towards private interests remains therefore relative. Big businesses such as car dealers, mining and construction enterprises as well as tourism and environmental agencies are said to have strong ties with the ruling party and to contribute to its financing, with party executives directly involved in business (Sebudubudu 2014). High-level corruption scandals erupt periodically. One area particularly prone to irregularities has been the allocation of state land: cases have been reported of allocations to private business persons and members of the political elite. Another series of scandals occurred in 1993, when newspapers revealed that government politicians (and other members of the elite) had accrued huge repayment arrears with the state-owned National Development Bank, which nearly led to the bankruptcy of Botswana's largest public lending institution (Good 1994: 511; Tsie 1996: 602). Then-president Masire was among the loan defaulters. These cases were documented in reports by various presidential commissions to demonstrate the government's capacity to control corruption. Institutions for executive control were also created, the most prominent of which were the Directorate of Corruption and Economic Crime (launched in 1994) and the position of ombudsman (launched in 1995) (on the directorate, see Olowu 1999; on the ombudsman, see Fombad 2001). Their achievements and reputations, however, are controversial, as the president appoints the heads of both offices.

The judiciary, on the other hand, is independent and actively reviews the executive's decisions; it has become the main accountability instrument within Botswana's political system. The institutional framework underpinning this branch of government does, however, leave open the possibility of political influence as it grants the president discretion to appoint the highest judicial authorities (Transparency International 2007). Except Botswana's first president, under whose tenure a minister committed suicide when suspected of corruption, it is not clear that the presidency has objectivity enough to fulfill this role. The last president appointed his brother over more qualified MPs as minister and the cabinet has far too many blood relatives, again giving the impression of an enlightened monarchy rather than of a republic. By and large, it seems that the first generation of postcolonial leaders put the country on the right path, allowing legal constraints to develop, but their inheritance should not be taken for granted under new, less idealistic politicians (Sebudubudu 2014).

Normative constraints are indeed less impressive and might become a concern if good governance flows less in a top-down manner as previously. Over the last two decades, civil society in Botswana has grown greatly, but it is concentrated in the public health sector and dependent on public funds – it is not active in a watchdog role (Transparency International 2007). Freedom of the press has shown signs of deterioration in recent years: Freedom House downgraded Botswana from a "free" to "partly free" press in 2005, and it has not evolved since. Among the reasons cited for the decline are a rise in political influence over state-owned media and the government harassment of journalists and private media outlets, both through formal and informal channels. In August 2012 the ruling BDP stifled a vote on a proposed freedom of information bill, and access to public information remains a major problem for journalists (Freedom House 2013).

Cases of corruption have recently surfaced again across all areas of the public sector, from public procurement, recruitment, land and housing allocation, to transport and road licensing services, management of state agencies and local government services, mining, and tourism licensing; not even the allocation of student loans and the distribution of medicine in health facilities are spared. Party membership and position – especially but not exclusively – in the ruling party have become an important ticket for accessing jobs, business loans, opportunities, and government contracts (Sebudubudu 2014). The increased frequency of media reports on corruption-related court cases involving ministers, senior politicians, and public officials might signal the effectiveness of the anticorruption mechanisms but also a genuine increase in corruption reflected in the public perception.

Acemoglu, Johnson, and Robinson (2003) argue that Botswana's development success lies in institutional arrangements that adequately protect the property rights of actual and potential investors. With law and order maintained, diamond revenue wisely managed, and an efficient, meritocratic bureaucracy, the country grew economically between 1965 and 1998 at an annual rate of 7.7 percent. This economic prosperity made many things easier, and presently Botswana is overperforming on governance. However, it would be difficult to argue that Botswana's equilibrium is based on ethical universalism, even if the choice of the political elite after independence was to organize the state as an autonomous defender of property rights, rather than as a source of continuous spoils (Von Soest 2009).

The Botswana path is thus close to the historical Danish path, through a mix of traditional authority and top-down reforms by enlightened leaders, but present Botswana society is not similar to present Danish society, even if control of corruption is to an important extent achieved in both cases.

Taiwan and South Korea

Corruption scholars have for many years marveled why corruption in sub-Saharan Africa is so detrimental to development while in Asia it seems to have fewer effects. The obvious answer, discussed quite a while ago by Barrington Moore Jr. (1966) in a book less quoted today, is that at different levels of societal development predatory behavior by elites can meet different degrees of resistance. Where there is no resistance at all because the population is helpless, famine results from corruption. Where some normative constraints exist and society can fight back, rulers will posit a commission on general economic activity for their self-enrichment, with fewer detrimental effects on society as a whole. This seems to have been the Asian situation for the most part, but being superior to the world's most disenfranchised and poor countries was not really a measure of Asian performance. Only recently has demand for good governance stepped up in importance on the continent as traditional achiever, West-emulating Japan, was joined by two new achievers, South Korea and Taiwan, and countries such as Indonesia and India have started more important anticorruption activities. The average across the region is personified by China, India, or Thailand, who perform quite poorly, though in comparison to Afghanistan and Pakistan do reasonably well. The achievers, however, do twice as well or more. Four of them are atypical polities and therefore will not be discussed here (Hong Kong, Singapore, Bhutan, and Brunei Darussalam), though the story of each of them is fascinating in itself. Leaving aside city states and monarchies, traditional or atypical, we are left with only two recent performers, still struggling to evolve from borderline to full control of corruption status: Taiwan and South Korea.

Taiwan's goodness of fit to the modernization model is very good; therefore, it is a predictable performer: a well-developed, educated, homogenous nation. However, its governance improvement only started after 2000 (Göbel 2014) and its fit to the equilibrium model is less than ideal. The country underwent a successful and peaceful transition to democracy, although it is somewhat controversial whether this transition also led to a better governance regime. Corruption has been indicated as the most pressing political issue in many opinion surveys over the years, and Taiwan's democratization in 1992 worsened the perception of corruption, because of more transparent deals on party finance and political support. During the authoritarian period of Kuomintang (KMT) rule, corruption was practically institutionalized, and the party was able to build a real-estate and business empire (Hsueh 2007: 11). Companies bribed the government for preferential policies and public contracts. During the period of democratic transformation, corruption dominated the electoral agenda. In fact, the DPP's (Democratic Progressive Party) anticorruption campaigns in the 1990s were a critical factor in terminating the single-party authoritarian regime controlled by the KMT for over fifty years (Yu *et al.* 2008).

In May 2000, when the KMT peacefully turned over the presidency to the DPP, Taiwan was regarded as a textbook case of successful democratization. Yet in the short run, the political changes led to an increase in corrupt exchanges, as political campaigning became competitive and more expensive and there was greater dependence on resources from the business sector (Hsueh 2007: 12). Challengers proved just as vulnerable to corruption as incumbents, and privatization added to older, existing rents. Some government officials made use of insider information to "secure interests in profitable enterprises for themselves, party supporters, or their family members" (Hsueh 2007: 17).

Despite swings in government, power discretion remains high, with semipresidentialism granting significant power discretion to the president, who appoints the prime minister without approval by the legislative. Additionally, the president has the power to appoint the members of the Control Yuan (main oversight body), Judicial Yuan (Taiwan's highest judicial body), and constitutional judges (Huang 2006) – which contributes to the view that the judiciary is not particularly independent (Freedom House 2010; Polity IV 2010). The Control Yuan, constituted as an independent government branch, has auditing and investigative powers and also exercises the function of an ombudsman (Shin and Chu 2004: 34). Bureaucrats in Taiwan are a class in their own right – well educated, protected, and paid. Unlike other young democracies, in Taiwan it is unheard of for there to be high turnover in the bureaucracy following elections, or for positions to be assigned to party-affiliated incompetents. Civil servants must pass a merit-based exam with the historical examination committee, established in 1925 when China became a republic. Taiwanese civil servants have among the most secure jobs in the world, with a monthly pension and 18 percent preferential bank interest, giving them the world's best income replacement ratio (the percentage of the working income needed to maintain a desired standard of living in retirement) (Cho-shui 2011; Khan 1998).

Taiwan began building an anticorruption framework in the 1990s. The 1993 Public Functionary Assets Disclosure Act required the disclosure of assets by high-level officials and elected representatives (Bertelsmann Stiftung 2009); later, President Chen (2000–08) pushed the issue to the forefront of the political agenda and, shortly after winning the 2000 elections, mapped out an "Action Plan for the Elimination of Corruption and Organized Crime." In 2004 a Political Contribution Act was passed, which imposed limits on political donations and attempted to make political financing more transparent. A Freedom of Government Information Law was also passed in 2005.

The main factor motivating the key reforms was the change in the ruling party after the DPP's electoral success. As the previous regime was based on engrained political corruption the survival of the DPP depended to a large extent on a change to the rules of the game: anticorruption policies were the best way to enfeeble their political opponents (Göbel 2014). The crackdowns on bribery, embezzlement, money laundering, and vote-buying removed many top bureaucrats who had been loyal to the previous regime. Popular support to remove what was perceived as a corrupt regime preceded the DPP's anticorruption agenda and indeed contributed to the swing in government.

But democratization simultaneously brought more resources for corruption and greater normative constraints. The latter are apparent in the popular movement against President Chen and the low trust in government institutions even after the implementation of new anticorruption legislation. Non-governmental organizations and think-tanks have a very active presence in the country. Legal constraints are among the highest in the world, with harsh penalties against corruption, even at the top levels of power, and they are enforced. However, early into President Chen's second term his administration's anticorruption efforts were largely discredited, due to the eruption of numerous scandals involving top-level officials, the President himself, and some close family members. The general public is still unconvinced that particularism as a regime is finished and that anticorruption is impartially implemented.

South Korea is the favorite case in Asia for economists studying development, as Chile is in Latin America. Like Uruguay, Korea has experienced positive change in all four dimensions of the equilibrium model over the last decades. The immediate trigger for good governance reforms was the financial crisis in 1997, which led to a change in policy toward the institutionalized rents of *chaebols* (large industrial conglomerates) and a gradual opening up of economic competition. There are older roots for Korea's control of corruption, however, as well as for external support for its improvements in governance that economists tend to neglect (You 2012).

South Korea gradually achieved important milestones, including a major land redistribution (1950s), the creation of a meritocratic and efficient bureaucracy (1960s to 1980s), industrialization, and the creation of an educated and financially independent middle class (1960s to 1990s) and, finally, democratic elections and a free press (since 1987). Particularism persists around South Korea's *chaebol*, which exert their influence through political financing, family ties, and public relations campaigns, but bribery and petty corruption are quite uncommon. More recently, there have also been gradual improvements on the constraints side: some anticorruption policies were adopted in the early 1990s and there has been increasing anticorruption activism within civil society since 1996. Legal constraints continued to increase with the implementation of a comprehensive anticorruption agenda by Kim Dae-Jung (1998–2002), the first opposition leader to be elected president, whose policies also contributed to the reduction of material resources. Although the judiciary has proved its independence since at least 2003, and has convicted many politicians and businessmen on corruption charges, some individuals have still received light sentences or even presidential pardons.

While Korea's control of corruption ratings are inferior to the other countries described above, it is the most populous country among contemporary achievers, which makes its progress even more significant. The suicide in 2008 of former President Roh Moo-Hyun due to corruption allegations shows how strong normative constraints have become. South Korea is doing significantly better than regional averages on all components of the modernization model: it is nearly three times richer, better educated by half, and more ethnically homogeneous than many other countries in the region. Similar to other Asian countries, its economy grew well (at 9 percent) for two decades during relatively corrupt years (1970–92); corruption became an issue following the Asian financial crisis in 1997, when the IMF insisted that the deep linkages between *chaebol* and the state must be brought to an end. Economists argue that Korea's model of state-led capitalism actually played a positive role in its development and that stable rents, conditioned by the overall country's performance, generated incentives for growth (Khan 1998). You (2012) argues that normative constraints played a far larger role in building Korea's progress to an open access order than economists allow: first, the land reform promoted by American occupation allowed the massive increase in educated people and a rise in the middle class; second, protest movements in the cities, especially by students, played a large role in the development of an accountable government in Korea.

Borderliners: Georgia

Georgia has been labeled by the World Bank as the country that has made the greatest progress in controlling corruption, jumping over 50 percentiles in the control of corruption global rankings in just a few years, and has intensively promoted this label in the international media for several years. Georgia ranks between 50 and 60 in the list of over 160 countries surveyed by Transparency International: its score has climbed over the years much higher than its neighbors Armenia, Russia, and Azerbaijan to surpass Greece and Hungary, among other EU members, although it remains well below the other "achievers" presented here. Georgia's improvement started in the aftermath of the 2003 Rose Revolution, and since then the country has successfully managed to reduce petty corruption through several high-profile anticorruption campaigns, including the prosecution of senior corrupt officials, police reform, deregulation, and the liberalization of the business environment, as well as public sector reform. If Georgia has not managed to climb further than six on our recoded 1–10 World Bank scale despite overperforming in its modernization determinants, it is due to major challenges that the other achievers lack. Georgia has important state building problems, does not control a part of its territory where Russian-speaking minorities seceded in the early 1990s following its independence, with the resulting destruction and impoverishment unleashed by civil wars. Its income, despite growth during the regime of Mikheil Saakashvili, its reform minded president (2004–13), remains below US$4,000 per capita. In other words, Georgia has the poorest fit with the modernization model possible. Its rapid progress is also noteworthy given corruption's deep roots in the country's Soviet past: In Soviet Georgia there was no distribution of financial and material resources without bribery and nepotism. According to non-market rules of life and business, personal and intellectual qualities and hard work did not guarantee material well-being. Rather, one needed a special ability (the so called "mariphathy") to find a corrupt bureaucrat and/or to offer bribes (Jandieri 2004). Yet although Georgia recorded very poor goodness of fit in our control of corruption model, its strides forward are the greatest. What explains its success?

In 2003, mass protests prompted by fraudulent parliamentary elections resulted in the so-called Rose Revolution – the resignation of President Eduard Shevardnadze, a revamp of the governing elite, and the election of opposition leader Saakashvili in January 2004 by an overwhelming margin. The three leaders of the reformist faction campaigned on an anticorruption platform, calling the country to rid itself of the destructively corrupt Shevardnadze leadership and to follow a path of modernization. Once in power, Saakashvili cracked down on high-level officials from the former regime and on Shevardnadze's affiliates, including his family members. Those indicted were often summoned to the prosecutor's office for questioning, charged with corruption and embezzlement, and arrested. They were asked to repay the allegedly stolen amounts, sometimes totalling several million US dollars, but were then released without standing trial. While the media reveled in the spectacle (these proceedings were often broadcast live on national television) and most of the public felt vindicated, the practice was actually in breach of Georgian legislation. These heavy-handed tactics did, however, allow the government to quickly mobilize enough revenue to repay the outstanding arrears in pensions and wage payments for public sector employees. After losing elections in 2013, some of the top executives who implemented these reforms were sentenced for power abuse by their successors, who had accused Saakashvili of authoritarian tendencies.

Fighting corruption did not stop with chastising the associates of the old regime. In 2004 the entire staff of the country's traffic police, which was notorious for its incompetence and penchant for bribe-taking, was fired and replaced by a well-equipped and newly trained patrol police. Another major achievement was an overhaul of the thoroughly corrupt system of university admissions, which became centralized and standardized for the first time in 2005, replacing the previous policy of individual university admissions. Safeguards were put in place to make corruption or favoritism all but impossible (Anderson and Gray 2006). These two reforms had particular impact on ordinary citizens, given their regular contacts with these institutions. The other reforms that were introduced were mostly aimed at easing the business environment and reducing excessive red tape. These included changes in the areas of licenses and permits: the number of legally required licenses fell by 85 percent (from a previous level of about 900 licenses) and the introduction of "one-stop shops" not only sped up the bureaucratic procedures, but also dramatically reduced the opportunities for corruption. Authorities also promoted the principle of "silence means consent," forcing time limits for approvals from the administration on the penalty of automatic granting of requests in case of delays. With only four procedures and four days necessary, Tbilisi is the most expeditious city in the world for foreigners wishing to register a business.

Critics argue that rampant petty bribery was eliminated to be replaced with more subtle and high-level state capture. This manifested itself through a discretionary distribution of public services by the state, whereby decisions about resource allocation were made in order to secure the loyalty of powerful groups or individuals to maintain political control (Kupatadze 2011). There were also allegations that the media had been captured by the new regime, both through changes of ownership and the censorship/self-censorship of journalists. However, the yielding of power by reform champion President Saakashvili indicates that he was a genuine reformer who might have cut some corners to get things done and not a new dictator in the making.

On the legal constraints front, Georgia has everything – a Freedom of Information Act, an ombudsman, and whistleblower protection legislation – and has ratified the UNCAC. Following Saakashvili's election as president, the anticorruption council created in 2001 under former President Shevardnadze disbanded itself, and no new national strategy has replaced it. The country had made its improvements without the usual plan cherished by the anticorruption industry, one that so frequently remains only on paper.

Georgia's improvements can be attributed to changes in all four dimensions of the equilibrium model. Resources were drastically curtailed by reductions in red tape, and policies promoting economic liberalization were even stronger than those enacted in Estonia. Legal and normative constraints created a new equilibrium through a "big bang" change – the 2003 Rose Revolution – followed by top-down reforms. Civil society played a large role in bringing down the Shevardnadze regime, but was later weakened by its participation in Saakashvili's government (Tsitsishvili 2010). Independent monitors of the government existed under all regimes, although the third sector overall is still quite weak in fighting corruption in Georgia. The few civil society organizations dedicated to fighting corruption engage in heroic deeds with little volunteer support from the grass roots and practically no funding from Georgia's business sector. The judiciary remains the most problematic part. As it showed in particular after the second change of regime the interference of the judiciary is more to be feared than welcomed. Saakashvili himself has been harassed after his peaceful departure from power in November 2013 for the accidental death of an ally nearly ten years earlier. The judiciary is not independent enough from political control to exercise impartial legal constraints.

Discussion

The contemporary achievers differ from one another on many dimensions (see Table 5.1), including the number of years since independence and current trends in control of corruption (e.g., the most advanced among them have been stagnating or even regressing slightly). The two borderline cases – South Korea and Georgia – are more advanced than their neighbors and show a positive trend toward control of corruption, but some challenges remain, in particular for Georgia due to its less-than-ideal fit to the model. Botswana is a remarkable achiever

Table 5.1 *Contemporary achievers at a glance*

Country	Evolution Type	"Goodness of fit" to model	Sequence	Trend	External triggers and influences
Botswana	Gradual	Poor	Control of corruption preceded genuine pluralism	Stagnant	Southern African Customs Union
Chile	Gradual	Good	Control of corruption preceded pluralism	Stagnant	Economic crisis prior to first good governance reforms; American model emulation
Estonia	Big-bang revolution	Good	Pluralism preceded control of corruption	Positive	EU accession; Scandinavian emulation
Georgia	Big-bang revolution	Poor	Pluralism preceded control of corruption	Stagnant	Some diffusion across former republics; American emulation
Slovenia	Gradual	Excellent	Control of corruption preceded pluralism	Negative	Austrian emulation, investment
South Korea	Gradual, confrontational	Good	Partial control of corruption preceded pluralism	Positive	American and IMF conditionality; Japanese emulation
Taiwan	Gradual, confrontational	Good	Partial control of corruption preceded pluralism	Stagnant	Important American assistance in the past
Uruguay	Gradual	Good (highest literacy rate in Latin America)	Control of corruption preceded pluralism	Positive	European influence always important, European descent

considering the sub-Saharan context, but with a more narrowly defined control of corruption than ethical universalism, which remains far off and may be slipping even further away.

Estonia and Georgia needed a revolution, top anticorruption leaders, and popular participation to achieve their progress. South Korea and Taiwan have experienced gradual but confrontational evolutions, with each step forward fought back, leading to an oscillating progress curve – though many individuals contributed to their advance, there is no one clear leader having led the evolution to open access. Chile and Uruguay transitioned gradually as well, but with less confrontation. Chile had leaders aware of the need to build open access – but the final product had many contributors. As a member of the EU, Estonia is in the safest position of all the cases examined here, as it has now joined a club based on good-governance rules – a good omen for its further consolidation. External factors are strong in other cases as well: South Korea and Taiwan were both on the front lines of the Cold War and received assistance at critical moments, part of it conditional upon reforms. Emulation of foreign models, in particular the Anglo-Saxon liberal model, played a role in Chile, Estonia, and Georgia, where local elites in charge of the economy were frequently educated in the United States. Uruguay had a Swiss model and its population descends from immigrants from various European countries, a far more diverse background than other Latin American countries. A similar dynamic is at play in South Korea, where a considerable number of local elites were educated in Japan. Estonia has benefited from its emulation of the Finnish control of corruption model as well as assistance from the Scandinavian countries.

Across the contemporary achievers, control of corruption was reached by changes in no less than three dimensions of the model. The legal constraints developed gradually and following changes in the balance of power and other good governance policies – even in Chile, the best-placed achiever, people do not credit the judiciary for control of corruption and do not fully trust it. The anticorruption institutional equipment in these countries is quite varied. Only Botswana has an agency which prosecutes anticorruption, but no Freedom of Information Act; all other countries have FOIAs. Some, however, were adopted fairly late and therefore have had a negligible impact on control of corruption measures thus far (e.g., Chile). Audit and controlling institutions carry some weight in Chile, Uruguay, Taiwan, and South

Korea. Having an autonomous, merit-based, and prosperous civil service prior to democratization was a positive factor in all but the post-Soviet cases that had to do without and therefore replaced nearly all civil servants from Soviet times. All countries had some type of anticorruption policy coordination committee with no direct prosecution power; these may have played a role in the formulation of cohesive control of corruption policies but no clear evidence exists.

Liberal economic policies with simplified taxation systems and low levels of red tape played a role in five cases: Estonia, Georgia, Chile, Botswana, and South Korea. Democratization played an important and positive role everywhere: corruption was high on the public agenda and candidates had to champion integrity, sometimes to their peril, as in the Taiwan case. The seven cases examined here have presidential, semi-presidential, or parliamentary systems (Estonia, Uruguay), all possible types of electoral systems and legislature organization, different types of party financing legislation (party financing is actually still a sensitive area in most of them), and varying types of judicial organization. In almost all the selected cases, the executives are strong compared to the other tiers of government: if power discretion is low, it is mostly due to strong accountability mechanisms and a functioning system of checks and balances, but these states are not federal.

Press freedom and collective action by civil society played a considerable role in all these countries, except Botswana but including Georgia, where civil society's roots are still fairly superficial. In South Korea and Estonia, the role of civil society seems to have been greater than elsewhere: Estonia's governing elite is its former civil society opposition from Soviet times. Media pressure is a key factor, but the media itself seems to have sustainability problems in some of these cases. Political leaders played a role everywhere, except in Uruguay where its recent transformation has been so gradual – however, Uruguay now has a model president for anticorruption, one who lives in his old apartment and drives in his old Beetle to the office. The tenure of a successful anticorruption leader needs to be short in order to avoid the onset of favoritism and disillusionment.

Contemporary achievers have managed their performance at different speeds and by different paths, but all cases confirm that progress is only achieved through a change in the equilibrium involving all four dimensions (see also Mungiu-Pippidi *et al.* 2011). Some arrived at control of corruption over decades of gradual build-up, others mixed gradual evolution with big-bang approaches. Half of the selected countries built control of corruption on the rule of law and sound economic policy inherited from a previous authoritarian regime; half started with pluralism and competition for power and then turned to control of corruption. Most of them have a reasonable fit to the basic modernization model, and some, like Estonia and Uruguay, have an excellent fit. This makes those cases distant from the model – such as Georgia – quite remarkable indeed. A stake in and commitment to change from some part of the elite, either political or professional, was essential. While crises and existential threats (present in the post-Soviet and Asian cases) occasionally provide a window of opportunity to move to another norm of governance, and popular demand helps to challenge the existing governance order, the sustainability of control of corruption is due to elite groups who become committed to changing the status quo either by a build-up of critical mass (as in Uruguay and Estonia) or by using their disproportionate power (as in Chile and Georgia) in politics, the legal profession, civil society, and the media. How these evolutions are achieved would need far more detailed process tracing than this chapter can allow and would certainly deserve a whole book in themselves. But the cases do teach us important lessons even at a more summary reading. All these cases outperform their modernization goodness of fit, although none of them is currently a poor country. And it is telling that Slovenia, which started on the top with an income close to nearby Austria and a large middle class, ends being a questionable achiever. Leaders and groups in society emulating a clear governance model, sometimes with help and guidance from the countries they were emulating, changed the governance in their countries, profiting from further legitimacy and prosperity. Other reasons for growth might exist in this interval – but as even the history of these cases shows, nothing sustains better growth than a gradual build-up of ethical universalism as one's governance principle.

6 Domestic collective action capacity

What are normative constraints?

In Chapter 4 we found evidence that a society can constrain those who have better opportunities to spoil public resources if free media, civil society, and critical citizens are strong enough.[1] We also found that elections in and of themselves do not offer sufficient empowerment, even in the absence of political violence. In competitive particularistic regimes (see Chapter 2), ethical universalism fails to take hold as the main rule of the game despite the presence of political pluralism and contested elections, and winners of the political process, in their turn, treat the state as the major source of spoils, feeding off the public resources they divert toward their clients. In many electoral democracies this type of governance context has developed and stabilized, and citizens of those societies seem uninterested or unable to change this state of affairs. Indeed, many of them contribute to it.

Where do normative constraints come from? In his book *Development as Freedom,* Amartya Sen (1999) famously argued that individuals, in order to achieve their potential, must be free from one-sided social domination and must combine their resources to pursue their collective interests and provide public goods to the many. It has never been obvious, however, that the end goal of freedom is to distribute public resources equally and fairly to everyone. In other words, liberty does not necessarily result in a governance regime based on ethical universalism. Elites, clans, tribes, political parties, and groups of every denomination may in fact use their freedom to advance their own narrow interests rather than those of society at large. Indeed, in the 100-plus countries that currently hold regular elections yet lag behind in controlling corruption, pluralism has delivered particularism rather than ethical universalism. The reason seems

[1] A reduced version of this, Chapter 6, was published as Mungiu-Pippidi (2013c).

to be the absence at the grass-roots level of an active and enlightened citizenry able to build normative constraints for elite predatory behavior; instead we find dependent clients or disempowered individuals.

The literature on good governance frequently addresses normative constraints on corruption by discussing such concepts as "civil society," "moral values," "the media," and sometimes "culture." In recent years, awareness of the importance of collective action has increased within the development community, yet many of its approaches to collective action remain disconnected both from theory and from one another. In an attempt to rectify this problem, in 2001 the World Bank devoted an entire *World Development Report* to "empowerment" and later proposed the concept of "social accountability," and in 2002 the United Nations Development Program established the Oslo Governance Center. Yet only the United States Agency for International Development (USAID) and later the US Millennium Challenge Corporation, along with private foundations such as George Soros' Open Society Institute, have started to fund civil society groups and, to a lesser extent, the media as main priorities of their good governance programs. The founding of Transparency International and the proliferation of local chapters in more than a hundred countries have helped to channel a steadier flow of funds toward anticorruption initiatives and to create a genuinely international anticorruption NGO community, though results at the national level are not yet encouraging.

Various streams of academic literature mention four distinct components of normative constraints:

- Values: a prevailing societal *norm* of ethical universalism based on values such as fairness and honesty;
- Social capital: a *widespread habit* of engaging in formal or informal collective action around shared interests, purposes, and values;
- Civil society: a dense *network of voluntary associations*, including NGOs in the Western understanding of the term, but also unions, religious groups, and the like;
- Civic culture: sustained *participation and political engagement* of the people, for instance through media or social movements.

Some virtuous combination of these four factors seems to enable societies to overcome competing tendencies toward violence, cronyism, and social domination and to generate normative constraints that empower ethical universalism. All four elements are necessary and no smaller combination is sufficient for the development of normative constraints capable of ensuring sustainable good governance. It seems that ethical universalism becomes an institution (a widespread norm endorsed by the majority) rather than a mere ideology of the enlightened when a significant part of society shares the belief in the superiority of ethical universalism over particularism as a mode of governance, *and* enough individuals are also willing to act on this belief to make it a reality. This does not necessarily require an absolute majority, but rather a majority of active public opinion, including a fraction of the elite.

The only source for examining the development of normative constraints remains historical. Two examples are frequently quoted and worth analyzing: the Dreyfus affair in France at the turn of the twentieth century, and the extension of the franchise in early nineteenth-century Britain. The story of Captain Alfred Dreyfus, the Jewish scapegoat unjustly sentenced by a military court to life imprisonment for treason is well known, as is Emile Zola's public denunciation of the trial, "J'Accuse!," published in 1898 on the front page of the newspaper *L'Aurore*. Less well known is the extensive public mobilization in favor of impartial justice: young writers such as Marcel Proust joined Zola in collecting 1,482 celebrity signatures, including that of painter Claude Monet, against the Dreyfus verdict. Zola's manifesto on the "civic crime" committed by the military tribunal initiated a long cycle of contestation and political realignment that led to Dreyfus' exoneration – and to a change in public norms – twelve years after the original trial and eight years after the publication of "J'Accuse!" Zola was perfectly aware that he was defending ethical universalism, not a simple miscarriage of justice, when writing that "It is a crime to poison the small and the humble, to exasperate passions of reaction and intolerance ... from which, if not cured, the great liberal France of humans rights will die ..." (Zola 1898). But in order to get a majority of the public agreeing that justice should be universal and impartial, regardless of patriotic appeals or the background of the defendant, it needed several press campaigns, considerable civil society activism, and many years. A clear threshold was in the end crossed in the Dreyfus case, and normative constraints at that point became institutionalized. Civil society and the press played the main roles, but the supporting cast included rising politicians and honest officers and bureaucrats. Many new democracies have not yet had their Dreyfus affair.

While the Dreyfus case is often cited as an example of the power of public opinion and the media, the British political reform a half-century earlier is frequently described as a major institutional change (Acemoglu and Robinson 2006). In 1832 a reform-minded aristocracy concerned with avoiding a French-style revolution extended the franchise in England and Wales. There had been widespread and sustained collective action prior to the bill's passage. Ongoing pressure, including riots and strikes, came from the working class and was sometimes harshly repressed. At the same time, an irrepressible and unauthorized press not only advocated change but singled out for blame those who opposed it. Moreover, there was continuous advocacy for further extending the franchise to the middle class and for abolishing royal sinecures.

For the reform to succeed, the Crown and the existing voters (the "institutional winners" in today's institutional jargon) had to agree to extend electoral rights to more people. Game theory predicts that they would have defended their privileges and fought to maintain the status quo. Yet when reform stalled, voters enfranchised under the old system returned the reformers to power by a wide margin and a clear mandate for change, underscoring that the bill itself merely mirrored a change that had already taken place in the collective mind of British society (Halévy 1961: 43–45). Thus it was the voters themselves who extended the rights that they already enjoyed to their disenfranchised compatriots, bringing about positive change. What appears to be a textbook example of political development driven by an elite strategic decision aimed at averting a potential revolution was actually far more than that, as both bottom-up and top-down elements were present. The change was grounded in collective action at the grass-roots level on many fronts – from the trigger of the French Revolution across the Channel to the activity of various groups at home.

By and large, republican thought has always argued that good government rests on a virtuous, enlightened, and engaged citizenry. The republican tradition insists on both civic virtue and participation in the city's affairs as a recipe for good governance. Machiavelli (2009) was highly skeptical about the former and suggested that free government is unachievable if the citizenry is corrupt. His doubt seems now confirmed in the many cases of electoral democracies unable to control corruption – hence the need to better clarify how citizens can bring about, or not, ethical universalism as the main governance norm.

In his depiction of American society Alexis de Tocqueville was the first modern writer to explain the mechanisms that yield good governance and an engaged citizenry (Tocqueville 2006). He argued that civil society, political participation, and media all serve the same purpose: to empower collective action on behalf of society, rendering it better equipped to solve common problems. He noticed that in all the countries where political associations are prohibited, civil associations are rare. Civil associations, he noticed, facilitate political association; but, on the other hand, political association singularly strengthens and improves associations for civil purposes.

He worried that as men become more equal, individualism is more to be feared and the costs of aggregating interests become higher. Here he saw the newspapers' main role:

> To suppose that they only serve to protect freedom would be to diminish their importance: they maintain civilization. I shall not deny that in democratic countries newspapers frequently lead the citizens to launch together into very ill-digested schemes; but if there were no newspapers there would be no common activity. The evil which they produce is therefore much less than that which they cure. (Tocqueville 2006: 73)

And he was perfectly aware of the difficulties of collective action and the need of practice for successful aggregation to occur:

> When men are as yet but little versed in the art of association and are unacquainted with its principal rules, they are afraid, when first they combine in this manner, of buying their experience dear. They therefore prefer depriving themselves of a powerful instrument of success to running the risks that attend the use of it. (Tocqueville 2006: 76)

Tocqueville offered a comprehensive answer to most, if not all, of the questions about civil society that have been widely debated in recent years, including the relationship between engaged civil society (pro-transparency activists, for instance) and nonengaged civil society (such as bowling leagues or book clubs) and between political and nonpolitical society. Once cooperation and the habit of association exist, it becomes easier to use the social capital these produce for any purpose of collective action. Tocqueville acknowledged that people can organize for any purpose, good or bad, but he viewed the capacity to act collectively as undeniably positive and as the only possible path to good governance. A society capable of collective action is capable of controlling its most violent or selfish tendencies. In short, the capacity for collective action is a public good that derives from extensive social interaction.

The link between collective action and control of corruption

Was Tocqueville right? The explanations he offers can be tested empirically. First, if civic and political associations both draw on the same capacity for collective action, we should find a positive relationship between them. Second, if civil society or the independent media – proxies for normative restraints – in fact limit corruption, we should find a positive relationship between their presence and success in controlling corruption. Despite the imperfections of data on corruption, we have enough material to test Tocqueville's theories and even to test the weight of normative constraints in a model of control of corruption.

The first hypothesis is easily confirmed. Regressing political-party membership on the total number (national aggregates) of civic voluntary associations (including recreational, artistic, charitable, environmental, and consumer groups) recorded by the World Values Survey (WVS) between 1995 and 2008, we find a relationship of high explanatory power. A similar finding was reported on WVS 2000 data by Baer (2007). Party membership in a country can be predicted on the basis of membership in general associations. The results (based on data from 54 countries and over 68,000 observations) are statistically significant at both the national and individual level, with controls for GDP, religion, experience of democracy, education, age, and income (Mungiu-Pippidi 2012). In other words, the propensity toward association is consistent across political and nonpolitical activity. The collective action capacity of civil society draws on people's habits of solving problems together. Results are robust with all tests. If we find low political participation, we also find few civic associations; hence, predatory elites can monopolize politics and engage in state capture with little opposition from society.

The association between collective action capacity and control of corruption was further tested in Chapter 4 (although the absence of time series data on civil society remains a setback), using the number of civil society associations per 100,000 inhabitants in a cross-sectional model; the number of internet connections per 100,000 inhabitants as an indicator of enlightened and informed citizens; freedom of the press; and the social openness index as proxy for normative constraints in the time series (see Table 4.5).

There is a significant positive relationship between control of corruption and the number of associations (CSOs) per capita that explains 54 percent of the total variation, controlling for either human development (HDI) or GDP per capita. A robust association also exists with the other proxies for normative constraints: freedom of the press (explains 67 percent), the number of internet connections (71 percent), and living in a country where Protestantism is the major religious denomination (61 percent), each with the HDI control. Both freedom of the press and the number of CSOs per capita are stronger determinants of control of corruption than Protestantism (when controlling for human development). Protestantism is one of the oldest references to the role of normative constraints in creating an ethical society and government. It has been tested often and has proven significant in relation to control of corruption (for instance, in Treisman 2000). Yet the relationship between Protestantism and good governance is probably more rooted in history than in present-day practice. Today many nominally Protestant countries are *de facto* secular, while quite a few non-Protestant countries tackle corruption quite efficiently. The influence of Protestantism seems to stem from its egalitarian ethos, which may have worked indirectly to support a general orientation toward ethical universalism, literacy, and the promotion of individualism. Its main historical role was probably in the early spread of literacy (a Bible for each constituent), which led in time to the consolidation of a critical mass of "enlightened citizens." This does not mean that other religious traditions are incompatible with good governance, but simply that at the "right" historical moment they did not initiate such a virtuous circle.

The test of civil society's impact on governance, drawing on a larger number of cases than tested before, thus confirms both Tocqueville's observations and the findings of more recent studies (Baer 2007: 67–125; Grimes 2008). A panel regression using corruption-risk data from the ICRG as the dependent variable (see Table 6.1) also confirms the importance of freedom of the press for 133 countries and 1077 observations, confirming earlier reports (Brunetti and Weder 2003: 1801–24). A two-stage least square regression with press

Table 6.1 *Effect of press freedom on corruption: panel regression*

Dependent variable	Pooled OLS		Fixed effects		Random effects
ICRG risk of corruption[a]	1	2	3	4	5
Freedom of the press (Freedom House)[b]	–0.0327***	–0.0239***	–0.0141***	–0.00952**	–0.0216***
	(0.00345)	(0.00286)	(0.00356)	(0.00359)	(0.00238)
HDI[c]		2.064***		–5.137***	1.346***
		(0.354)		(0.888)	(0.356)
Constant	4.100***	2.381***	3.288***	6.399***	2.746***
	(0.194)	(0.294)	(0.156)	(0.559)	(0.289)
Number of observations	1,077	1,077	1,077	1,077	1,077
Number of countries	133	133	133	133	133
R^2 – Overall	0.41	0.48	0.41	0.22	0.47
R^2 – Within			0.02	0.05	0.01
Hausman test (Chi^2 based)					64.47***

Time series cross-section estimations for yearly data between 2000 and 2008, using the corruption measure of the International Country Risk Guide as the dependent variable. Models 1 and 2 show pooled OLS results with cluster robust standard errors in parentheses. Models 3 and 4 report fixed effects estimation results, while model 5 shows random effects estimates (standard errors in parentheses). Significant Hausman test suggests random effects to be biased. Significance levels: * $p<0.1$, ** $p<0.05$, *** $p<0.01$.

[a] Values range between 0 and 6 (higher values indicate less risk of corruption).

[b] Values range from 0 (best) to 100 (worst).

[c] Human Development Index (UNDP), values range from 0 (low development) to 1 (high development).

freedom and corruption using ethnic fractionalization as an instrument seems to confirm earlier findings that causality runs from press freedom to corruption, but when controlling for GDP the instrument loses significance. The normative constraints proved also fairly robust in more complex variants of the model, when tested alongside pluralism, natural resources, ethnic fractionalization, independence of the judiciary, and various economic policies, as shown in Chapter 4 of this book. Altogether, this group of variables seem to measure one latent variable, normative constraints: the collective action capability of a society to censor the behavior of its powerful elites.

The data shows that in countries where control of corruption works we find numerous political and civic associations as well as an active media, and an increase in the freedom of the media in time leads to greater control of corruption. To understand the mechanism of their influence, however, and in particular how they could be made to contribute to better governance in other countries, we need a more in-depth look at both civil society and the media in the problematic countries.

Civil society as watchdog

Alongside statistics, the historical examples provide support for the theory, but introduce concerns as well. London in the 1830s, Paris at the end of the nineteenth century, and New York after the Civil War likely had higher capacities for collective action in support of ethical universalism as a main governance norm than many developing countries do today. A modern-day Tocqueville visiting capitals such as Accra, Kiev, Manila, New Delhi, or Moscow, where anticorruption efforts have been raging for many years now, would not remark on the density of voluntary associations, but rather on the isolation, exhaustion, and underfunding of a few dedicated groups and individuals who have not managed to reach a critical mass. Prague and Sao Paolo might do better. But the widespread picture shows insufficient collective action alongside occasional outbursts and over-reliance on external donors due to insufficient support (cash and volunteer work) from a country's own society. People from Brazil to Sofia who took to the streets in 2012–13 in a remarkable wave of new anticorruption "revolutions" refused to be represented by established NGOs and political oppositions, considering them all part of a corrupt establishment. Yet without any organization such spontaneous movements cannot bring about sustainable change.

In recent years, attempts were made to document the role of civil society in promoting good governance (Armstrong 2007; Boussard 2003; Diamond 1999; Grimes 2008; Park 2003; White 1995). Successful case studies in promoting ethical universalism are not many, but they do exist: Central Europe, Georgia, the Baltic States, and South Korea are the most well known. New social media revolutions are still ongoing and it is too early to assess them (although the number of Facebook users per country does associate with control of corruption). There are some commonalities, as democratization in South Korea, Central Europe, and the Baltics originated in civil society movements that had started as grass-roots protests and loosely organized social movements and evolved after transition into more institutionalized and specialized NGO communities. These anticorruption actions span many years and are extremely diverse. Two comparable short-term campaigns allow us to illustrate the mechanism triggering the change in norms.

In January 2000, 473 South Korean NGOs from across the country formed the Citizens' Alliance for the 2000 Elections with the goal of fostering electoral reform. The main complaint against political parties was their organization on the basis of cronyism – the nomination of candidates according to monetary or personal relationships – resulting in governments captured by private interest and plagued by favoritism. A list was researched and compiled with 114 names of politicians who were found unsuitable for nomination.

A similar situation happened in Romania in 2004, when the EU asked the country to show commitment to anticorruption in order to be invited to sign the EU accession treaty. A small but representative coalition comprised of NGOs and individual journalists created the Coalition for a Clean Parliament, which started negotiations with parties on integrity criteria for screening their candidates on the closed lists for parliament, practically blackmailing them to drop unsuitable candidates or face a naming and shaming campaign. The criteria were not very different between the two countries, despite the lack of awareness by the Romanians of the Korean action: profit from conflict of interest, cooperation with the previous authoritarian regime, unaccountable personal fortune. Based on the findings on these points, some candidates were blacklisted. Media not under government control closely followed the negotiations and the parties' responses, escalating public attention and creating a snowball effect. Political parties that stood to gain from the campaign cooperated publicly with civil society in Romania, increasing the costs of noncooperation for the other parties and making everyone pledge publicly the integrity of candidates. There were attempts to obtain court orders in both Romania and Korea to restrain publicity of any form and legal battles during and after the campaigns, as some candidates sued for libel. However, with slightly different sequences between the two countries both actions were successfully pursued. In Korea, the parties' reaction was to largely ignore the Alliance's blacklisting of candidates and forty-six candidates on the blacklist were nominated nonetheless. The Alliance kept up the movement and campaigns were made in every district, leading to fifty-nine candidates (out of eighty-six blacklisted) losing elections. Forty-two percent of incumbent parliamentarians were voted out, and 106 new candidates were elected.

The Romanian situation went equally well. Parties all stepped into the trap of negotiations: smaller ones knowingly did so to gain advantage over a corrupt, dominant party which had been in government for most of the transition; the latter cooperating because it could not afford to be seen as the only corrupt one. The blacklist included nearly 200 names – more than one-third of the two chambers. Opposition parties had far fewer names on the list than those then in government. The campaign pushed corruption as the main agenda topic and within a few weeks caused the governing party to lose its original twenty percent lead in opinion polls. The party leader who fully cleansed his party of controversial people won the presidential elections, for which he had started as an outsider. About a hundred candidates did not make it to parliament: half were retired by their own parties and half were rejected by voters. One of the civil society leaders became minister of justice after the elections, and better legislation was passed.

Despite these "big bang" successes, preceded by a general feeling of personal frustration due to corruption from the general population – shown in public opinion surveys – corruption scandals and popular perception of widespread corruption in politics did not disappear in the next years. The two "big bangs" worked in similar ways, helped by the media and extensive mobilization due to elections. By 2011, however, the feeling of sustainable accomplishment was somewhat greater in Korea than in Romania, despite the latter's successful EU admission. Although in the short run the two campaigns look nearly identical, the level of civil society in the two countries is very different. According to the WVS 2000, voluntary membership in South Korea, which has the highest percentage of Protestants in the region, is higher than anywhere else in Asia: religious associations enroll about 40 percent, educational 25 percent, and professional 9 percent. By contrast, in Romania, a Christian-Orthodox country experiencing a religious revival, less than 10 percent were enrolled in any sort of associations in 2000, growing to 12 percent ten years later. An online publication written by the public and including many disclosures is extremely popular in South Korea, enjoying millions of views per week. In Romania, the most popular civil society publication is hosted by a major news agency and has about 25,000 viewers a week. Romania's population is 20 million and Korea's is 48 million.

The success of these two campaigns, once significant coalitions managed to cooperate and ally with a part of media, is worth studying but hardly surprising. After all, they came close to reproducing what seemed to have been the historical mechanism of building normative constraints in historical achievers. Significant disclosure campaigns in modern times existed in Sweden, Britain, and the United States, all related to politics, elections, and leading to some ulterior deep reform. The question is why so few "big bangs" exist, and why their positive results are so difficult to sustain once results are achieved.

Daniel Kaufmann (1997) offered the formula that successful anticorruption programs are dependent on knowledge and information plus leadership plus collective action. Indeed, the World Bank has argued that "civil society and the media are crucial to creating and maintaining an atmosphere in public life that discourages fraud and corruption. Indeed, they are arguably the two most important factors in eliminating systemic corruption in public institutions" (PREM Network, World Bank 1997: 44; Stapenhurst 2000). However, few donor programs, including the World Bank, offer programs designed to foster collective action, leadership, and media activity.

The factors hindering the effectiveness of donor-sponsored civil society become apparent when evaluating a significant number of civil society anticorruption projects. Few resemble the grass-roots-intense campaign described here. Eastern Central Europe, for instance, was rich in civil society programs dedicated to good governance in the twenty years following the fall of the Berlin Wall. A research team in an Open Society Institute project collected and examined 471 anticorruption civil society projects from sixteen Eastern European countries, from the "good governance" decade (2000–10).[2] This is an interesting period, as in this interval the region did not progress further, unlike in the previous decade. Most of these projects were funded by Western donors. A handful only (2.5 percent) had a volunteer or community contribution; though these first began to appear at the end of the decade in Hungary, Czech Republic, and Poland. The USAID and other American foundations using American public funds sponsored the largest number of projects (23 percent), followed by the European Union (19 percent), and the Soros Foundation (18 percent). Other donors, including the UN (less than 3 percent), and EU member countries through bilateral projects compose the rest. About half of these projects were run in direct cooperation with governments at various levels, though civil society directly managed them in over 90 percent of cases. However, the other half was not made of projects exposing corrupt activities or practices: less than 10 percent of "engaged" projects dealt with disclosing corruption, and in some countries such projects did not exist.

Most projects were dedicated to research, information, training, consultancy, and advocacy; and their most frequent outcomes were the adoption of legislation, the writing of a report, or the organization of training or conferences. Such projects can only be judged by output indicators (the number of investigative journalists trained), as impact was not sought from the design stage (such as, for instance, the resignation of a corrupt official due to reports by investigative journalists).

The projects that seem to produce traceable impact and particularly those with the highest number of quotations in local media (less than a third) share a number of characteristics. Firstly, they target corruption directly and concretely, proposing a change of norms or people in a limited framework in a limited interval of time. Secondly, they are based on cohesive (so not all-inclusive) coalitions including journalists and the media as active participants (not only involved in dissemination), and are in general broader than just NGOs. Involving media in NGO projects, not just as dissemination agents but as full-fledged participants, exponentially increases the effectiveness of such projects. The more diverse the coalition, the more effective the project becomes: those coalitions including NGOs that each have a specific

[2] The webpage www.againstcorruption.eu and its repository of civil society good governance projects is the product of this research conducted by the author in 2009–10.

task (not just formal, nominal coalitions) as well as unions and other civil society actors seem to work best. Thirdly, the most successful coalitions were not set up by donors, but were grass-roots endeavors sponsored by donors, and also included voluntary work. Fourthly, projects that managed to unearth incentives for groups and targeted individuals worked the best, particularly when linked with natural competition. Some projects managed to create an integrity "market," where actors had to compete to brand themselves as noncorrupt in exchange for avoiding public exposure. Eastern Europe had a few successful projects of this kind, all with a strong dissemination component: compiling rankings of government agencies, municipal services, or public universities on integrity, administrative transparency, and responsiveness. Such rankings inform voters of the quality of public services and encourage the demand for good governance.

Some factors hindering the effectiveness of donor-sponsored civil society become apparent when considering the projects with less impact or whose impact cannot be evaluated. The first problem is insufficient concreteness of anticorruption projects. Far too many projects dealt with corruption in general or with "raising awareness," and only a handful directly attacked corruption in a specific organization or branch of government (see also Spector 2005; Tisne and Smilov 2004). Their basic assumption seems to be that corruption is a natural calamity, like a volcanic eruption, and not a vicious public resource allocation perpetuated by individuals in their own, – or their group's – best interest. It is then deemed sufficient to inform people – for instance, the civil servants who profit from corruption – with a booklet and the risk would magically decrease. Such an approach is far from what donor-sponsored anticorruption aims to achieve when funding civil society anticorruption projects, namely the replication of the normative constraints exercised in societies that have historically managed to control themselves. This objective requires concrete and very public projects addressed at changing behavior: building rule of law and control of corruption is like staging a response to the Dreyfus affair. Some people are bound to lose from anticorruption; thus, exposing and targeting predators is essential for success.

The second frequent source of inefficiency is getting the objectives wrong. To challenge corruption one must understand how it works in its specific environment. Importing objectives from anticorruption efforts in developed countries that do not suit postcommunist countries was a common error. In almost every country projects existed inspired by the debate on US party finance reform, which addressed only a marginal problem in postcommunist countries, and missed the real problems such as politicization of the administration, government favoritism of specific firms, and capture of administrative resources by the governing party. Both the Global Corruption Barometer, a global survey, and Eurobarometer, an EU survey, ask questions about the perceived efficiency of anticorruption government strategies, which are as a rule viewed critically in countries where corruption is a problem, despite different performances across these governments. People strongly perceive the inadequacy of anticorruption strategies and become increasingly skeptical.

The third problem with many anticorruption projects stems from the confusion between the two roles of civil society. This is a widespread problem: global civil society actors such as Transparency International engage in large-scale consultancy for governments and companies, teaching them how to comply with the increasing number of laws and regulations (adopted after their own lobbying). Having the same organization working as a watchdog of government and business and as a deliverer of services for the same government raises conflict of interest issues. If civil society is financed from the government funds it is supposed to monitor, it risks jeopardizing its critical censorship role and a client–patron relationship may emerge instead. This faulty model is copied by many smaller organizations who see in anticorruption a source of funding and does not contribute to the development of normative constraints. If we take Rwanda, for instance, which has progressed considerably on paper due to top-down reforms in recent years, but still has a president elected with over 90 percent of the vote, it becomes clear that civil society needs to play the role of a real watchdog, not merely an adviser to government.

The fourth category of problems is the insufficient domestic support enjoyed by engaged civil society. Watchdog NGOs are often an isolated vanguard in a society with low association capacity that does not really follow behind. Most types of watchdog activities in Eastern Europe were supported by external donors. EU funds do not target corruption, and civil society can access them only through cooperation with the government: hence the backslide on corruption scores in quite a few new Eastern European member countries after EU accession, when most external funds disappeared and contribution from

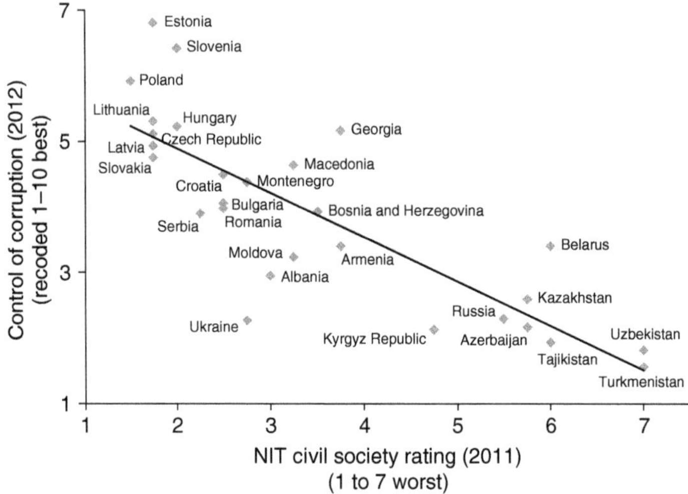

Figure 6.1 The association between civil society and control of corruption in post-Soviet states
Source: Worldwide Governance Indicators and Freedom House

their own societies remained very low. People complain loudly about corruption in public opinion surveys, but in practice businesses do not often engage in any good governance promotion activity, though they are the main ones to profit from it. This is an indicator that such activities are still too costly for businesses in an environment where government favoritism is high and control agencies often extort and repress. This is a vicious circle; if the main profiteers of good governance (competitive companies) do not fund such activity, then it is unclear whence the money should come. Volunteer work is also scarce and often unnecessary, since most projects concentrate on expertise rather than participation. Many coalitions initiated by donors disappeared once the donor money was spent. Outsiders cannot really protect whistleblowers from conformity to local rules of the game, exercised as peer pressure; normative constraints in particularistic societies are rather exercised against whistleblowers, not the corrupt, so their numbers remain low despite the adoption of whistleblower protection acts in many countries.

If this is the situation in Central Europe and the Balkans, the countries of the former Soviet Union fare much worse. They have almost no associations of any kind and mostly authoritarian governments, therefore their control of corruption is inferior to that of less developed sub-Saharan Africa. They also have the largest gap in the world between estimates of corruption by development (Central Asia, Azerbaijan, and Russia in particular) and their real situation, on account of their weak civil society, as Figure 6.1 shows. As watchdog NGOs develop in capital cities, we might see occasional outbursts of sheer heroism, like the winter 2011 Russian election protests (led by anticorruption activists) or the 2012 *Chesno!* Ukrainian campaign. If a couple of years later we see their activists harassed by the same authorities, it is because such vanguards have strayed too far from the passive society behind them.

Media as watchdog of ethical universalism

Civil society exercises normative constraints both indirectly, by creating a general capacity for collective action, and directly, through groups and individuals promoting public interest and ethical universalism. What about the media? On the one hand, freedom of the media allows a plurality of voices and interests to manifest themselves openly in a society. This alone is insufficient, however, because such voices could simply promote private interests, often to the detriment of others, if not society as a whole. As Hallin and Papathanassopoulos put it: "The notion of journalistic professionalism, which forms the basis for journalists' claims of autonomy, is connected with the idea that journalists serve a public interest that transcends the interests of particular political parties, owners, and social groups" (2002: 185–86). Therefore, the media must be more than plural in order for it to generate normative constraints by performing effectively and credibly its public watchdog function over the conduct of public officials (Pope 2000: 120). The media must promote ethical universalism as governance's chief principle, and denounce a government captured by private interests. This simple definition shows the difficulty of the task. Why, in a society where particularism is the rule of the game, would the media be different and promote ethical universalism, or, in media jargon, fairness and accuracy in reporting? When Zola was denouncing military courts, the majority of other newspapers sided with the establishment. Some were openly nationalistic and anti-Semitic: opinions are diverse in a society, and most media are private and cater to groups of different persuasions. If resources would be found to analyze the whole global media today, only a minority would be found to aspire to "objectivity," a norm of American journalism that has distinguished it from the dominant model of continental European journalism for more than a century (Donsbach 1995). Though many journalists around the world emulate this norm, being socialized into the values of American journalism, they do not comprise the majority even in Europe. Quite the contrary, alternative models exist.

"Objectivity" could once be defined as a moral ideal, a set of reporting and editing practices, and an observable pattern of news writing (Tuchman 1972). Its foundation is the norm of ethical universalism, permeating the attitude of journalists toward journalism itself, before becoming an attitude oriented toward the rest of the world. One must be fair to demand fairness. Techniques exist that measure the degree of impersonality and nonpartisanship in news stories through content analysis of newspapers and news broadcasts. The few media systems where objectivity is the dominant norm have developed it very gradually, in the late nineteenth and early twentieth centuries in the United States, and to a smaller extent in Europe (Schudson 1998; Tuchman 1972). Early media was wildly partisan, living off blackmail (an effective way of coercing advertising) or government or partisan subsidies in exchange for slandering opponents and promoting propaganda more than readership.

An accurate depiction is offered by one of the best-documented corruption stories ever, that of Tammany Hall, which dominated New York City politics at the end of the nineteenth century. Although the "Ring" of corrupt local administrators (who were also running the local Democratic Party and who controlled the judiciary) was eventually brought down with the help of the media, it was the media that also helped them to survive so long. Most New York newspapers seem to have been on the Ring's payroll. The minority market-oriented media, personified by *The New York Times* and *Harper's Weekly*, fought against them for years, but it was not until, due to a stroke of luck, they were able to publish the financial accounts of the city on their front pages, that they succeeded in curbing the Ring's power. Eventually, a few Ring members were jailed, and very slowly the city moved away from corrupt politics. It took far more, however, for the media to become professional, through a mixture of economic incentives and legal repression.

> On some sheets ... there were six or eight staffers who drew stipends from the city ranging from $2000 to $2500 a year. Their jobs were to write blurbs in the guise of news stories. Some specialized in writing letters to out-of-town papers extolling the accomplishments of Mayor Hall's administration. (Miller 1996)

This PR disguised within journalism is all too familiar to many media producers in many countries of the world. Alena Ledeneva sketches a similar picture of the post-1989 Russian media. She describes a landscape where the main goal of most media is not information, but public relations, particularly "black and gray" PR, which frequently amounts to disinformation. This is the source of a whole array of pathologies that she describes in her book, such as disinformation campaigns, "kompromat" (blackmail targeted at politicians), and so on. (Ledeneva 2006). This model is referred to as "media capture" (Mungiu-Pippidi 2012). A captive media is a media where private interests and not objectivity shape the content. The definition is grounded in the American model of media, relying on the presumptions that "objectivity" has to be the benchmark, and that objectivity is a reachable ideal – and beyond controversy.

A media landscape where most media is captive can be found in nearly all limited-access order regimes and can be diagnosed by some clear features. For instance, we would find far more media sources than the advertising market would predict in such countries, mostly unprofitable but heavily subsidized by their owners. The reason is that captive media has a business model of its own: it may lose money, but generates other types of profit for its owner. We would not find fully functioning media market institutions. Advertising from private sources would not be very well correlated with circulation, for instance; and tax breaks, monopolies, advertising, or other forms of subsidy distorting the media market would exist in abundance. Though a plurality of sources exist, as in presently unconsolidated democracies, the media owners would in all likelihood belong to vested interest groups and/or negative social capital networks linking business and politics. Frequently, no de facto separation would be found between the business of media, politics, and business more generally, and the most powerful would own media, either directly or through intermediates. In this landscape, one would be hard pressed to find an investor who makes a profit from media alone. More frequently, one finds businessmen owning media in order to promote their other business or political interests through blackmail or intimidation. Such media owners act as a cartel directly opposed to the autonomy of the journalistic body, which is unable to oppose very effective collective action due to the presence of so many mercenaries or plain "disinformation" agents accountable only to media owners. As the general picture is so removed from the standards of quality journalism, a wide range of other individual acts of corruption can be found, too. Ethical norms simply would not exist. Guests would pay producers to be invited to talk shows to promote their ventures, and reporters would be organized to cover events.

Jeremy Pope acknowledged that corruption exists within the journalism profession and even that its character can reach systemic proportions:

> In Mexico and India, many reporters, for example, earn a stipend from the institutions they cover to supplement their meager salaries. Journalists in various other countries, such as Indonesia, are also known to accept such pay-offs. This creates a powerful disincentive to explore misdeeds in high places. (Pope 2000: 120)

The existence of systemic corruption greatly perverts the media system, and its analysis in classic terms of the repressive action of government becomes inadequate. The model of "media capture" can range between the ideal of Anglo-Saxon journalism and the plain authoritarian model. The latter has evolved due to democratization, even if partial in the last three decades: governments unable or unwilling to resort to direct media control contribute to media capture either directly or indirectly. State subsidies, debt bailouts, preferential distribution of state advertising, and tax breaks for media owners are traded in exchange for favorable treatment by the media. The government once controlled the media through formal regulations, but as those can become the focus of international attention, it increasingly resorts to less overt means of control. Governments, as well as other powerful actors, pervert as well as repress. If we know where a country stands on corruption we can predict how its media would operate, not only the other way around. Again in the words of Hallin and Papathanassopoulos (2002: 189):

Clientelism tends to break down the autonomy of social institutions, and journalism is no exception. It forces the logic of journalism to merge with other social logics – of party politics and family privilege, for instance. And it breaks down the horizontal solidarity of journalists as it does of other social groups.

The existing statistical evidence shows the reciprocal impact of media and corruption. In their report *A Free Press Is Bad News for Corruption,* Aymo Brunetti and Beatrice Weder (2003) found evidence of a significant relationship between more press freedom and less corruption in a large cross-section of countries (125) and suggested that the direction of causation runs from higher press freedom to lower corruption. Evidence of a strong statistical association was also found in the research for this book, but reverse causation remains. A 2009 World Bank report also introduces some caution, warning that the relationship was weak in authoritarian countries and nonexistent in intermediate categories: only consolidated democracy displayed a clear and strong association (Norris 2010). A large survey on media freedom and development in 134 countries also warned that the media was used quite successfully to perpetuate the status quo in government and the economy (Weaver *et al.* 1985). Running a two-stage least square regression on a panel of postcommunist Europe (28 countries) with ethnic fractionalization as instrument, the causation is clearly reciprocal.

The picture is more complex than what naive anticorruption and media freedom promoters believe. As electoral democracy expands, the government monopoly of ownership and direct censorship are less and less the main cause affecting media freedom (Djankov *et al.* 2001). By and large, how can a media landscape be any better than the general state of market relations in a society? In their classic *Four Theories of the Press*, Siebert, Peterson, and Schramm (1956: 1–2) claimed that "the press always takes on the form and coloration of the social and political structures within which it operates. Especially, it reflects the system of social control whereby the relations of individuals and institutions are adjusted." So why should media be an exception when particularism is the dominant norm in a society? Although some media outlets may try to combat it, the media system as a whole will accurately reflect the state of affairs in that society. Other authors may claim, as Paolo Mancini does, that this state of affairs, although indeed more widespread than media scholars acknowledge, is in fact a form of pluralism in its own right which should not be equated with corruption. Describing Italy's institutionalized particularism of the 1980s, when public TV channels were divided, from management to journalists, between the three main political parties (Christian Democrats, Socialists, and Communists), Mancini praises *lotizzazione* and compares it favorably with majority domination (Mancini 2009). Under this model, however, journalists would only report corruption in parties other than their own, and objectivity would result from an intersection of viewpoints rather than in the individual news stories or investigations.

Can such a media successfully exercise the role of watchdog and serve as a "pillar of integrity," as the design of Jeremy Pope and Transparency International would expect? The answer is not plain and illustrates the difficulties faced by anticorruption activists and honest journalists in such environments. The media can be the main accountability actor, but also a vulnerability when it comes to countering corruption. As the civil society favoring ethical universalism and rule of law has to impose itself gradually against negative social capital civil society, we can also encounter free versus less free media, and corrupt versus noncorrupt, as in the Tammany Hall story.

The unilateral perpetrator model, with the government as culprit and the media the victim, relies on the presumption that media is by default "good" and the government "bad." The model fit well a world where the majority of countries were plainly defined as nonfree by Freedom House. But what about the world past the fourth wave of democratization, when the number of plain authoritarian countries has diminished in favor of electoral democracies, hybrid regimes, and competitive particularistic countries? The "partly free" media category, to which most countries rated by Freedom House have come to belong, hides a widespread phenomenon of "captive media," a media whose main role is not to inform or entertain the public, but to serve as a means of trading influence and favors for its owners.

Who then can shake this suboptimal equilibrium of corrupt press and corrupt society, and how can they initiate the virtuous circle? Various types of external influence vary greatly across countries; such influence is generally regarded as a positive attribute for the media, as socialization into "objectivity" as the main universal professional norm is sometimes the only factor balancing domestic particularism.

Postcommunist European media, for instance, was greatly influenced by external factors in three ways: firstly, by receiving an accessible cultural model from Western media to be followed by journalists and politicians alike; secondly, by the political conditionality related to Council of Europe, NATO, and EU accession, which all included some media freedom promotion elements; thirdly, through the permanent channels of communication between professions, contributing to the resocialization of Easterners according to Western standards. This third type of influence was in most cases exercised directly on the media, through grants, training, and assistance programs.

Journalists exist in every country who are professionally motivated to emulate quality investigative journalism from the most competitive and professional media environments. They may be in the minority in their profession, but they are an asset. The problem is the lack of autonomous media outlets to publish their stories or organize anticorruption campaigns. Online publications and socialization networks seem increasingly the solution, as in Mexico, where anonymous bloggers fight organized crime more than established publications. But they also need support. Very few donor programs cater for the media or ensure the survival of such outlets, which cannot be economically viable in countries dominated by particularism. Training investigative journalists is more popular, but of limited utility, as each country has its own data-gathering problems. Locals are bound to know better than outsiders how to obtain and check their data. What is solely missing is support for dissemination and widespread watchdog activity, by bloggers or simply citizens armed with their own mobile phones and long-term support building them into a critical mass. In other words, while an Emile Zola is not easy to find, nearly all societies produce Zola types. The difficult part is in building some sustainable collective action around them until a reasonable level of normative constraints is reached, so that they do not remain isolated and exceptional, until finally defeated within their own societies.

Can collective action be fostered? An open question

Since a level of normative constraint sufficient to enforce an open-access order has emerged in so few countries, it is clear that this socially optimal equilibrium is difficult to reach. Examining the matter from a developmental perspective helps us to understand why the odds against moving from weak to strong normative constraints seem so high. As Eisenstadt and Roniger (1984) have noted, clientelism is frequently in competition with more open forms of exchange. Similarly, the development of civil society and rule-bound associations does not advance in a vacuum, but rather in opposition to groups benefiting from particularistic arrangements and seeking to advance their own interests against collective ones.

In a society dominated by particularism, it is frequently more convenient for individuals to try to accede to the privileged group or to become clients of influential patrons than to engage in a long-term battle to change the rule of the game to ethical universalism. In such societies, there is no tradition of association between equals, since trust is particularistic and is built on clans, patrons, and clients. Attempts to change this are bound to have high costs with few immediate returns. Any progress toward ethical universalism would threaten the existing order, and the predators and patrons who would fight against such progress are likely to be greater in number, richer, and better placed in society than new, horizontally structured associations.

Finally, the political mobilization of public opinion in support of ethical universalism is also difficult to achieve. More than a century has passed since Zola's manifesto, yet such instances remain memorable chiefly because they are rare; they have become routine in only a handful of societies. For a society to reach the optimal equilibrium that maximizes social welfare, there must be some sort of critical mass that favors governance based on ethical universalism. Societies must reach the permanent capability to exercise normative constraints, and not be forced to rely solely on the vertical accountability provided by elections. Otherwise, even when successful "big bangs" exist (like an Orange Revolution), the newcomers to power will end up behaving similarly to those ousted, and the vicious circle will be closed again.

But why, a social psychologist might ask, would individuals associate to promote ethical universalism rather than narrow self-interest in the first place? If we look at historical developments, we find instances when competitive groups, such as traders, were better able to expand their private profits under universal rather than privilege-based rules. They allied with more altruistically minded people, who advocated virtue and civism, like the Scottish Enlightenment philosophers, or practiced it – philanthropists, journalists, a few barristers. Thus, good governance was brought about not by the most disenfranchised and powerless, but by merchants, politicians, and intellectuals who engaged in collective action against privilege and in favor of fair competition and a level playing field, an alliance of utilitarianism and altruism.

People's behavior is shaped by their expectations about the future consequences of their actions. If they perceive particularism as a widely accepted general norm, they are unlikely to engage unilaterally in altruistic, cooperative, and honest behavior. They know that their action will have little effect if undertaken alone rather than collectively. The problem is thus one of inducing a sense of efficacy that will mobilize individuals in favor of changing the rules of the game (Bandura 1997; 1999) and then build a critical mass of such individuals. Fostering collective action at such a level amounts to an exercise in society building, if the traditional small-scale communities have already been merged into unwieldy cities and large states, an overextension Adam Ferguson saw as a main cause of weakening civil society and rising corruption (1996: 257).

Nevertheless, attempts to build this critical mass – helped greatly by social media tools – have become very visible all around the world in a new generation of protests raging since 2010 in both crisis-hit and economically prosperous countries. The demand for good governance is on the rise, but the capacity of long-term collective action in favor of new rules of the game is bound to vary greatly across these countries.

7 International agency and its anticorruption impact

The previous chapter explored the domestic mechanisms of generating normative constraints on behavior. But international factors in controlling corruption should be discussed as well, given the growth of an international anticorruption community and the creation of aid conditionality in this regard. Is the international community able to create serious constraints impacting the national level? The equilibrium pictured in this book is reached – or not reached – there only. Any influence, either on resources or constraints, needs to have a national impact to be defined as such. Can external agency influence this domestic equilibrium – for the worse, but especially for the better?

The international influence on governance of interest in this chapter is not the side effect of international trade or development aid. Deliberate effort is made by the international community to support domestic control of corruption. The fall of the Berlin Wall unleashed an international process without precedent in ambition and depth: the peaceful democratization and transformation of countries by external actors represented by the international community. The lessons of 1989 were well learned and seemed to indicate that sufficient external pressure (in the form of economic and political conditions) combined with domestic agency of sufficient proportions can change political regimes. It worked marvelously in Central Europe and the hope was that an action model had been created that could be applied further to great effect. Compared to this grand drive to change undemocratic political regimes, improving governance might seem a mere addition, a far less ambitious side goal. But while evidence existed that externals can play some role in democratizing a country (Huntington 1993), next to nothing was known about influencing governance from outside. It was largely presumed that some formal institutional transfers in the fields of civil service or the judiciary targeted by donor programming could improve a country's governance. The first serious academic accounts sounded the alarm, however, that areas such as justice and administration reflect closely the existing power equilibrium in a society and with their high transaction costs and high discretion are quite difficult to influence from outside (Carothers 1998; Fukuyama 2004). By transferring institutions, international donors are attempting to change governance orders after having tried – and, to some extent, succeeded – with political regimes. But can governance contexts, if understood in terms of this interplay of formal and informal institutions balancing one another to determine the allocation of public resources, be affected at all from the outside? In other words, what elements of the opportunities versus constraints formula can be influenced by donors? What specific strategies have donors developed to push the agenda of anticorruption to recipient countries (for instance, tying foreign assistance to improvements in governance) and what impact did they manage to achieve? The fourth chapter of this book has already examined the performance of a few institutional transfers by comparison across countries, finding that they perform poorly by themselves: this chapter presents evidence of external impact on control of corruption, focusing on three aggregated sets of transformation experiences: Millennium Challenge Corporation Threshold Grants, a pilot project offering countries grants to improve their control of corruption rating (among others); the European Neighbourhood Policy, an EU policy targeted at Mediterranean and Eastern European countries; and the EU accession process, which made control of corruption a condition for the admittance of the eight new postcommunist members, as well as to a host of aspiring candidates in the Balkans.

Before going into the systematic evidence collected on these three areas, a brief review might be useful. The years since 1990 have seen a range of multilateral agreements fighting corruption enacted, engaging states, international organizations, and a range of non-state actors, such as multinational companies and civil society organizations. These agreements have aimed to address corruption in three ways: first, by overcoming collective action problems that might limit cooperation in efforts to increase international constraints to corruption; second, by developing and codifying anticorruption legal norms internationally; and third, by promoting and establishing legal constraints and good governance norms at the national level (Johnsøn *et al.* 2012). The key international agreements with regard to anticorruption are:

- the Financial Action Task Force, established in 1989 to combat money laundering;
- the 1997 OECD Anti-Bribery Convention (41 signatories by June 2015);
- the 2002 Extractive Industries Transparency Initiative (EITI), to improve transparency and reduce corruption in resource-rich countries;
- the 2003 United Nations Convention Against Corruption (UNCAC), counts as of April 2015 175 parties, which includes 172 UN member states, the Cook Islands, the State of Palestine, and the European Union;
- the 2007 Stolen Asset Recovery Initiative of the World Bank and the United Nations Office on Drugs and Crime.

However, these strictly international acts only follow earlier efforts, either unilateral or continental. The oldest anticorruption act with an international reach was the US-sponsored Foreign Corrupt Practices Act (FCPA) of 1977, which criminalized bribery of foreign officials and extended jurisdiction of American courts to include the country where the alleged felony had been committed. Enforcement varies greatly across these international acts, some relying mostly on individual agency (as in the case of the FCPA), others on the political will of governments. Seeing the great effort that went into legislating, one would expect more effort in assessing results. However, very little work has been undertaken on the impact of the new international legal framework or external intervention in anticorruption more generally (Johnsøn *et al.* 2012; Mungiu-Pippidi *et al.* 2011). Some work (Carr and Oouthwaite 2008; Cuervo-Cazurra 2006, 2008; Segal 2006; Tarullo 2003–2004) seems to suggest that international bribery acts are underenforced for various reasons, ranging from judicial cooperation difficulties to plain conflict between policy goals of states, with international anticorruption losing to national interests. Escresa and Picci (2014) found that the number of cases filed under the FCPA in US courts correlates with corruption perception indicators per country, which seems to validate both perception measurements and enforcement of the FCPA: most cases are filed from more corrupt countries. But such evidence seems also to suggest that enforcement, even in the rare situation when enforcement exists, contributes to control of corruption more in the developed country in which firms are based than in the developing country. Applying a game theory approach, researchers also found that the optimal strategy for proponents of strong anti-bribery enforcement through the OECD Anti-Bribery Convention is to convert the play into an assurance game, thus forecasting that enforcement will be weak (Tarullo 2003–2004). Signatories of the OECD Convention on Combating Bribery of Foreign Public Officials in international business transactions presented relatively lower foreign direct investment (FDI) afterwards (Cuervo-Cazurra 2006). Such evidence means that enforcement of laws against bribery abroad might work primarily by discouraging business engagement in notoriously corrupt countries: prudent investors have always invested more in developed and noncorrupt countries. In short, international antibribery legislation may reduce resources for corruption, but its direct impact is felt mostly by international firms with no evidence as yet that recipient countries are in any way affected. Seeing that a country like China with low control of corruption is also a major foreign investor and can easily use domestic resources to replace any affected Western companies and that FDI in Brazil, Russia, India, and China has only grown in recent years, the overall impact of OECD's convention on domestic control of corruption for developing countries becomes quite questionable.

The impact of other conventions where enforcement is ensured only by peer-review mechanisms (UNCAC, GRECO) is also seldom measured. In a recent paper, David-Barrett and Okamura (2013) found some evidence that countries that implemented the EITI standards attracted additional aid, and they argue that governments see EITI membership as a way of building a reputation for seeking to improve governance with the international community. This suggests that conditionality related to EITI implementation might work.

It is the United Nations Convention Against Corruption (UNCAC) on which most hopes are pinned, as it is the world's first global, comprehensive, and legally binding anticorruption instrument. The idea of a specific international instrument addressing corruption was born amidst negotiations for the United Nations Convention Against Transnational Organized Crime. UNCAC came into force in 2005 and includes provisions for preventive measures (Chapter II) as well as criminalization and law enforcement (Chapter III). To date, the convention numbers 149 signatories and 171 parties. A review mechanism was adopted in 2010. The adoption of an effective follow-up monitoring mechanism for UNCAC implementation is considered to be one of the biggest challenges ahead. Few developing countries have transposed the provisions of UNCAC into national law, to say nothing of the challenges of implementing them in practice. Considering the reputational costs (international and domestic) for a country that does not adopt UNCAC, it may be that a similar mechanism as EITI can work with countries competing to gain a better reputation. However, by 2009 there was no evidence that countries adopting UNCAC progressed more than those that had not (Mungiu-Pippidi *et al.* 2011). Once every country has adopted the UNCAC – a moment fast approaching – variation will disappear, eliminating the value of testing UNCAC impact through regression analysis, because too little diversification in the dummy variable will exist. In 2009, when 129 ratifications had taken place, the before and after test showed no significant improvement, and the regression tests showed no significant association between adopting UNCAC and progress toward better control of corruption.

The international normative framework is completed by other actions of developed countries or "donors." Presuming corruption is an effect of poverty, aid should have a positive impact on building control of corruption. Conditioning aid on reforms or effective implementation of EITI or UNCAC would also make a lot of sense. By the end of the 1990s, however, academic studies increasingly supported the view that donors had little control over how a recipient government financed its projects and that foreign aid was rather an incentive for corrupt practices. With the embrace of a "selectivity" approach by the United States, enough variation was created across donor strategies to assess how conditionality and selectivity perform in the field of good governance promotion, if at all.

Alesina and Weder (1999) reported that more corrupt governments receive more aid and they could not find any evidence that an increase in foreign aid reduces corruption. Other authors found that more aid had a negative impact on corruption, rule of law, and bureaucratic quality (Bräutigam and Knack 2004; Knack 2001). However, evidence pointing to the contrary also exists, showing that foreign aid generally reduces corruption (Tavares 2003), and its reduction effect is greater in less corrupt countries. Moreover, this effect varies by donor country (Okada and Samreth 2012). The variation in results can be explained by authors using a variety of country samples, aid types, and controls. Data on aid is often scarce and incomplete. The bottom line remains the one emphasized by Burnside and Dollar (2004), the authors of the most quoted and contested paper from this literature: "We found these results quite intuitive: a corrupt, incompetent government is not going to use aid wisely and outside donors are not going to be able to force it to change its habits."[1] The evidence on conditionality is also perplexing. Conditionality is a set of requirements that must be implemented *prior* to disbursement of a loan or grant (Johnson and Zajonc 2006). But if donors know a country is corrupt, do they also know the recipe for helping it out, or do they rely on the aforementioned "monocropping," neglecting the local context? What seemed an ideal anticorruption prescription, such as privatization, for instance, turned into a major source of corruption in many countries (Hoff and Stiglitz 2005). Such international prescriptions might not only be too poorly linked to the local context, but risk being adopted only formally, resulting in a void of responsibility. The conditionality of the international financial institutions' structural adjustment programs of the 1980s and 1990s, for instance, were highly criticized for poor impact on stabilization and economic growth and blamed for a worsening of social indicators. However, authors such as Nicholas van der Walle (2001) have argued that the formal conditions contained in financing agreements were seldom implemented in practice, and this was, in fact, the main reason why such reforms were ineffectual. Conditionality makes governments less accountable for their own failures or, as Collier (1999) argues, "Conditionality is often dysfunctional because it implies a transfer of sovereignty that undermines the domestic political process."

Finally, inconsistent enforcement of conditionality is blamed on "exit failure" – the donors' incapacity to make credible threats to stop aid in the case of noncompliance (Birdsall 2004). There are examples of donors who have repeatedly imposed the same reforms on recipient countries or paid for reforms that never materialized or that were soon reversed. In such cases, the breach of promises was rarely sanctioned by donors such as the World Bank (Mosley *et al.* 2004; Radelet 2005; Svensson 2003). Conditionality fails because recipients do not regard the conditions as binding and most donors are reluctant to stop the flow of aid even when conditions are not met. This results in low compliance, but continued high release rates of loan installments (World Bank 2001). Because aid continues flowing, poor governance is perpetuated. Against this backdrop, performance-based aid, based

[1] See Collier and Dollar (2002) for a synthesis of the debate.

on the selectivity principle, emerged as an alternative to the traditional approach. In performance-based approaches, donors make aid dependent upon on the actions and performance of recipient countries and give more aid to countries that have already, for example, implemented policy and institutional reforms to improve their governance. The main proponents of performance-based allocation of aid were Collier (1997; Collier *et al.* 1997) and Svensson (2000; 2003), who called for a fundamental change in donor behavior to reward reform-minded recipient countries. Aid allocation would be based on retrospective performance appraisals rather than conditional on reform promises. This approach proposed a radical shift of strategy. As Radelet (2005) put it, "In the language of the principal–agent problem, donors should spend less time trying to write contracts that force an alignment of incentives and instead give more aid to countries that on their own demonstrate similar motivations and objectives."

In recent years, corruption has become the major theme of conditionality and/or selectivity. Changing governance is no longer only a side condition for the effective disbursement of aid, but is specified by the United States and the EU at the core of their assistance. The following three sets of cases analyzed further will review this approach and its impact so far on national control of corruption.

Millennium Challenge Corporation

Established by the US Congress in 2004 with the deliberate purpose of promoting more efficient and accountable foreign assistance, the Millennium Challenge Corporation (MCC) has adopted an approach that emphasizes the careful selection of aid recipients rather than the imposition of restrictive conditions on the use of aid. The corporation addresses corruption in three ways: the selection process itself incentivizes countries to adopt tough anticorruption reforms, as corruption control is an essential eligibility criterion; its Threshold Grant Program (designed to help candidate countries become eligible for an MCC Compact) is used to scale up and accelerate reform-minded governments' anticorruption programs; and the MCC's underlying premise that foreign aid should be a two-way street is advancing the global anticorruption agenda by institutionalizing the notion that if donors are to provide more assistance, recipient countries must provide greater accountability and deliver results (Braga 2011). As a response to critics of one-size-fits-all development policies, MCC works according to the principle that successful anticorruption programs must be tailored to local institutions, knowledge, culture, social structures, and technologies. Every country's history of governance is different and each policy intervention needs to be tailored to these particularities.

The MCC's Threshold Grant Program grew out of a concern that too few countries would meet the eligibility criteria for an MCC Compact Grant and that, as a result, those countries most in need of MCC aid might end up permanently excluded. Even if there is political will, it is difficult in the absence of targeted resources for an impoverished nation to raise health or education standards to a level high enough to meet the eligibility criteria. The Threshold Program is intended to support countries in focusing on the very deficiencies that make them fail to qualify for a Compact Grant in the first place. Using the incentive of a potential MCC Compact, the Threshold Program is meant to encourage partner countries to design and undertake a challenging reform program (Millennium Challenge Corporation 2010). In order to qualify for assistance, countries must submit concept papers identifying where and why they failed to meet specific indicators, proposals for reforms that would improve these indicators, and the types of assistance required to implement these reforms (US Congress 2007). By 2011 MCC had funded twenty-three Threshold Programs worth over $495 million. Control of corruption is the only "hard" indicator that must be satisfied in other to classify for MCC Compacts and 54 percent of Threshold Program budgets are directed toward fulfilling this indicator. By 2011, all but four Threshold Programs (Burkina Faso, Guyana, Jordan, and Sao Tome and Principe) had focused on control of corruption and two countries (Paraguay and Albania) had already signed second Threshold Programs, both to continue battling corruption.

Improvements in policy performance in countries that are either seeking to become eligible for MCC assistance or that have already been selected and are continuing the reform process are presumed to be related to the MCC. As the former MCC CEO John J. Danilovich put it, "The incentive of becoming MCC eligible has prompted many countries to reevaluate their policies, regulations, and legislation related to good governance, health, and education, and their business climate ... This is a welcome result of something I call the MCC effect" (Millenium Challenge Corporation 2006). In a working paper, Harvard economists Doug Johnson and Tristan Zajonc (2006) checked for such an effect during the early years of the MCC's existence in a sample of 102 possible recipient countries and found that potential recipients of MCC funds improved 25 percent more on indicators after the MCC was created than before it. A more recent study focusing specifically on control of corruption (Öhler *et al.* 2010) also finds that the MCC was successful in promoting better control of corruption. Yet given the absence of statistically significant and undisputed evolution in nearly all the cases, more in-depth research is needed.

Rather than looking at all potential recipients, we examine the MCC effect on the threshold countries only – that is, on the part of the program that combines conditionality with selectivity and stresses corruption in particular – assessing their performance on the CoC indicator. Taking the period 2004–09 as reference interval, we find no significant effect at the 90 percent confidence interval; if the time interval is extended backwards to 2000, Tanzania progressed significantly. Relaxing the confidence error to 75 percent to increase sensitivity of CoC to change, I find some improvement during the threshold period in Albania (but later backsliding), Indonesia, and Paraguay, and regression in Kyrgyzstan, while Peru, Uganda, Ukraine, Zambia, Malawi, the Philippines, and Timor-Leste register no evolution. Paraguay registers the largest change, partly due to its low starting point.

Despite this, really successful cases are missing – including those that might, at first glance, appear to be likely candidates. The most telling example is Ukraine, targeted with massive sums by both the European Neighbourhood Partnership and a $44 million-dollar MCC Threshold Program grant – probably the largest good governance grant on record – which failed to deliver essential legislation, let alone implementation. The anticorruption laws that were finally passed after great delay in 2009 were repealed by the new parliament in 2010; in 2011 the Cabinet of Ministers also terminated the Government Agent on Anticorruption Policy, a position created at the donors' request. The politicization of anticorruption, with two sets of offices created by two different regimes, reached unprecedented heights. The prosecution of high-profile political corruption cases was severely politicized, leaving Western donors in a difficult position. They had to defend the former Prime Minister Yulia Tymoshenko when she was accused by the new regime, but discovered that her former constituency was not rallying in her favor, as many believed she was indeed corrupt, though unjustly sentenced. Ukraine's CPI rating before and after the Threshold Program grant is very telling: in 2011 Ukraine ranked 152nd out of 183 countries and territories, down from 134th (out of 178) in 2010 and 118th place (out of 179) in 2007. Donors shifted gradually their strategy to civil society in 2012, but progress was still lacking by that time.

EU enlargement

Despite the general difficulty in changing governance, the EU has a privileged position. In the early twenty-first century the EU was largely perceived as a very successful club that many countries queued to join despite very demanding conditions. Even countries without any accession perspective, such as Ukraine or Tunisia, started contemplating adopting parts of the EU legislation in the hope that this would open the door to favorable treatment, from visa liberalization to EU assistance. In other words, the EU had the greatest leverage in the world on its candidate countries and even some neighbors, making the lessons learned from this experience all the more important. "Europeanization," the process of domestic change under EU influence, is a grass-roots process, not a top-down one, as integration is driven by national entrepreneurs who take advantage of the European regulatory framework to advance their interests. In theory, the EU has important instruments that confer leverage: significant preaccession, accession, and assistance funds (the largest donor in the world), and conditions attached to membership and association agreements. How have these performed in recent years? Let us examine separately the impact within the enlargement process and outside it.

Although new member states had undergone important reforms to reorganize their governments after communism (Goetz, Partridge and Deller 2009), this was largely an unfinished job by the beginning of the "big bang" wave of EU enlargement negotiations. As early democracies, these countries could not escape competitive particularism, shown, for instance, in the division of spoils across party lines (Grzymała-Busse 2007; O'Dwyer 2006). During negotiations with the EU, reform of the judiciary, administration, policy-making structures, and civil service were important issues. Despite the EU not having an acquis per se in these areas, the European Commission, with the help of other international organizations, invested a considerable amount of assistance, monitoring, and coaching in these areas. Conditionality was also strong, particularly for the "laggards" Romania and Bulgaria, and a safeguard mechanism in the area of justice and corruption control (Mechanism of Cooperation and Verification) was created for the three immediate postaccession years, in case the new member countries would not meet their commitments in the area of corruption, home, and justice affairs more generally. After the big bang enlargement was completed in 2007, when Romania and Bulgaria joined the first eight postcommunist new member states (the Baltic States, Slovenia, Poland, Hungary, the Czech Republic, and Slovakia) the applicants from the Western Balkans (Croatia, Serbia, Macedonia, Bosnia, Montenegro, and Albania) became the target of increased focus in this area, as the postwar Balkans were associated with organized crime and human trafficking.

A review of control of corruption in the accession and postaccession area of Central Europe and the Balkans in 2012 showed three stable clusters. There are good governance achievers with scores between 6 and 7, namely Estonia and Slovenia; there are five borderline cases with scores between 5 and 6: Poland, Czech Republic, Hungary, Latvia and Lithuania; and finally, we see a group of laggards with scores lower than 5 (scores run from 1 to 10). This last group includes Albania, Kosovo, Bosnia and Herzegovina, Montenegro, Serbia, Romania, Bulgaria, Croatia, Slovakia and the Republic of Macedonia. Croatia and Slovakia are on the top of this group. Serbia, Croatia, Macedonia and Latvia have all seen significant improvement at a confidence error of 5 percent over the whole interval (1996–2012), but despite this positive perception still face important challenges. This is reflected in a measure computed by Global Integrity called the "implementation gap," reflecting the difference between the score for legal equipment and the score for practice. Romania, Serbia, Macedonia, and Montenegro, countries that adopted the most extensive anticorruption legislation in the world during negotiations with the EU, have huge implementation gaps (scores between 30 and 40 on a scale of 1–100, where 100 is the complete split between law and practice), followed by Bulgaria, Hungary, Croatia, and Albania with scores in the 20s. Most countries surveyed by Global Integrity are assessed to have backslid between 2008 and 2010, including frontrunners such as Poland. In the words of Global Integrity, "Poland's aggregate data also point to a widening implementation gap, suggesting that in a post-EU accession environment, enforcement of anticorruption laws and institutions on the books has deteriorated" (Global Integrity 2010).

The trend analysis, as reflected in the World Bank CoC indicator at three points in time (1998, 2004, 2008) and separately on the ICRG Corruption Risk and Freedom House Nations in Transit, shows two clear facts. Firstly, the good scores of Central European "achiever" countries already existed at the start of the EU accession process, so their governance evolution was largely completed by that time. However, since the average of Eastern Europe (excluding the former Soviet Union) is still far lower than the OECD average, the expectation was that conditionality and technical assistance would cause further improvement during EU negotiations (starting in 2000) and after accession (completed in 2007 for Romania and Bulgaria and 2004 for all others). Secondly, none of the eight new EU member countries recorded any significant progress after being invited to join between 1998 and 2000. In fact, most of them registered insignificant regress (at 5 percent confidence error). Once the EU membership offer has been made, progress seems to slow down, and once countries have joined, they actually backslide, as political elites show decreased restraint. The current accession countries in the Western Balkans, countries whose accession perspective (with the exception of Croatia) is still in the future, have been progressing, creating larger implementation gaps – similar to Romania and Bulgaria in the years prior to accession. Croatia is the case to watch on stagnation and backslide following its accession in 2013.

Poland, the EU's largest and most successful new member state, illustrates a typical trajectory, allowing us to observe how political and governance regimes are different conceptual entities. Figure 7.1 shows the evolution of democracy versus governance since 1984, illustrating that the governance regime remains fairly stable through major political changes including the dramatic improvement of pluralism in 1989, until 1998, when it actually starts declining slightly, remaining at a lower level throughout EU accession and after membership. Poland seemed to enjoy relatively good governance (scoring 5 out of 6) even under Communism, where democratization, transition, and EU integration seemingly affected this equilibrium very little; after briefly touching one another in 1989, the two trend lines again go

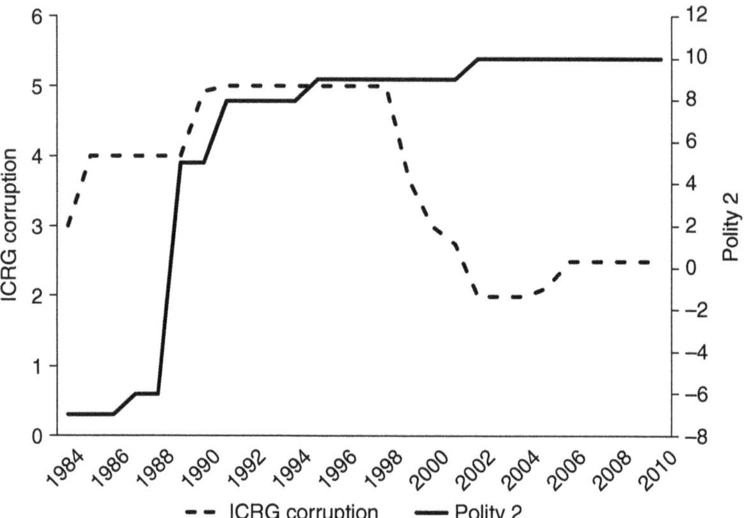

Figure 7.1 Democracy and governance in Poland, 1985–2010
Source: The PRS Group and Polity IV data

their separate ways, the gap smaller than in the past, but nevertheless growing. The period of EU impact is where the ICRG line drops dramatically.

A review of facts country by country confirms the scores: the anticorruption institutional framework built during EU accession years and not yet properly implemented began to be dismantled the day after EU accession. Many anticorruption agencies saw their budgets cut and their leaders put under threat of removal, if their existence altogether was not put into question.[2] In Romania and Latvia anticorruption "heroes" were fired after accession, just when their anticorruption agencies had started to make significant arrests. In Slovenia the anticorruption prevention agency, which was monitoring the assets of politicians, was saved *in extremis* by the Constitutional Court, while in Poland and Romania the same courts were dealt serious blows when anticorruption legislation was declared unconstitutional years after it had been enacted. In Slovakia the anticorruption court was significantly weakened by the government, and in the Czech

[2] Focus group with regional experts from GRECO, USAID, OECD, Freedom House, and civil society at the Hertie School of Governance in Berlin, November 18, 2009.

Republic the anticorruption unit was closed down. The second day after accession domestic elites thus recuperated some of the control lost during EU accession and secured their immunity. The EU showed its greatest muscle in the prosecution of Croatian Prime Minister Ivo Sanader, who was forced to resign during accession negotiations. This gesture showed the great potential of EU political as opposed to technical intervention and the lessons learned from the Central European disillusionment, as Croatia joined nine years after the first wave. The mechanism which seems to have worked here is what is called in development aid "selectivity" rather than "conditionality": countries with a chance to join emulate good institutions in order to achieve progress and be selected. Countries already invited to join – an irreversible mechanism – slow down reforms, even when tough conditionality is in place.

That governance and not just individual corruption is at stake is shown in a 2013 survey question asking people to choose between the following options: "In the public sector most people can succeed if they are willing to work hard" (rated 0), and "Hard work is no guarantee of success in the public sector for most people – *it's more a matter of luck and connections*" (rated 10). All new Central European member countries surveyed leaned toward connections, with scores over 5, keeping company only with Italy, Greece, and Portugal. Bulgaria and Slovakia, two new member states, rank at the bottom, with only Serbia and Croatia underneath them, showing how far these two societies are from creating a merit-based system. Hungary, which used to be perceived as one of the cleanest countries in the region (GRECO 2003: 3), showed worrying signs of institutional corruption after EU accession. Here, political parties are perceived as the most corrupted sector in the country (Transparency International 2009: 28–31) and favored companies thriving on public contracts turn over radically at each electoral change of government. After Romania joined the EU in 2007, only companies with domestic connections started winning public tenders for EU funds, with famous European giants being cut out entirely. Bulgarians revolted against favoritism in public procurement in 2013 after numerous reforms failed to take root. The top Slovenian businessman was uncovered to have made his fortune through his relations to state-owned companies – as is the case with most successful transition business people, an entire generation of capitalists who grew rich on state rents. A Czech Prime Minister, himself a profiteer after a previous electoral revolution directed against party corruption, had to resign in 2013 amidst allegations he was using the secret service for private ends. Bulgaria and Romania were both sanctioned by the European Commission after accession in 2007; EU funds were largely cut as evidence of massive conflict of interest was uncovered – this despite governance indicators showing progress. A 2012 dedicated Eurobarometer (European Commission 2012) showed that EU citizens from new member countries were highly skeptical of the efforts of their governments in fighting corruption, especially in Lithuania (81 percent), the Czech Republic (87 percent), Latvia (85 percent), Slovenia (91 percent), Hungary (73 percent), Slovakia (79 percent) and Romania (79 percent).

What factors explain this situation? For the postcommunist candidate countries, conditionality was the key mechanism that the EU relied upon: a mixture of conditional positive incentives (closure of negotiation chapters) as well as negative (delaying negotiations closure, delaying accession date, safeguard mechanisms, withholding of EU funds). Conditionality is supposed to be smart power. It offers an incentive to shape behavior. But it may well be that a general incentive (EU integration) is insufficient to motivate all the social groups that need to change their behavior. The fundamental alteration of rules of the game for politicians, bureaucrats, and magistrates in the Central and Eastern European countries, for instance, presumes that they would stand to win more than they would lose from the change. But is this accurate for everyone, and are the gains from particularism (mainly privilege) matched by what EU membership has to offer? In other words, for such an institutional transfer to be successful, it has to incentivize key groups and not just rely on the presumption that what is good for the country is also good for everyone. Supportive constituencies of EU accession are not the same as key groups for reforms. Those directly concerned, from bureaucrats to magistrates, displayed considerably less enthusiasm than the general public or democracy-minded NGOs. A review of every significant area in the field of governance reforms shows that motivating agents to change was extremely difficult. Incentives for local elites in the accession process seem to have been often wrong, confusing, or absent, leading to an overall effort very much shaped like an old communist plan.

Furthermore, to understand how EU policies do or do not affect corruption we can systematically match the control of corruption formula to the EU's enlargement policies. EU accession is a heavily bureaucratic process that relies on the presumption that rule of law and high implementation capacity are already there. If they are imperfect, as was the case in the eastern Balkans, some Central European countries, and the western Balkans, then accession increases significantly the distance between formal rule and informal practice. Transparency and red tape are never stressed as main parts of the administrative reforms undertaken during accession: transparency is low and red tape increases instead of decreases, unintended consequences in the negotiation and EU acquis adoption processes. The EU also brings in new funds tied to very bureaucratic rules and outputs that are difficult to measure, thereby unintentionally increasing resources for corruption. This is particularly true after accession, when the role of cofunding from national sources increases (EU funds require some matching contribution from recipient governments). One explanation for new member country regression is this new resource for corruption: we actually find that in more corrupt EU countries, more structural funds only generate additional corruption (Mungiu-Pippidi 2013a). Furthermore, in the enlarged EU, the more a government invests, the more corrupt it is. It is not general expenditure that is correlated with corruption, but the discretionary funds (such as social entitlements) not tied to some clear objective that a government has the freedom to allocate. This explains a case such as Kosovo, a country praised by the EC's 2011 Progress Report for improvement on its procurement legislation but which nevertheless exhibits increasing corruption. Even further legal improvements would not help build control of corruption in Kosovo as long as the value of public procurement contracts awarded yearly remains at around 20 percent of Kosovo's GDP, 482 million euros (2009 estimation by Global Integrity Report), opening up huge opportunities for corruption.

Moreover, the European Commission puts all its energy into building legal constraints, which limits its impact from the very start, as this is less than a quarter of what control of corruption entails and is the most difficult element to influence from outside. Judicial Councils, the self-ruling bodies of magistrates, are a telling example. Since their adoption there has been less direct political intervention on the judiciary, but indirect influence and especially corruption remain rife. In many countries the judiciary has become plainly unaccountable since judges rule themselves. The European Commission first advocated the introduction of Judicial Councils everywhere, then had to fight to bring them to some order: accession does not create equal incentives, and judges who see their discretion curtailed (and their corrupt income as well) might be less supportive of EU integration than students expecting more Erasmus mobility grants. In an environment of institutional corruption, repressive and preventative agencies are permanently engulfed in political conflict, seldom impartial, and always threatened by politicians. Still the EU continues a strategy in the western Balkans that has already failed in Romania and Bulgaria, prescribing steps such as Judicial Councils and Anticorruption Agencies and rating countries positively if they adopt them instead of leaving national governments the freedom to organize their reforms and measure their impact themselves. Considerable importance is also attributed to party funding, although in EU-27 we find no evidence that a specific formula of party funding is currently associated with better control of corruption; countries have a variety of arrangements. The evidence shows only that full transparency of party funding and reasonably low thresholds for donations are sufficient guarantees as long as they can be enforced, but stress on transparency has always been a secondary issue. Due to poor fiscal transparency, parties manage to allocate funds using their discretion when in government, so the supervision of party coffers does not pay: a variety of ways that cannot be controlled for politicians to collect (from businesses or individuals) still exist, while the far simpler oversight of returns to favorite businesses (through public resource allocation) has not been a reform priority in any accession country so far. Moreover, there was little or no assistance from EU for free media, civil society watchdogs, transparency, or red tape reduction reforms before and after accession. Only recently in the western Balkans has the EU started to invest modestly in the watchdog capacity of civil society.

Earlier studies argued that the EU has sizable effects on democracy promotion (Schimmelfennig and Scholz 2008), that new member countries comply more with EU regulation than the old (Sedelmeier 2008), and that governance reforms are sustainable after accession (Levitz and Pop-Eleches 2010). Such conclusions are not consistent with basic facts (negative evolutions in many countries, most notably Hungary and Romania) and show the risk of preferring econometrics to facts, seeing the lack of dependent variable sensitivity in the fields of democracy and governance, the absence of time series for most relevant independent variables (for instance, data on the civil service), and the lack of a consistent theory explaining the relationship between democracy and governance. The use of panel regressions must necessarily be checked with other more concrete and verifiable policy indicators that can be measured before and after a clear policy intervention, as well as an understanding of each country. When assembling such evidence, we find limited EU impact on governance and counter-intuitive findings on the relationship between EU assistance and governance reforms. Our conclusions reinforce some previous studies on Europeanization, which argued that "the conceptual discussion [on the impact of the EU in the accession states] tends to overestimate and generalize the effects of EU conditionality vis-à-vis domestic factors" (Sasse 2008: 300) and warn that compliance can prove purely formal once incentives change after joining the EU (Falkner *et al.* 2008).

European Neighbourhood Policy

Leaving enlargement aside, the European Neighbourhood Policy is also tied to good governance in its partner states and its impact can be assessed. A survey of the governance performance of partner states since its initiation shows that the influence of the EU in initiating change has also been limited (Kleemann 2010). Countries that had received more per capita funding by 2010 did not improve more – most of them actually regressed. With the exception of Lebanon, where regression can be explained by the 2006 war with Israel, countries such as Tunisia or Jordan that have received high per capita funding above €40 have in fact regressed during the investigated period, and the uprisings in the winter of 2011 should not have been a surprise. Moreover, countries with relatively low amounts of per capita funding such as Georgia have progressed substantially. Higher per capita funding does not seem to produce any statistically significant improvements in the governance scores of the partner states. This observation reinforces previous studies, which have shown that higher aid levels lead to worse governance outcomes in neopatrimonial or competitive particularistic contexts. In a previous study on the relationship between aid levels and the quality of governance, Knack (2004) found that "periods of higher aid levels coincide with periods of lower-quality governance." However, countries that received higher amounts of funding tied to good governance programs have shown a little more progress. On average, Eastern European states have received governance-related per capita funding of €6, while Mediterranean/Middle Eastern countries, which progressed less, received only €3.10. Important aid recipients such as Egypt had only 5 percent of total funds dedicated to good governance, compared to 4 percent in Jordan and 7.5 percent in Tunisia during the 2004–08 period (Kleemann 2010). The data shows that per capita good governance funding, although modest, has been more effective in initiating governance change than overall funding. However, countries that have received higher per capita good governance funding have probably been more willing to implement reforms to start with. Finally, the impact of Governance Facility, a new and innovative instrument, is too early to assess, as it has only been in place since 2007, but its level of funding is extremely limited, and prior reports are not encouraging (Youngs 2010).

The situation has not improved in recent years. A report of the European Court of Auditors in 2013 focused on public finance management, anticorruption, human rights, and democracy-related conditionality for the period 2007–13 for €1 billion in aid allocated by the EU to Egypt found that democracy programs had been a complete failure and that most of the money was simply untraceable due to a lack of budgetary transparency, an ineffective audit function, and endemic corruption of the Egyptian government. Furthermore, "The Commission and the EEAS [European External Action Service] did not react to the lack of progress by taking decisive action to ensure accountability for considerable EU funds" (European Court of Auditors 2013). The European Court of Auditors also issued a sobering assessment that the European Union Rule of Law Mission in Kosovo is not efficient enough for the €700 million in assistance provided by the EU between 2007 and 2011. Kosovo is a special case, having been directly ruled by the international community, especially the EU, with some transfer of sovereignty to the national government in recent years. The report found considerable political interference with the judiciary and police and rampant corruption (Wulf 2012).

The absence of impact of the EU's good governance promotion in the European neighborhood can be explained by several unrelated contributing factors. First, conflicting interests exist between the EU's priorities in the neighborhood, leading to a trade-off between fearing immigrants and aspiring to improve governance; obviously the latter was the weaker priority in the policy toward North African countries, so it is rather doubtful if any good governance promotion worthy of the name has ever taken place. The EU supported neopatrimonial dictators such as Tunisia's Ben Ali until the very last moment. Second, good governance promotion policies are often merely replicated EU accession policies without adjustment for local conditions and lacking the primary accession "carrot," thus offering even fewer incentives for key reform groups than enlargement does. Civil society was entirely neglected, and there was simply too much reliance on front-loaded aid (Kleemann 2010).

Conclusions

A review of all three models – MCC, European Union enlargement, and the European Neighbourhood Policy– casts serious doubt on the effectiveness of conditionality and finds some moderate support for selectivity. Real successes, such as Estonia or Georgia, seem to be determined by domestic agency, not outside promotion. Selectivity works better than conditionality, but the sustainability of reforms is a challenge, as shown in the example of Eastern and Central European countries after EU accession. The failure of conditionality in general seems to have had less to do with countries and more to do with the donors themselves. Otherwise it is difficult to explain why conditionality fails so uniformly across different goodness of fit equipment of recipient countries, from modern Central Europe to premodern sub-Saharan Africa. Georgia, a country with poor modernization fit and no conditionality, managed to progress, while Hungary, a country with an excellent fit and greater EU conditionality, regressed: this clearly shows how important domestic agency is. But can donors incentivize it through selectivity or a cash-on-delivery approach from outside, as advocated by the Center for Global Development (Birdsall and Savedoff 2011) for assistance policies more generally? To take a simple counterfactual example, it is certain that Ukraine would have progressed further if cash had been delivered not at the promise of a good conflict of interest law, but rather after its adoption. The great theoretical advantage of selectivity is that it empowers rather than constrains local agents of change and creates a new domestic political dynamic. In cases where the modernization fit is really poor, with high informality and low life expectancy, agency might be severely constrained. Thus far, threshold countries simply have not managed to make the governance progress necessary to get a compact and EU accession countries have not yet reached sustainability in their control of corruption, so the question remains open.

But the real key to having an impact and not just spending money on anticorruption efforts remains elusive. Experience in trying to identify plausible actors who can initiate virtuous circles in order to empower them is either very recent among donors or does not exist. Sometimes called a "political economy approach," this should be the main starting point when building control of corruption from outside.

8 From critical mess to critical mass: some tentative policy conclusions

"The most practical thing in the world is a good theory."
Hermann von Helmholtz

Current state of play

The Anti-Corruption Resource Centre, U4, concluded its 2011 evidence review by stating that "most anticorruption initiatives in developing countries fail" (Heeks and Mathisen 2012). In the same year, the World Bank evaluation team made a similarly laconic acknowledgment in its evaluation of good governance programs: "The evaluation's desk reviews and case studies showed that the Bank's record in helping to achieve countrywide governance improvements was limited" (World Bank 2011). European donors (the Swedish International Development Corporation; NORAD; the UK's Department for International Development; the Danish Development Corporation) also sponsored a joint evaluation of their anticorruption projects, which checked on selected countries such as Bangladesh, Nicaragua, Tanzania, Vietnam, and Zambia, to conclude that: "Although donors have helped to strengthen country institutions and systems in support of [anticorruption] in all five countries, these intermediate results have not translated into reduced levels of corruption at national levels" (ITAD 2011). Thinly veiled in this assessment is the recognition of the huge ambition of international donors to have an impact on national governance. Another evaluation indicated that there is no country to point to as a successful example of the deployment of the international anticorruption toolkit – in addition to having no statistical evidence to substantiate the impact of anticorruption tools (Mungiu-Pippidi *et al.* 2011). By and large, the evaluations piling up after the first fifteen years of anticorruption work showed great expectations and humble results.

Yet, how could donor-sponsored good governance deliver satisfactory results to such ambitious goals? If the theory and evidence presented in this book seem convincing, most of the anticorruption industry could only have walked into what the U4 authors call a design-reality gap (Heeks and Mathisen 2012). Most anticorruption approaches by Western donors (the so-called zero-tolerance approach, for instance) presume that ethical universalism is a default state of governance, so corruption must be a deviation from it. But in developing countries corruption is not a deviation, but rather the norm – with the consequence that norm-infringing anticorruption instruments had been adopted that failed to promote norm building. Legal repression of deviance does not work where rule of law has not been historically reached: the underprivileged risk becoming the deviants. The theory and evidence presented in this book argue that particularism is an *alternative* social allocation mode, more widespread and closer to some sort of "natural" default state than ethical universalism. Approaching it as social pathology is not useful as it leads directly to unsustainable strategies. If we believe that freedom of the press, a purely Western concept presuming objectivity and impartiality as some inborn journalistic quality as the norm, we simply do not understand the media in most countries of the world. This is not to argue that more insightful theories did not exist from which the anticorruption industry could have devised inspiration; these existed in plenty – in the sociological tradition, at least – but somehow they did not manage to influence the mainstream approach to anticorruption, which remained confined to counting bribes, repressing "deviation," and finding "incentives" for spoilers to become honest, in a flawed attempt to prove that integrity is more rational than cheating.

The inadequacy of popular anticorruption methods to meaningfully address reality was also due to earlier generations of empirical work, particularly work based on big N and scarce data. Scholars have compared the shared characteristics of countries now largely free of corruption with those that were not, presuming "causes," "consequences," and "costs" without sound counterfactuals or a causal theoretical model. One example is the erroneous interpretation of numerous scholars that women are less corruptible than men, ignoring the conclusion-altering fact that particularistic societies favor the most powerful and discriminate against the rest, women among them (Sung 2003). Such an approach ended up basically recommending countries to be rich, Protestant, common law-based former British colonies and old democracies (see also Pritchett and Woolcock 2004). The only desirable condition missing from the list was island nation status, uncovered in this book. This experience inspired various waves of criticism (Andrews 2008; Huther and Shah 2000; Treisman 2007), as well as the control of corruption model outlined in this book, one that considers goodness of fit, but departs from it. As evidence clearly exists that agency matters, there must be better avenues to real policy options. In struggling with these issues, this book resorted to a blend of statistical method and history as each alone returned imperfect evidence. And while none of the case studies contradicts the theory sketched here, it is beyond question that even more evidence – especially historical – would be useful, to the extent that a grand theory such as North, Wallis, and Weingast's "violence and social orders" (2009) can be tested at all.

Finally, what kind of agency works? The third conceptual flaw in contemporary anticorruption work is to conceptualize corruption in a particularist context as a principal–agent problem when it is more often than not a collective action problem. This book argues that individual behavior is strongly bound by context (most people simply follow the "rules of the game" in their own societies) and only to some extent by individual status (individuals who believe in merit-based competition tend to be intolerant toward a distribution system based on favoritism and corruption). Where particularism is the main allocation norm and no domestic agents are pushing for change, generally because those willing and able to challenge the rules of the game are too few, societies reach a suboptimal equilibrium. Rules of the game in social allocation result from a given society's distribution of power resources and are reflected in the model of corruption as an equilibrium between resources and constraints. Transition from a corrupt regime to one where ethical universalism is the norm is therefore largely a political rather than a technical-legal process: the main issue is power inequality, which can hardly be overcome only through "training" and building "technical expertise." Some power sharing (among other means of deeper democratization) is indispensable in successfully controlling corruption (Johnston 2013). But as a consequence of the principal–agent approach, donors frequently presume that anticorruption efforts are win-win policies and entrust various implausible principals with the task of controlling corruption. This ambiguous and inconsistent role of the international anticorruption community largely "sabotaged its own efforts" (Mungiu-Pippidi *et al.* 2011: xv). An attempt to promote a political economy approach based on drivers of change was found to be too political and was discarded, despite a passing fancy for it with some donors (Fisher and Marquette 2014). The concept of building "critical mass" is for many donors dangerously close to political regime change and the whole paradigm of democracy promotion. In Tunisia, Brazil, India, Ukraine, Bulgaria, or the Philippines, an anticorruption critical mass has grown in parallel with donor efforts to develop good institutions, expressing public exasperation with official anticorruption policy. Public demands in all of these countries are targeted at particularism rather than the legal definition of corruption, blending social justice concerns with open cries for good governance: protesters ask for less favoritism, better spending priorities, the abolishment of discretionary MP funds. Their problems are in no way captured by the anticorruption toolkit currently promoted by the industry. How can whistleblower protection acts assist people in contexts where the majority are complicit in a particularistic system where public pressure is focused not on the corrupt, but rather on the system's dissenters? There is little wonder that such laws alone, now adopted in many countries, have never delivered a change in public norms.

Finally, while globalization has turned corruption into a global phenomenon in need of a global response, the battlefield upon which this war is won or lost remains national. Globalization may have brought more money into poor and developing countries, thereby feeding corruption, but it also brought freedom of trade and communication, enabling people around the world to inform themselves and associate with one another. The more globalized a country is, the better is its control of corruption, we find in Chapter 4, and this impact is stronger than the negative effect of increasing resources. Nevertheless, this war cannot be fought and won internationally, although it might help if we conceptualize international anticorruption assistance as the empowerment of domestic forces: the optimal equilibrium is finally built (or not) nationally, on the domestic battlefield. For example, consider the current, highly commendable international effort to recover assets amassed by deposed neopatrimonial rulers. While neopatrimonialism persists or is succeeded by competitive particularism, the next leader will amass spoils as great as the first, so that in the absence of major national governance change, the long sought and expensively paid proceeds of such efforts will vanish like water in the sand upon their return. Increasing international constraints, particularly in the field of bribery, have led to some progress. But as long as constraints at the national level remain low and particularism continues to be the rule of the game in a given country, increasing the costs for international businesses will not by itself result in fair competition as long as a suboptimal equilibrium stays the same in the country itself. Bribes are frequently paid by international businesses in order to even their chances with domestic favorites, and they will disappear when there is enough pressure on those granting favors (who are largely static) in addition to the bribe givers (who change all the time). Risk-averse investors such as the Japanese simply do not invest in countries below seven on the 1–10 CPI scale, as they value knowing what to expect.

The model of particularism as the default social allocation model in this book explains why after nearly two decades of unprecedented good governance efforts in the international arena change is so scarce and remains so controversial. It also opens up new avenues for diagnosing governance contexts on the basis of second-generation indicators and – hopefully – for drawing more realistic plans, based on lessons learned from successful cases of control of corruption. Far more development of indicators, diagnostic tools, and lessons learned is needed, but my hope is to have contributed a solid foundation. This approach, therefore, has important policy implications, but as it rests on governance contexts, it cannot offer any universal recipe. Instead the rest of these conclusions are devoted to a methodology on grounding any good governance strategy from a donor perspective in evidence, ending with a reflection on how fit the present anticorruption industry is for this challenge.

Steps to a strategy

Societal control of corruption is reached as a balance between opportunities (resources) and constraints. A forecast based on this model suggests that change in governance order can occur only gradually and through a succession of radical actions and disequilibria until a new equilibrium is achieved with a superior control of corruption. That explains why so few success stories exist and why they seem to result more from domestic agency and broad reforms following exceptional circumstances, such as democratization after a dictatorship, than from typical internationally assisted anticorruption strategies focused on the civil service and the judiciary. From a donor perspective, therefore, a few logical steps need consideration before any context-sensitive intervention on good governance is developed.

The first step is full diagnosis of the governance context. What is the exception and what is the norm in social allocation (ethical universalism or particularism)? How advanced is public–private separation? How is power distributed? Who reaps most of the social benefits and who faces the losses? How transparent and democratic is this process (programmatic policies decided electorally) versus insidious and informal? How many social allocations are de facto rents? Is the law treating everyone equally? Is the governance order perceived as legitimate? Differentiating between traditional patrimonialism, neopatrimonialism, and competitive particularism opens the door to alternative, tailored strategies, as shown in Chapter 3. Even if a country score from the World Bank or Transparency International offers by itself synthetic answers to the above questions, we need to document in full both resources and constraints to assess not only where control of corruption stands in a given society, but also why it is so. Governments may be lobbied to reduce red tape, but civil society, demanding citizens, and a functional judiciary cannot be built in the space of a few years; they presume long-term investment and require tolerance of an interval of time when particularism would reign.

The second step is charting the position of actors in favor of or against the status quo in order to establish if a plausible principal exists at the domestic level who can be the main actor in a good governance coalition. A principal should never be taken for granted. If, for instance, the minister of internal affairs in a semiauthoritarian country receives commissions from every informal payment extracted by subordinate control agencies, grounding a technical assistance program at his level would not help in the least nor yield any positive results. Only the status quo is in the interest of the minister and his staff. Who, then, are the plausible agents of change, and how long would they remain so if they were to gain power? Do we find professional groups who can be both sustainable allies of good governance, serving their own best interest (egoists), and promoters of ethical universalism (altruists)? What is the potential of such groups and individuals once identified to form a stable, goal-oriented coalition? In the past, merchants motivated by profit and lawyers and journalists motivated by the need to have access equal to the privileged classes were in the vanguard of historical good governance. "Achiever" countries all had professional elites engaged in changing governance regimes: South Korean lawyers trained in the United States and bureaucrats trained in Japan; Chilean and Georgian economists trained at American universities. The co-optation system of particularistic regimes frequently manages to deter such coalitions, but not always – it would take tremendous resources to distribute payoffs to everyone so there are no losers of corrupt rules of the game. The historical examples in this book suggest (but no more) that in democratizing contexts a critical mass unable to be accommodated by old networks of power and privilege is built gradually, as in the Dreyfus affair. Can we observe or even plan such a build-up? These are preliminary questions to the decisive diagnosis on the (near-future) existence of sufficient domestic agency, as evidence shows that in the absence of educated and autonomous professional groups fighting for good governance, sustainable development does not exist and advocacy by external agents remains fruitless.

Such realizations, however, do not mesh easily with existing donor programs. Most international donors are governments or intergovernmental organizations, assisting in principle other governments. But constitution writing and training civil servants or magistrates deprived of fundamental autonomy (financial and otherwise) by their country's center of power are poor palliatives. Such dependent groups evolve when the demand for change increases in society, matching the power influence they are subjected to. Creating collective action – and providing political support – at the level of strategic groups within society seems to be the only good governance change strategy that has worked in the past. And while such attempts are seen today, they are scarce. For instance, the American Bar Association, an organization helping lawyers organize and articulate their professional interests, has developed a grass-roots rule of law program complete with indicators and top-quality volunteers ("ABA Rule of Law Initiative"). The charity Oxfam organizes genuine consumer surveys for public services that deter corruption far better than pure anticorruption programs, while also increasing collective action capacity (Ahmad 2014). These are genuine society-building programs, which surpass in ambition the typical anticorruption programs preferred by most international donors that produce meagre results (Mungiu-Pippidi 2006b; Persson *et al.* 2013).

Presuming that some principals can be found, the timing of the intervention (when it should begin) should be assessed as a third step. Evidence from the cases of historical and early "achievers" indicates the important role of certain contexts in promoting good governance. Windows of opportunity are offered by crises of any sort; elections (when actors need to compete to prove their integrity); revolutions; or status upgrade perspectives (joining an international club or a free trade agreement). Changes in equilibrium are greatly helped by such circumstances, and smart support should make the most of them. Aid selectivity or cash-on-delivery are methods of engineering such natural circumstances, with weaker impact but the right goal. We should always ask if it is a good moment to intervene to build ethical universalism in a given governance context. For instance, are major stability and political violence problems in check? Corruption should be a concern only when a polity is free of major violence and has no essential stability threats. When groups can obtain what they want by violent means, different strategies, including offering them privilege in exchange for laying down arms, unfortunately might be necessary. Bosnia is corrupt because it is no longer violent: Ethnocracies exist there because the price of disarming them was to allocate the country among ethnic groups. While the international community starts considering good governance strategies for Bosnia, it needs to understand that particularism was one of the chief foundations of the Dayton Peace Accords. Particularism was built into the Bosnian Constitution and it flows into the entire governance context. A radical change at this stage is bound to be very difficult (Mungiu-Pippidi 2013).

The fourth step is an assessment of the donors' influence itself. It seems that the *Star Trek: The Next Generation* dictum never to intervene in the life of other civilizations is wisdom confined to fictional contexts only: many international donors intervene today in the governance of other countries. Nevertheless, outside donors should at least assess thoroughly how their intervention will affect the balance, both on the side of resources and on the side of constraints. There are many borderline situations where the intervention might be worthwhile, but it can be argued that these are the least challenging situations. For the others, expectations have to be severely curtailed, and the main concern should be not to produce more harm than good. For instance, the creation of a strong anticorruption agency where power is highly asymmetrical may simply provide another repressive tool.

The pouring of a large quantity of money into discretionary investments versus clear, universalistic allocations may simply bring new resources that stabilize rather than change a suboptimal equilibrium. Some people argue, for instance, that EU funds would be better used to pay unemployment benefits than go into infrastructure programs with high costs and poor returns, used primarily by local elites for their clienteles, thus consolidating their power (Fazekas *et al.* 2014). But this observation applies to contexts that are highly developed and exhibit reasonable goodness of fit, such as Italy or Greece – what about Zambia or Bangladesh? Below a certain level of income, set at approximately US$2,700 per capita (Collier 2011), corruption can be seen as a survival strategy and an alternative to violence (with each example needing its own diagnosis). In such cases donors should simply organize their assistance funds to make sure it reaches targets, but dedicated programs on anticorruption alone would make little sense.

Once intervention has been decided upon (when a country has reasonable domestic agency showing the will to change, exhibits a growing demand for change, has understandable local power relations and rules of engagement, and is approaching a favorable circumstance pressuring the government to show goodwill), then and only then are the questions of what to do and which tools to select worth answering.

In the case of traditional monarchies, the path is that of the King of Denmark: top-down reforms, elite control agencies, build-up of a solid, merit-based bureaucracy, taking care that all categories are represented to check the privileged class and their rents, gradually reducing them. Technical assistance in this case might help to direct reforms to the key elements affecting the balance: Qatar, the United Arab Emirates, and Bhutan are moving in this direction independently.

In the case of neopatrimonial systems, the situation is different. Their leaders and cliques are generally far more predatory and authoritarian. Assisting them in anticorruption efforts results in little more than a credibility transfer from donor to ruler, thereby risking both uselessness and immorality. Entrusting them with tough anticorruption legislation and agencies (which they will control) is dangerous for their opponents. It is unrealistic to hope they will reduce the administrative discretion from which they profit. Solutions should therefore be sought in the areas of increasing demand for good governance, empowering citizens, and fostering collective action – and where such programming risks being too political, investing in alternative (new) media and development of civil society (regardless of the field). A village with an internet cafe is connected to both news and similar places elsewhere, thereby increasing its potential to contribute to good governance than a village without. The strategy of building an enlightened citizenry with collective action capacities is a long-term one, but this is the basis of sustainable development, though few donors pursue this path presently (Alsop and Heinsohn 2005; McNeil and Malena 2010).

But frequently such a strategy is unrealistic as political barriers prevent such programming. The best strategy for donor engagement in such situations is to ensure some form of direct aid provision through charities working directly at the grass-roots level in cooperation with targeted recipient communities, applying both external and community-based mechanisms of audit and control (with the great advantage of simultaneously developing local organization and collective action capacities). Premodern, community-based mechanisms described in this book (Chapter 3) can hopefully be a source of inspiration here: downsizing aid to the community level can allow participatory audit and oversight mechanisms to be built even in premodern societies and contexts. Direct organization of aid procurement by donors themselves could also be a solution where evidence exists that spoiling would otherwise be dramatic and aid would only increase resources for corruption.

Combining assistance in neopatrimonial or competitive particularistic contexts with good governance/state modernization strategies has been attempted on the largest scale during the past twenty years, yielding disappointing results (De Maria 2010; Mungiu-Pippidi *et al.* 2011). Good governance strategies were not implemented and conditionality was either not enforced or caused program termination due to their failure to fulfill requirements. Evidence in this book shows that achievers (Estonia, Georgia, Uruguay) do their own state building by emulating proper models when necessary and that non-achievers (e.g., Zambia, Bulgaria, and Ukraine, three countries topping the list of highest donor investment on anticorruption) do not – this regardless of external help and conditionality, since elites are not constrained enough to accept the destruction of their spoiling machines. If Georgia managed to reform its notoriously corrupt traffic police and Ukraine did not despite receiving far more international grants than Georgia over the same period, it is clear that only domestic agency matters.

Finally, in the case of competitive particularism, donors could identify plausible principals, assist their coalition building, and support an increase in demands for anticorruption measures more generally. These countries have both pluralism and freedom: what they lack is the capacity for collective action, the sort of social organization allowing for permanent government accountability, not only at the polls. Magistrates, clerks, policemen, and voters all need to become far more autonomous and change-oriented. They cannot be organized from outside: donor-sponsored coalitions, such as USAID in Albania in the early 1990s, are frail and disappear once financing is gone, as discussed in Chapter 6. But genuine coalitions need support. External conditionality or selectivity might not succeed in building good governance directly, as shown in Chapter 7 of this book, but any form of international pressure can work in a piecemeal way, leading to the gradual adoption of institutional weapons that domestic civil societies can use: e-government, freedom of information, fiscal transparency, red tape reduction, participatory budgeting, and auditing (see Table 8.1). A successful mechanism cuts across state and society, positively affecting the equilibrium: FOIA actively used by civil society, tax simplification and tax collection outsourced to private collectors (as in Uruguay), e-government and its oversight through media watchdogs, civil society, or ombudsmen. Participation and social accountability have great potential, as shown in famous experiments such as participatory budgeting in Brazil. Attempts in the Czech Republic and India to build anticorruption-based political parties have shown in recent years that while Facebook may be a great means to gather people for a protest rally, using such momentum to build stable alternative organizational forms on the basis of ethical universalism and ideology that are electorally competitive with client-based party machines remains a daunting task. However, parties may reform at a faster pace if challenged by alternative political formations with an integrity-building agenda: both of the aforementioned countries are evolving case studies worth watching in this respect.

There are also situations in which the international community has a strong influence in a given country – from the Balkans to Taiwan to Namibia. When violence is not the paramount problem, as in Iraq or Afghanistan, donors can take advantage of their privileged position to intervene in institution building: by correcting the initial institutional endowment, as in the case of US-sponsored land reforms in South

Korea and Taiwan; through greater accountability, as in the case of the general controller in Chile; or through radical reform and socialization of judiciaries and magistrates, as lawyers trained in British, US, or Japanese law schools have made a difference in Botswana, Chile, and India, among other cases.

Borderline countries present the best opportunity for the international anticorruption industry to make a serious impact, as they already have the necessary societal preconditions – in other words, a critical mass demanding good governance. This is where donors generally fail by promoting one tool or another without regard for the specific context. A sound good governance program in countries where sufficient conditions exist for an intervention should be built on the lines of this classic elementary strategy: reduce opportunities and increase constraints (see Table 8.1; also Huther and Shah 2000). Rather than monitoring the rather insensitive CoC or CPI measures or doing general population surveys, agencies promoting good governance should monitor indicators on robust independent variables for control of corruption or organize targeted surveys for users of certain significant public services (customs, for instance).

The policy menu in Table 8.1 has two advantages over the ordinary consultant's toolkit. First, each variable is tested and is robustly significant. We know that each one affects control of corruption in a context with all relevant controls. Second, each strategy or policy action was tried in some previously borderline country and was successful. On the weak side, administrative and judicial reforms depend on the government – if no genuine principal exists, it is unlikely that reforms will go deep, even if pushed as part of a conditionality package. The table is not a universal recipe, but rather a checklist, an evidence-based instrument tracing reforms and measuring progress toward an optimal equilibrium. It cannot replace the kind of political economy strategy described earlier in this chapter – it must still come after the "who" question has been solved.

Formalization, cutting red tape, building civil society capacities, supporting media, and partnering with the private sector are also worth doing in more challenging governance contexts. After all, the border of "borderline" is fuzzy: whenever the political will exists to promote such reforms or assist them, the above checklist applies. Donors who invest in any of these areas contribute indirectly to good governance even if their primary target might be media development or computer

Table 8.1 *Checklist of good governance progress-tracing indicators for borderline countries*

Factor	Action	Indicator	Benchmark country
Reduce opportunity			
Natural resources	Private management with public share of proceeds established by broad consultation; transparent spending	Public report on spending revenues from natural resources	Botswana (EITI)
Ethnic fractionalization	Cross-ethnic national public institutions based on proportionality	Equal access indicators for schooling and other cultural activities in different languages	Switzerland
Administrative discretion	• Reduce red tape and enforce equal treatment	• Ease of doing business; indicators of equal treatment	Georgia
	• Ombudsman also auditor and controller	• Cases solved administratively; cases solved through prosecution	Chile
	• Make resources transparent through e-government	• E-services as percentage of total public services	Estonia
Public spending	Public spending concentrated on areas such as health, education, research, and innovation, with infrastructure funded mostly through private–public partnerships (FDI)	Existence of e-portal for tracking expenses from national and local government procurement	Uruguay
Formalization	Tax simplification; tax collection also by private agents; e-payments facilitation	Time spent filing taxes; percentage increase in annual collection rate	Uruguay

Table 8.1 (*cont.*)

Factor	Action	Indicator	Benchmark country
Increase constraints			
Judicial independence	Tenure, appointment, and sanctioning of magistrates entrusted to magistrates' bodies only with validation by two-thirds of upper chamber	WEF judiciary independence measurement (perception of businessmen) Successful litigations against government	Chile, Botswana, and Taiwan
Civil society	Ease of registering; "sunshine" laws for public consultations; civil society component in every donor program, separate or combined with assistance to governments; conditions on participatory budgeting; auditing or evaluations	Number of NGOs; percentage of public consultations on total new legal drafts or policies; existence of and traffic on watchdog websites; number of Facebook users	Estonia
Media freedom	No government regulation of media except antitrust or cartel legislation; political conditionality of international community related to media freedom	Media sustainability indicators; news readership/audience	Estonia
Empowered citizens	IT investment in education and training for educators; internet freedom	Internet connections per household; Facebook users per country; percentage of citizens using e-services	South Korea and Estonia

literacy. Such indirect help may at times prove far more effective than direct action. Developing a country's communications infrastructure is a universal goal and less openly a political program: but it nevertheless greatly contributes to good governance.

Is the anticorruption industry up to the task?

A real industry around anticorruption came into being following the adoption of UNCAC. For instance, the Conference of the States Parties to the United Nations Convention Against Corruption that assembled in Panama City in 2013 for its fifth session counted no fewer than 168 country delegations out of 193 UN member states, not including the civil society, private sector, and international organizations that also attended – nearly one thousand participants. Panamanian President Ricardo Martinelli Berrocal was asked to address the participants. In his message, President Martinelli Berrocal recalled that Panama had ratified the convention in 2005 and that his country's review report provided evidence of good practices and achievements as well as challenges that were now being addressed, and that, by and large, Panama had "an effective anticorruption regime." Panama is, indeed, a typical country, which, nearly ten years after the adoption of UNCAC, has not budged in the charts – a very problematic fact since it is placed below 4 (3.8, ranked 90 of 174) on Transparency International's Corruption Perception Index, a 1–10 scale where 10 is the best control of corruption. Transparency International, the international watchdog, had checked nearly all the reviews of UNCAC completed by November 2013 (60 of 69) and found that in 60 percent of countries, governments made no public announcement of the review, while in 40 percent not even the contact details of the country's UNCAC coordinating body had been made available to domestic NGOs (Transparency International 2013). Internationally, the situation is not much better, as the same sources indicate that NGOs have been denied entry to meetings of the Implementation Review Group (the body that oversees the review process) and the Intergovernmental Working Groups on Prevention and Asset Recovery. It is up to individual countries whether the UNCAC implementation review process is public or not: a "firm" EU request that civil society participation in the review process, reviewer country visits, and publication of full country review reports become mandatory has not yet been accepted (Marquette *et al.* 2012).

In a parallel but related development, the International Association of Anticorruption Authorities (IAACA) announced its establishment on October 22, 2006, with the official aim of "facilitating implementation of the United Nations Convention Against Corruption." The IAACA held a string of annual conferences, general meetings, and seminars in Beijing (2006), Guangzhou (2007), Bali (2007), Chongqing (2008), Kiev (2009), and Macau (2010), with local heads of states opening the ceremonies. The association has grown meanwhile to more than 300 organizational members, including nearly every law enforcement agency for national institutions and bodies entrusted with the task of fighting corruption across the world. It also fundraises from member countries and private sources with the goal of spreading knowledge about and increasing cooperation in anticorruption efforts, mainly through an Anticorruption Academy it set up in a palace on the outskirts of Vienna.

The IAACA should not be confused, however, with the International Anticorruption Conference (IACC) series, which has been jointly organized since 1996 by the IACC Council (with Transparency International serving as its secretariat). The IACC meetings are great fundraising events and draw over 1,500 participants and guests. The leaders of countries under the 50th percentile in the Control of Corruption ratings are invited to speak at the conference, where they pledge to implement the UNCAC, receiving awards and other incentives. While the heads of many anticorruption agencies have lost their jobs since 2005 (with Nigeria the most famous case), the institutionalization of the global anticorruption movement has progressed energetically. On its fringes are many well-meaning activists: not professional consultants funding themselves through anticorruption efforts, but real stakeholders in their countries' progress. Therefore some diffusion of negative and positive anticorruption lessons learned is bound to take place – but anything more seems a distant prospect for now.

It is therefore hardly surprising that countries that have adopted UNCAC have not progressed more significantly in controlling corruption than countries that have not (Mungiu-Pippidi *et al.* 2011). Frequently, the industry seems to be driven by its own need to expand (and find funding), rather than by the task of problem solving. The environment is also changing fast. Take Transparency International, for instance. It has been the world's leading force for increasing awareness of corruption, in fact introducing this taboo world into public debate, since its founding by retired World Bank official Peter Eigen in 1993. It had an ambitious self development program from the onset, which led in time to the franchise of over one hundred chapters around the world. However, while making its chief contribution – awareness raising – through research and international advocacy, it refrained from the start from any work at the domestic level which could be interpreted as a challenge to national governments, even the most predatory. As Eigen explained,[1] the goal was to protect Transparency International's activists from coming to harm. The original charter was revised in 2012, but at present it still centers on awareness raising, shying away from litigation, name shaming, calls for resignation or other more decisive protest actions (Transparency International 2011). Meanwhile, anticorruption protests and movements have developed and literally exploded in many countries. However, Transparency International will not be found behind the anticorruption protests in Brazil, India, Turkey, or Ukraine. Grand, "big bang," domestically organized anticorruption coalitions in South Korea, Romania, or Ukraine also do not have Transparency International activists among their ranks. Instead, Transparency International creates frameworks for action such as the Transparency Aid Initiative, or Extractive Industries Transparency Initiative, monitors global treaties, and keeps the topic of corruption on the agenda of all world summits – all remarkably useful things, yet on the national level, despite a great variety of chapters, it seldom challenges governments. In many countries it receives public funding from the government it monitors. Its budget needs have grown exponentially: in 2014 the central secretariat alone accounted for €25 million. Its perfectly transparent audits and accounts can be consulted on its website.

One may argue that not enough time has passed since UNCAC's adoption for a meaningful evaluation to be made. After all, it has been more than 50 years since the adoption of the Universal Declaration of Human Rights and 57 percent of the world's population still live in countries where human rights are observed only imperfectly (an evaluation based on Freedom House's 2012 political and civil rights index). The UNCAC is not just a declaration, however: it not only sets targets,

[1] Answer by Peter Eigen to the author's public question at a conference at the New School for Social Research, New York, November 22, 2013, www.newschool.edu/cps/corruption/.

but also gives prescriptions and calls for implementation. Compared to the human rights covenants it was ratified very quickly. In fact, many countries signed the Convention Against Corruption precisely during the interval in which their citizens reported a perceived increase in corruption in the Global Corruption Barometer.

The human rights progress made since 1948 would not have been possible without growing demands for freedom and the increasing mobilization of freedom fighters worldwide. If UNCAC is to work in the future, it has to encourage similar developments – ones that go beyond international meetings and peer reviews among states. As a result of UNCAC, many countries have formally adopted ethical universalism as a norm, which simplifies the work of anticorruption advocates. But we are unlikely to see significant progress without greater domestic demand for new rules of the game and public participation in a sustainable mechanism which would prevent the eternal reproduction of privilege. Strategies must be adapted according to needs: UNCAC is a collection of institutional tools, not all similarly effective or useful. Some of them have the potential to become effective weapons, depending on the context. This is true, however, only if local actors choose and wield them. Let us imagine UNCAC ratification as the act of throwing an arsenal over a prison wall. Some arms require a high degree of specialized training, and, thus, no one knows how to use them; others are not fit for use in confined spaces. But among all these weapons is a handful of grenades that could bring the wall down – if only enough people are willing to pull the pins and throw them.

The extent to which UNCAC can address grand and political corruption – arguably the most significant types of corruption within limited access orders – is thrown into question by a recent report examining implementation in three countries (Hechler *et al.* 2011). The authors argue that "the Convention could have addressed the nexus between power relations and corruption more clearly" and "the fact that UNCAC is a government-driven and government-owned convention against corruption that also implicates politicians and public officials at all levels poses difficult barriers to genuine implementation and bottom-up reform." Their case studies show that a review process is far more useful when it is conducted in a participatory manner – that is, involving a broad range of relevant national stakeholders – and when the convention is considered within the context of the specific country, avoiding simply becoming an exercise oriented toward external actors (Hechler *et al.* 2011).

What the international community should do to increase its impact is to think of UNCAC implementation and review as mechanisms for stirring collective action. It can have an impact only if society as a whole contributes to being a check on the government. Domestic review of UNCAC implementation should play a far more important role than international review. For example, if a corrupt Ruritania were to ratify UNCAC, the international community should push for an annual meeting of a national stakeholders' commission, including media, unions, local community leaders, and anticorruption NGOs, to reinforce implementation. Those in charge of Ruritania's UNCAC implementation should report back to this body and make their report public. Accountability to society as a whole on UNCAC implementation is a minimum requirement in the process of building much-needed government accountability. In this context, the Paris Declaration's "ownership principle" should be interpreted as ownership by society, not government.

But the need to control rent seeking no longer refers to Ruritania-like places only. Evidence has piled up that rent-seeking behavior is on the rise and that globalization has been used by "shadow elites" to amass "plutocratic fortunes" in the developed as well as the developing world: there is widespread acknowledgment that political connections have become the most important capital, subverting both markets and democracy (Freeland 2012; "Planet Plutocrat" 2014; Wedel 2009). *The Economist*'s ranking of crony capitalists puts on top not only obvious suspects whose economies are dominated by crony sectors, such as Russia, Ukraine, and Malaysia, but also the textbook control of corruption cases of "institutional monocroppers" such as Singapore and Hong Kong. The methodology perhaps needs further refinement; nevertheless, this seems to be further evidence that particularism can flourish legally alongside "successful" anticorruption agencies, and that control of corruption can come under threat anywhere if scrutiny is relaxed.

One might believe that the highly developed EU, with a CPI average far superior to the rest of the world, would find it easier to organize itself than the broader international community where anticorruption is concerned. But not even the EU has an easy time building collective action against corruption. The Stockholm European Council called upon the European Commission to develop new instruments to monitor control of corruption and financial crime in all member states (European Council 2010). This led to the idea of monitoring corruption across old and new EU member states alike, which materialized in 2014 in the first pan-EU anticorruption report. Such a development would have been inconceivable prior to the Greek crisis; and even after, it has been a serious challenge for the European Commission to find a mechanism acceptable to all member countries. While the elimination of double standards toward old and new members is obviously a gain for the legitimacy of the process (Estonia, for instance, scores better than both Greece and Italy in all governance charts), similar monitoring indicators across countries where corruption is under control to where it is the norm opens the door to other controversies. Reviewing the first report, the European Council already asked for a change of methodology highlighting objective indicators collected at the country level rather than reliance on public opinion polls (Council of the European Union 2014).

The demand for effective anticorruption has therefore never been greater. It strains not only the political will of many governments, but also the capacity of political science to measure, map, and offer valid instruments for effective policy intervention. Respondents may well be critical and pessimistic in surveys: these times can be seen equally as the most exciting and the most challenging.

Appendix 1
Explaining bribery

	(1)
Variables	Model I
% of respondents who are self-employed	0.44**
	(0.18)
% of respondents employed in the private sector	–0.54**
	(0.247)
% of male respondents	1.67***
	(0.507)
Perception of importance of personal contacts	0.10*
	(0.051)
% of respondents with low income	0.27
	(0.22)
% of respondents with secondary education	0.01
	(0.135)
Constant	–0.87**
	(0.371)
Observations	97
R–squared	0.31
Adj. R–squared	0.27

Source: Transparency International 2013
Legend: Linear regression with dependent variable % bribers per country. Robust standard errors in parentheses.
*** $p<0.01$, ** $p<0.05$, * $p<0.10$.

Appendix 2
List of variables and sources

Variable	Variable description/measurement	Scale	Time period	Country coverage	Source
% of respondents who consider civil servants/public officials corrupt	Percentage of respondents who answered the question: “To what extent do you see public officials/civil servants to be affected by corruption in this country?” with 4 (corrupt) or 5(extremely corrupt)	%	2012	110	Global Corruption Barometer 2013 (Transparency International 2013)
% of respondents who have paid a bribe at least once	Percentage of respondents who answered Yes to any of the following questions: “Have you or anyone in your household paid a bribe in any form in the past 12 months to: Education system?/Judiciary (courts)?/Medical and health services?/Police?/Registry and permit services?/Tax revenue or customs?”	%	2012	110	Global Corruption Barometer 2013

% of respondents who think that personal connections are important to get things done in the public sector	Percentage of respondents who answered the question, "In your dealings with the public sector, how important are personal contacts and/or relationships to get things done?" with "important" or "very important"	%	2012	110	Global Corruption Barometer 2013
Appreciation of competition	Answers to the question: How would you place your views on this scale? 1 means you agree completely with the statement on the left; 10 means you agree completely with the statement on the right; and if your views fall somewhere in between you can choose any number in between: (1) Competition is good. It stimulates people to work hard and develop new ideas vs. (10) Competition is harmful. It brings out the worst in people.	1 (competition is good) to 10 (competition is harmful)	2005–06	82,992 respondents (57 countries)	World Values Survey 2005
Average years of schooling in 1900	Average years of schooling among the population older than 15	Numerical (0 to ∞)	1900	74	Morrisson and Murtin (2009)

Variable	Variable description/measurement	Scale	Time period	Country coverage	Source
Civil society organizations	Data on the number of civil society organizations from CIVICUS, a global network of civil society organizations active in the area of social and economic development. The directory is compiled for the development community and does not purport to be an exhaustive register of all organizations. Marcia Grimes has tried to validate the data by comparing it to the results of a comprehensive analysis conducted at the Johns Hopkins University Center for Civil Society Studies of a much smaller subset of countries (Salamon and Sokolowski 2011).Though the latter employs a broader definition of civil society and measures civil society as the proportion of a country's workforce active in civil society, the Johns Hopkins and CIVICUS measures correlate respectably (Pearson's $r=0.63$, $p<0.001$, $N=35$).	Numerical (0 to ∞)	2000	191	Quality of Government dataset

Civil society organizations per million inhabitants	Number of civil society organizations per million inhabitants. For more information on the construction of the variable, see "Civil Society Organizations" above.	Numerical (0 to ∞)	2000	191	Quality of Government dataset
Corruption Perception Index (CPI)	The CPI focuses on corruption in the public sector and defines corruption as the abuse of public office for private gain. The surveys used in compiling the CPI tend to ask questions in line with the misuse of public power for private benefit with a focus, for example, on bribe taking by public officials in public procurement. The sources do not distinguish between administrative and political corruption. The CPI score relates to perceptions of the degree of corruption as seen by business people, risk analysts, and the general public.	0 (highly corrupt) to 10 (very clean)	2010	172	Transparency International
Democracy	Average of Freedom House (fh_pr and fh_cl) is transformed to a scale 0–10 and Polity (p_polity2) is transformed to a scale 0–10. These variables are averaged into fh_polity2.	0 (least democratic) to 10 (most democratic)	2010	158	Freedom in the World survey, Freedom House; Polity IV

Variable	Variable description/measurement	Scale	Time period	Country coverage	Source
Diversion of public funds	In your country, how common is diversion of public funds to companies, individuals, or groups due to corruption?	1 (very common) to 7 (never occurs)	2010	135	Global Competitiveness Report
Ease of doing business	Ease of doing business ranks economies from 1 to 183, with first place best. A high ranking (a low numerical rank) means that the regulatory environment is conducive to business operations. The index averages the country's percentile rankings on 10 topics covered in the World Bank's "Doing Business" report. The ranking on each topic is the simple average of the percentile rankings on its component indicators.	1 (best) to 183 (worst)	2010	183	World Bank database
Economic openness index	Economic globalization is characterized as long-distance flows of goods and services as well as information and perceptions that accompany market exchanges.	0 (least globalized) to 100 (most globalized)	1970–2010	207	KOF Globalization Index, Dreher (2006)

Electoral democracy	The designation of electoral democracy is assigned by Freedom House to countries that have met certain minimum standards. The numerical (0 to ∞) benchmark for a country to be listed as an electoral democracy is a total of 7 points or higher (out of a possible 12) for the three political rights subcategory questions on electoral process, as well as a total of 20 points or more (out of apossible 40) for all 10 political rights questions.	1 (electoral democracy) and 0 (other)	2012	195	Freedom in the World, Freedom House
Equal treatment by police forces	Please respond with agree, rather agree, rather disagree, or disagree: All citizens are treated equally by the police force in my area.	1 (agree) to 4(disagree)	2013	85,166 respondents (30 countries)	European Quality of Government Index 2013
Equal treatment in the public education system	Please respond with agree, rather agree, rather disagree, or disagree: All citizens are treated equally in the public education system in my area.	1 (agree) to 4(disagree)	2013	85,166 respondents (30 countries)	European Quality of Government Index 2013
Equal treatment in the public healthcare system	Please respond with agree, rather agree, rather disagree, or disagree: All citizens are treated equally in the public healthcare system in my area.	1 (agree) to 4(disagree)	2013	85,166 respondents (30 countries)	European Quality of Government Index 2013

Variable	Variable description/measurement	Scale	Time period	Country coverage	Source
Ethnic fractionalization	Reflects probability (0 to 1) that two randomly selected people from a given country will not belong to the same ethnolinguistic group. The higher the number, the more fractionalized a society. The definition of ethnicity involves a combination of racial and linguistic characteristics.	0 (no ethnolinguistic fractionalization) to 1 (total ethnolinguistic fractionalization)	2001	183	Quality of Government dataset
Experience of corruption	Percentage of respondents who answered Yes to the question, "Have you ever been asked to pay a bribe?"	%	2012	110	Global Corruption Barometer 2013
FOIA presence	Whether FOIA was in existence this year (1=yes; 0=no)	1 (FOIA present) and 0 (no FOIA present)	2010	189	Hertie School of Governance database
FOIA year	Year FOIA came into existence	Numerical (0 to ∞)	2010	81	Hertie School of Governance database
Freedom of the press	The press freedom index is computed by adding three component ratings: laws and regulations; political pressures and controls; and economic influences and repressive actions.	0 (most free) to 100 (least free)	2010	189	Freedom House

Fuel exports as % of merchandise exports	Fuel exports as % of merchandise exports (latest available data)	%	2008–2010	172	World Bank database
GDP per capita	GDP per capita (constant US$2,000)	Numerical (0 to ∞)	2010	176	World Bank database
GDP per capita (current $US)	GDP per capita (current $US)	Numerical (0 to ∞)	2010	178	World Bank database
GDP per capita PPP (constant international US$)	GDP per capita, PPP adjusted. GDP is the sum of gross value added by all resident producers in the economy plus any product taxes and minus any subsidies not included in the value of the products. It is calculated without making deductions for depreciation of fabricated assets or for depletion and degradation of natural resources.	Numerical (0 to ∞)	2010	166	World Development Indicators
GNI per capita, PPP (current international US$)	GNI per capita, PPP (current international US$)	Numerical (0 to ∞)	2010	168	World Bank database

Variable	Variable description/measurement	Scale	Time period	Country coverage	Source
HDI	Summary composite index that measures a country's average achievements in three basic aspects of human development: longevity, knowledge, and a decent standard of living. Longevity is measured by life expectancy at birth; knowledge is measured by a combination of the adult literacy rate and the combined primary, secondary, and tertiary gross enrollment ratio; and standard of living is measured by GDP per capita. The Human Development Index (HDI), reported in the Human Development Report of the United Nations, is an indication of a country's relative development. Countries with an index over 0.800 are part of the High Human Development group. Between 0.500 and 0.800, countries are part of the Medium Human Development group, and below 0.500 they are part of the Low Human Development group.	0 (lowest human development) to 1 (highest human development)	2010	185	UNDP database

HDI education index	The education component of the HDI is now measured by mean of years of schooling for adults aged 25 years and expected years of schooling for children of school entering age. The indicators are normalized using a minimum value of zero, and maximum values are set to the actual observed maximum value of mean years of schooling from the countries in the time series 1980–2010. Expected years of schooling is maximized by its cap at 18 years. The education index is the geometric mean of two indices.	Numerical (0 to ∞)	2010	186	UNDP database
Internet users	Internet users (per 100 people)	%	2010	192	World Bank database
Judicial independence	To what extent is the judiciary in your country independent from influences of members of government, citizens, or firms?	1 (heavily influenced) to 7 (entirely independent)	2010	135	Global Competitiveness Report

Variable	Variable description/measurement	Scale	Time period	Country coverage	Source
Justification of bribery	Answers to the question: Please tell me for each of the following actions whether you think it can always be justified, never be justified, or somewhere in between: Someone accepting a bribe in the course of their duties.	1 (always justifiable) to 10 (never justifiable)	2005–06	82,992 respondents (57 countries)	World Values Survey 2005
Life expectancy at birth,	Life expectancy at birth, total (years)	Numerical (0 to ∞)	2010	194	World Bank database
Literacy rate	Total adult literacy rate (% of people aged 15 and above)	%	2000–10	148	World Bank database
Mobile cellular subscriptions	Mobile cellular subscriptions (per 100 people)	%	2010	201	World Bank database
Natural resources rents	Total natural resources rents are the sum of oil rents, natural gas rents, (hard and soft) coal rents, mineral rents, and forest rents.	%	1996–2011	196	World Bank database
Natural resource dummy	Binary variable taking the value of 1 if a country is resource rich according to the IMF (2010, 2012) classification: A country is classified as resource rich if its natural resources contribute to at least 20 percent of its total fiscal revenues and/or at least 20 percent of its total exports.	1 (resource rich) and 0 (not resource rich)	2010–2012	196	International Monetary Fund (2010; 2012)

Open Budget Index (OBI)	The Open Budget Index rates countries on how open their budget books are to their citizens. It is intended to provide citizens, legislators, and civil society advocates with the comprehensive and practical information needed to gauge a government's commitment to budget transparency and accountability.	0 (scant or no information available) to 100 (extensive information available)	2010	100	Open Budget Survey 2010
Ombudsman presence	Whether ombudsman was in operation the previous year	1 (ombudsman is present) and 0 (no ombudsman is present)	2010	194	Hertie School of Governance database
Ombudsman year of creation	Year ombudsman started operating	Numerical (0 to ∞)	2010	131	Hertie School of Governance database
Paid a bribe for health or medical services	In the past 12 months have you or anyone living in your household paid a bribe in any form to health or medical services?	1 (yes) and 0 (no)	2013	85,166 respondents (30 countries)	European Quality of Government Index 2013
Paid a bribe in the last 12 months	Aggregates the questions, "In the past 12 months have you or anyone living in your household paid a bribe in any form to health or medical services/the public education system/the police forces/any other government-run agency?"	1 (yes) and 0 (no)	2013	85,166 respondents (30 countries)	European Quality of Government Index 2013

Variable	Variable description/measurement	Scale	Time period	Country coverage	Source
Perception of bureaucratic corruption	Weighted average of the answers to the question: “In your opinion, to what extent do you perceive the following categories in this country to be affected by corruption: civil servants/public officials?”	1 (not at all corrupt) to 5 (extremely corrupt)	2010	110	Global Corruption Barometer 2010
Perception of the extent of the use of bribery	Weighted average of the answers to the question: “In your opinion, how often do you think other people in your area use bribery to obtain other special advantages that they are not entitled to?”	0 (never) to 10 (very frequently)	2013	85,166 respondents (30 countries)	European Quality of Government Index 2013
Personal autonomy and individual rights	The variable evaluates the extent of state control over travel, choice of residence, employment, or institution of higher education; the right of citizens to own property and establish private businesses; private business freedom from undue influence by government officials, security forces, political parties, or organized crime; gender equality, freedom of choice of marriage partners and size of family; equality of opportunity and absence of economic exploitation.	0 (worst) to 16 (best)	2010	188	Freedom House

Physical integrity rights index	This is an additive index constructed from the Torture (ciri_tort), Extrajudicial Killing (ciri_kill), Political Imprisonment (ciri_polpris), and Disappearance indicators (ciri_disap). (Details on its construction and use can be found in Cingranelli and Richards (1999).)	0 (no government respect for physical integrity) to 8 (full government respect to physical integrity)	2002–2010	187	Cingranelli and Richards (2010)
Presence of Anticorruption Agency (ACA)	Whether ACA was in operation the previous year	1 (ACA present) and 0 (ACA not present)	2010	171	Hertie School of Governance database
Region	This is a politico-geographic classification of world regions adapted from the World Bank classification, which is based on a mixture of two considerations: geographical proximity (with the partial exception of category 5 below) and demarcation by area specialists. The categories are as follow: 1) Eastern Europe and the Baltics; 2) Latin America (including Cuba, Haiti, and the Dominican Republic);	Numerical (0 to ∞)	2010	189	Quality of Government dataset

Variable	Variable description/measurement	Scale	Time period	Country coverage	Source
	3) North Africa and the Middle East (including Israel, Turkey, and Cyprus); 4) Sub-Saharan Africa; 5) Western Europe and North America (including Australia and New Zealand); 6) Asia and the Pacific; 7) Former Soviet Union (and Central Asia); 8) The Caribbean (including Belize, Guyana, and Suriname)				
Respondents who paid a bribe to at least one public service,	Aggregates the total number of respondents who admitted paying a bribe to at least one public institution/service (education, medical, land, and/or registry services, customs, judiciary, police and tax authorities).	1 (paid a bribe) and 0 (did not pay a bribe)	2010	98	Global Corruption Barometer 2010

Risk of corruption	This is an assessment of corruption within the political system. The most common form of corruption met directly by business is financial corruption in the form of demands for special payments and bribes connected with import and export licenses, exchange controls, tax assessments, police protection, or loans. This measure takes such corruption into account, but it is more concerned with actual or potential corruption in the form of excessive patronage, nepotism, job reservations, "favor-for-favors," secret party funding, and suspiciously close ties between politics and business. In our view these insidious sorts of corruption are potentially of much greater risk to foreign business in that they can lead to popular discontent, unrealistic and inefficient controls on the state economy, and encourage the development of the black market.	0 (lowest risk of corruption) to 6 (highest risk of corruption)	1984–2012	139	The PRS Group

Variable	Variable description/measurement	Scale	Time period	Country coverage	Source
Rural population	% of total population living in rural areas	%	2010	210	World Bank database
Satisfaction with healthcare system	How would you rate the quality of the public healthcare system in your area?	0 (very poor) to 10 (excellent quality)	2013	85,166 respondents (30 countries)	European Quality of Government Index 2013
Satisfaction with police services	How would you rate the quality of the police force in your area?	0 (very poor) to 10 (excellent quality)	2013	85,166 respondents (30 countries)	European Quality of Government Index 2013
Satisfaction with public education	How would you rate the quality of public education in your area?	0 (very poor) to 10 (excellent quality)	2013	85,166 respondents (30 countries)	European Quality of Government Index 2013
Social openness index	Social globalization is expressed as the spread of ideas, information, images, and people.	1 (least globalized) to 100 (most globalized)	1970–2010	207	KOF Globalization Index, Dreher (2006)
UNCAC year of ratification	Year of UNCAC ratification	Numerical (0 to ∞)	2010	147	Hertie School of Governance database

WGI Control of Corruption (CoC) estimate	CoC measures perceptions of corruption, conventionally defined as the exercise of public power for private gain. The particular aspect of corruption measured by the various sources differs somewhat, ranging from the frequency of “additional payments to get things done,” to the effects of corruption on the business environment, to measuring “grand corruption” in the political arena or in the tendency of elite forms to engage in “state capture.” The recoded version of this variable to a scale of 1 to 10 was also used throughout this report.	-2.5 (weak control of corruption) to 2.5 (strong control of corruption) (Alternatively recoded to a scale from 1 (lowest control of corruption) to 10 (highest control of corruption)	1996–2011	200	Worldwide Governance Indicators
WGI political stability estimate	Reflects perceptions of the likelihood that the government will be destabilized or overthrown by unconstitutional or violent means, including politically motivated violence and terrorism.	-2.5 (weak governance performance) to 2.5 (strong governance performance)	2010	203	Worldwide Governance Indicators

Variable	Variable description/measurement	Scale	Time period	Country coverage	Source
Year of creation of the ACA	Year ACA was created	Numerical (0 to ∞)	2010	171	Hertie School of Governance database
Years since ACA was established	Years since ACA was established	Numerical (0 to ∞)	2010	171	Hertie School of Governance database
Years since FOIA came into power	Years since FOIA came into power	Numerical (0 to ∞)	2010	189	Hertie School of Governance database
Years since ombudsman started operation	Years since ombudsman started operating	Numerical (0 to ∞)	2010	203	Hertie School of Governance database

Appendix 3
Brief description of databases and surveys used

European Quality of Government Index 2013

Quality of Government Institute for ANTICORRP

This survey (EQI) on corruption and governance at the regional level within the EU was first conducted in 2010 and then again in 2013. The data focus on both perceptions and experiences with public sector corruption, along with the extent to which citizens believe various public sector services are impartially allocated and of good quality. It covers all 28 EU member states and two accession countries (Serbia and Turkey). The subnational regions are at the Nomenclature of Units for Territorial Statistics (NUTS) 1 or NUTS 2 level, depending on the country and, for 2013, the EQI was expanded to 206 regions and was answered by 85,000 citizen respondents.

Data provided by the Quality of Government Institute.

Freedom in the World and Freedom of the Press Index

Freedom House

Freedom in the World is an assessment of global political rights and civil liberties. It has been published annually since 1972 and covers 195 countries and 14 related and disputed territories. The Freedom of the Press Index is an annual survey of media independence in 197 countries and territories. The annual index contains the most comprehensive data set available on global media freedom. The index assesses the degree of print, broadcast, and internet freedom in every country in the world.

Data available at: www.freedomhouse.org/reports#.UzRBQYVK-A0.

Global Competitiveness Report

World Economic Forum

Since 2004, the Global Competitiveness Report ranks the nations according to the Global Competitiveness Index. The report is made up of over 110 variables, of which two-thirds come from the Executive Opinion Survey, and one-third comes from publicly available sources. The variables are organized into twelve pillars, with each pillar representing an area considered an important determinant of competitiveness.

Data available at: www.weforum.org/issues/competitiveness-0/gci2012-data-platform/

Global Corruption Barometer

Transparency International

Since its debut in 2003, the Global Corruption Barometer (GCB) has surveyed the experiences of everyday people confronting corruption around the world. The GCB 2013 is the biggest ever survey tracking worldwide public opinion on corruption. The survey was answered by over 114,000 people in 107 countries.

Data provided by Transparency International at: www.transparency.org.

Hertie School of Governance Database

Hertie School of Governance

This database was compiled by the Hertie School of Governance for NORAD in 2011 and updated for ANTICORRP in 2013. It contains data on several corruption measurements and anticorruption tools such as the existence of Freedom of Information Acts, ombudsmen, and anticorruption agencies in over 190 countries.

International Country Risk Guide

The PRS Group, Inc.

This database (ICRG) includes political, economic, and financial risk ratings for 140 countries since 1980. ICRG ratings form the basis of an early warning system for country-by-country opportunities and pitfalls. It provides the longest history of country risk data for analysis.

Data available at: http://epub.prsgroup.com/the-countrydata-gateway

Indices of Social Development

International Institute of Social Studies

The Indices of Social Development (ISD) bring together 200 indicators, synthesizing them into a usable set of measures to track how different societies perform along six dimensions of social development:

- civic activism, measuring use of media and protest behavior;
- clubs and associations, defined as membership in local voluntary associations;
- intergroup cohesion, which measures discrimination and ethnic and sectarian tensions;
- interpersonal safety and trust, focusing on perceptions and incidences of crime and personal transgressions;
- gender equality, reflecting gender discrimination in home, work and public life; and
- inclusion of minorities, which measures levels of discrimination against vulnerable groups such as indigenous peoples, migrants, refugees, or lower caste groups.

The indices are composed from 25 reputable data sources for 193 countries over the period from 1990 to 2010 and are updated as new data become available.

Data available at: www.indsocdev.org/.

KOF Index of Globalization

Swiss Federal Institute of Technology, Zurich

This database contains data on the KOF Index of Globalization, measuring the three main dimensions of globalization: economic, social, and political. Data are available on a yearly basis for 207 countries over the period from 1970 to 2010.

Data available at: http://globalization.kof.ethz.ch/.

Open Budget Survey

International Budget Partnership

The Open Budget Survey measures the state of budget transparency, participation, and oversight in 100 countries around the world. It consists of 125 questions and is completed by independent researchers in the countries assessed. A total of 95 of the questions deal directly with the public availability and comprehensiveness of the 8 key budget documents that governments should publish at various points of the budget cycle. The remaining 30 questions relate to opportunities for public participation in the budget process and to the roles played by legislatures and supreme audit institutions in budget formulation and oversight. The survey does not reflect opinion. It measures observable facts related to budget transparency, accountability, and participation.

Data available at: http://internationalbudget.org/what-we-do/open-budget-survey/

Quality of Government Institute Database

Quality of Government Institute

The Quality of Government Institute (QoG) offers a range of datasets on indicators of quality of government and related issues in both cross-section and time-series formats.

Data available at: www.qog.pol.gu.se/data/.

World Bank Database

World Bank

The World Bank database is one of the most reliable and comprehensive databases on developing economies. It provides a listing of 331 indicators for over 200 countries and territories.

Data available at: http://datacatalog.worldbank.org/.

Worldwide Governance Indicators

World Bank

The Worldwide Governance Indicators (WGI) project reports aggregate and individual governance indicators for 215 economies over the period 1996–2012, for six dimensions of governance:

- voice and accountability;
- political stability and absence of violence;
- government effectiveness;
- regulatory quality;
- rule of law; and
- control of corruption.

These aggregate indicators combine the views of a large number of enterprise, citizen, and expert survey respondents in industrial and developing countries.

Data available at: http://info.worldbank.org/governance/wgi/index.aspx#home

World Values Survey

The World Values Survey Association

The World Values Survey (WVS) is a worldwide network of social scientists studying changing values and their impact on social and political life. The WVS in collaboration with the European Values Study (EVS) carried out representative national surveys in more than 100 countries containing almost 90 percent of the world's population. These surveys show pervasive changes in what people want in life and what they believe. In order to monitor these changes, the EVS/WVS has executed six waves of surveys, from 1981 to 2013.

Data available at: www.worldvaluessurvey.org/

Appendix 4
Impact of anticorruption interventions on control of corruption: bivariate regressions

	All countries			Middle– and low–income countries		
Variables	–1	–2	–3	–4	–5	–6
FOIA	–0.014			0.008		
	(–0.34)			(0.18)		
ACA		–0.085**			–0.058	
		(–2.14)			(–1.31)	
Ombudsman			0.027			0.02
			(0.53)			(0.39)
Constant	3–0.339***	1.907***	1.565***	0.705***	0.405***	0.413*
	(–3.71)	(64.14)	(29.25)	(3.56)	(4.27)	(1.91)
N	2369	2175	2200	1825	1676	1712
Countries	184	169	171	153	140	143
Adj. R–squared	0.95	0.95	0.95	0.89	0.88	0.89

OLS regressions covering a sample period 1996–2011. The dependent variable is Control of Corruption from WGI. By country, clustered standard errors are used; t statistics in parentheses: * p<0.1, ** p<0.05, *** p<0.01. All regressions include country and year dummies as well as year dummies interacted with regional dummies.

Appendix 5
HDI differentials from Figure 4.1

Variables	(1) Model 1
Human Development Index	4.05***
	(0.307)
Constant	−2.72***
	(0.209)
Observations	184
R-squared	0.49
Adj. R-squared	0.49

OLS regression with WGI Control of Corruption as dependent variable.
Robust standard errors in parentheses.
*** $p<0.001$, ** $p<0.01$, * $p<0.05$.

Country	HDI	Control of corruption (real score)	Predicted value according to Model 1	Residuals
Afghanistan	0.394	−1.62	−1.12	−0.50
Albania	0.737	−0.43	0.26	−0.69
Algeria	0.696	−0.48	0.10	−0.58
Andorra	0.838	1.33	0.67	0.66
Angola	0.482	−1.33	−0.77	−0.56
Antigua and Barbuda	0.763	1.33	0.37	0.96
Argentina	0.794	−0.44	0.50	−0.93
Armenia	0.714	−0.67	0.17	−0.84
Australia	0.927	2.06	1.03	1.03

Country	HDI	Control of corruption (real score)	Predicted value according to Model 1	Residuals
Austria	0.883	1.64	0.86	0.79
Azerbaijan	0.699	−1.17	0.11	−1.28
Bahamas, The	0.77	1.35	0.40	0.96
Bahrain	0.805	0.25	0.54	−0.29
Bangladesh	0.496	−0.99	−0.71	−0.28
Barbados	0.791	1.43	0.48	0.95
Belarus	0.751	−0.82	0.32	−1.14
Belgium	0.885	1.50	0.86	0.64
Belize	0.698	−0.08	0.11	−0.18
Benin	0.425	−0.75	−1.00	0.25
Bhutan	0.518	0.83	−0.62	1.45
Bolivia	0.66	−0.48	−0.05	−0.43
Bosnia and Herzegovina	0.731	−0.32	0.24	−0.56
Botswana	0.631	0.97	−0.16	1.14
Brazil	0.715	0.06	0.18	−0.12
Brunei Darussalam	0.837	0.86	0.67	0.19
Bulgaria	0.768	−0.18	0.39	−0.57
Burkina Faso	0.329	−0.37	−1.39	1.01
Burundi	0.313	−1.08	−1.45	0.37
Cambodia	0.518	−1.21	−0.62	−0.59
Cameroon	0.479	−0.98	−0.78	−0.20
Canada	0.907	2.06	0.95	1.11
Cape Verde	0.566	0.77	−0.43	1.20
Central African Republic	0.339	−0.78	−1.35	0.57
Chad	0.326	−1.32	−1.40	0.08
Chile	0.802	1.50	0.53	0.97
China	0.682	−0.60	0.04	−0.65
Colombia	0.707	−0.39	0.14	−0.53
Comoros	0.431	−0.74	−0.97	0.24
Congo, Dem. Rep.	0.282	−1.38	−1.58	0.19
Congo, Rep.	0.528	−1.14	−0.58	−0.56
Costa Rica	0.742	0.67	0.29	0.38
Cote d'Ivoire	0.401	−1.15	−1.10	−0.05
Croatia	0.794	0.05	0.50	−0.45
Cuba	0.773	0.50	0.41	0.09

Country	HDI	Control of corruption (real score)	Predicted value according to Model 1	Residuals
Cyprus	0.839	1.07	0.68	0.40
Czech Republic	0.863	0.31	0.78	−0.47
Denmark	0.893	2.37	0.90	1.48
Djibouti	0.427	−0.31	−0.99	0.68
Dominica	0.723	0.74	0.21	0.53
Dominican Republic	0.686	−0.83	0.06	−0.89
Ecuador	0.718	−0.88	0.19	−1.07
Egypt, Arab Rep.	0.644	−0.56	−0.11	−0.44
El Salvador	0.672	−0.22	0.00	−0.22
Equatorial Guinea	0.534	−1.49	−0.56	−0.93
Eritrea	0.345	−0.46	−1.32	0.87
Estonia	0.832	0.91	0.65	0.26
Ethiopia	0.358	−0.70	−1.27	0.57
Fiji	0.687	−0.91	0.06	−0.97
Finland	0.88	2.15	0.84	1.30
France	0.883	1.39	0.86	0.54
Gabon	0.67	−0.76	−0.01	−0.76
Gambia, The	0.418	−0.55	−1.03	0.48
Georgia	0.729	−0.16	0.23	−0.39
Germany	0.903	1.70	0.94	0.76
Ghana	0.533	0.09	−0.56	0.65
Greece	0.862	−0.12	0.77	−0.89
Grenada	0.746	0.44	0.30	0.14
Guatemala	0.573	−0.53	−0.40	−0.13
Guinea	0.342	−1.19	−1.33	0.15
Guinea-Bissau	0.351	−1.06	−1.30	0.24
Guyana	0.629	−0.56	−0.17	−0.38
Haiti	0.449	−1.26	−0.90	−0.35
Honduras	0.623	−0.86	−0.20	−0.66
Hungary	0.814	0.33	0.58	−0.25
Iceland	0.896	1.92	0.91	1.01
India	0.542	−0.52	−0.52	0.01
Indonesia	0.613	−0.73	−0.24	−0.49
Iran, Islamic Rep.	0.707	−0.88	0.14	−1.03
Iraq	0.567	−1.32	−0.42	−0.90
Ireland	0.907	1.67	0.95	0.71
Israel	0.886	0.64	0.87	−0.23

Country	HDI	Control of corruption (real score)	Predicted value according to Model 1	Residuals
Italy	0.873	−0.04	0.82	−0.86
Jamaica	0.726	−0.37	0.22	−0.59
Japan	0.899	1.54	0.92	0.62
Jordan	0.697	0.04	0.10	−0.06
Kazakhstan	0.74	−1.00	0.28	−1.27
Kenya	0.505	−0.91	−0.67	−0.24
Kiribati	0.621	−0.05	−0.21	0.16
Korea, Rep.	0.894	0.42	0.90	−0.48
Kuwait	0.758	0.35	0.35	0.00
Kyrgyz Republic	0.611	−1.07	−0.25	−0.83
Lao PDR	0.52	−1.07	−0.61	−0.46
Latvia	0.802	0.21	0.53	−0.32
Lebanon	0.737	−0.84	0.26	−1.10
Lesotho	0.446	0.19	−0.91	1.10
Liberia	0.325	−0.51	−1.40	0.90
Libya	0.77	−1.26	0.40	−1.66
Liechtenstein	0.904	1.84	0.94	0.90
Lithuania	0.805	0.32	0.54	−0.22
Luxembourg	0.865	2.06	0.78	1.27
Macedonia, FYR	0.726	−0.06	0.22	−0.28
Madagascar	0.481	−0.27	−0.77	0.51
Malawi	0.395	−0.42	−1.12	0.70
Malaysia	0.758	0.12	0.35	−0.23
Maldives	0.658	−0.63	−0.06	−0.57
Mali	0.356	−0.68	−1.28	0.60
Malta	0.83	0.92	0.64	0.28
Mauritania	0.451	−0.68	−0.89	0.21
Mauritius	0.726	0.68	0.22	0.46
Mexico	0.767	−0.37	0.39	−0.76
Micronesia, Fed. Sts.	0.635	−0.13	−0.15	0.02
Moldova	0.644	−0.73	−0.11	−0.62
Mongolia	0.647	−0.71	−0.10	−0.61
Montenegro	0.769	−0.33	0.39	−0.73
Morocco	0.579	−0.16	−0.38	0.22
Mozambique	0.317	−0.40	−1.44	1.04
Myanmar	0.479	−1.68	−0.78	−0.90
Namibia	0.622	0.26	−0.20	0.46

Country	HDI	Control of corruption (real score)	Predicted value according to Model 1	Residuals
Nepal	0.455	−0.69	−0.88	0.19
Netherlands	0.909	2.15	0.96	1.18
New Zealand	0.908	2.36	0.96	1.41
Nicaragua	0.587	−0.78	−0.34	−0.44
Niger	0.293	−0.66	−1.53	0.87
Nigeria	0.454	−0.99	−0.88	−0.11
Norway	0.941	2.07	1.09	0.97
Oman	0.704	0.37	0.13	0.24
Pakistan	0.503	−1.10	−0.68	−0.42
Palau	0.779	−0.50	0.43	−0.94
Panama	0.765	−0.36	0.38	−0.74
Papua New Guinea	0.462	−1.14	−0.85	−0.30
Paraguay	0.662	−0.76	−0.04	−0.72
Peru	0.721	−0.23	0.20	−0.43
Philippines	0.641	−0.82	−0.12	−0.70
Poland	0.811	0.45	0.56	−0.12
Portugal	0.808	1.03	0.55	0.48
Qatar	0.825	1.52	0.62	0.90
Romania	0.779	−0.16	0.43	−0.59
Russian Federation	0.751	−1.07	0.32	−1.40
Rwanda	0.425	0.48	−1.00	1.48
Sao Tome and Principe	0.506	−0.38	−0.67	0.29
Saudi Arabia	0.767	0.15	0.39	−0.24
Senegal	0.457	−0.68	−0.87	0.18
Serbia	0.764	−0.21	0.37	−0.59
Seychelles	0.771	0.30	0.40	−0.11
Sierra Leone	0.334	−0.76	−1.37	0.61
Singapore	0.864	2.18	0.78	1.40
Slovak Republic	0.832	0.27	0.65	−0.38
Slovenia	0.882	0.84	0.85	−0.01
Solomon Islands	0.507	−0.46	−0.67	0.21
South Africa	0.615	0.09	−0.23	0.32
Spain	0.876	1.01	0.83	0.18
Sri Lanka	0.686	−0.43	0.06	−0.49
St. Kitts and Nevis	0.735	1.05	0.26	0.79
St. Lucia	0.72	1.23	0.20	1.03

Country	HDI	Control of corruption (real score)	Predicted value according to Model 1	Residuals
St. Vincent and the Grenadines	0.715	1.05	0.18	0.87
Sudan	0.406	–1.33	–1.08	–0.25
Suriname	0.677	–0.43	0.02	–0.45
Swaziland	0.52	–0.16	–0.61	0.45
Sweden	0.901	2.25	0.93	1.32
Switzerland	0.901	2.06	0.93	1.13
Syrian Arab Republic	0.631	–1.05	–0.16	–0.89
Tajikistan	0.604	–1.17	–0.27	–0.90
Tanzania	0.461	–0.49	–0.85	0.36
Thailand	0.68	–0.34	0.03	–0.37
Timor–Leste	0.491	–0.95	–0.73	–0.22
Togo	0.433	–0.97	–0.97	0.00
Tonga	0.703	–0.31	0.13	–0.43
Trinidad and Tobago	0.758	–0.35	0.35	–0.70
Tunisia	0.698	–0.13	0.11	–0.24
Turkey	0.696	0.01	0.10	–0.09
Turkmenistan	0.681	–1.44	0.04	–1.47
Uganda	0.442	–0.88	–0.93	0.05
Ukraine	0.725	–0.97	0.22	–1.19
United Arab Emirates	0.845	0.98	0.70	0.28
United Kingdom	0.862	1.48	0.77	0.71
United States	0.908	1.23	0.96	0.28
Uruguay	0.78	1.29	0.44	0.85
Uzbekistan	0.636	–1.32	–0.14	–1.17
Vanuatu	0.615	0.35	–0.23	0.58
Venezuela, RB	0.734	–1.24	0.25	–1.49
Vietnam	0.59	–0.58	–0.33	–0.25
Yemen, Rep.	0.46	–1.14	–0.86	–0.29
Zambia	0.425	–0.57	–1.00	0.43
Zimbabwe	0.364	–1.39	–1.25	–0.15

Appendix 6
Classification of countries by governance orders

Countries by Type of Governance Regime (2012)

Neo-Patrimonialism*	
Country Name	CoC Score 2012 (recoded)
Afghanistan	1.41
Algeria	3.38
Angola	1.67
Azerbaijan	2.17
Bahrain	5.48
Belarus	3.41
Brunei Darussalam	6.03
Cambodia	2.23
Cameroon	1.79
Chad	1.77
China	3.51
Congo, Dem. Rep.	1.65
Congo, Rep.	1.90
Cuba	5.27
Djibouti	3.75
Equatorial Guinea	1.07
Eritrea	3.13
Ethiopia	3.23
Gabon	3.35
Gambia, The	3.14
Guinea-Bissau	1.83
Iran, Islamic Rep.	2.75
Iraq	1.82
Jordan	4.75
Kazakhstan	2.60
Korea, Dem. Rep.	1.49
Lao Pdr	2.24

Neo-Patrimonialism*	
Country Name	**CoC Score 2012 (recoded)**
Mali	2.87
Mauritania	3.23
Myanmar	2.07
Oman	4.77
Russian Federation	2.30
Rwanda	6.07
Saudi Arabia	4.45
Somalia	1.00
South Sudan	1.58
Sudan	1.19
Swaziland	3.86
Syrian Arab Republic	1.94
Tajikistan	1.94
Turkmenistan	1.56
Uzbekistan	1.82
Vietnam	3.34
Yemen, Rep.	1.81
Zimbabwe	1.71
45 Countries	

* Countries ranked as "not free" in Freedom House's Freedom in the World index and with a recoded Control of Corruption score below 3.3.

Competitive Particularism**	
Country Name	**CoC Score 2012 (recoded)**
Albania	2.96
Argentina	3.50
Armenia	3.40
Bangladesh	2.64
Belize	4.61
Benin	2.53
Bhutan	6.46
Bolivia	3.00
Bosnia And Herzegovina	3.93

Competitive Particularism**	
Country Name	CoC Score 2012 (recoded)
Brazil	4.43
Bulgaria	4.06
Burkina Faso	3.42
Burundi	1.28
Cape Verde	6.42
Central African Republic	2.57
Colombia	3.61
Comoros	2.95
Costa Rica	5.91
Côte D'ivoire	2.55
Croatia	4.50
Czech Republic	5.11
Dominica	6.16
Dominican Republic	2.71
Ecuador	3.11
Egypt, Arab Rep.	3.30
El Salvador	3.73
Fiji	3.61
Georgia	5.17
Ghana	4.40
Greece	4.02
Grenada	5.51
Guatemala	3.20
Guinea	2.09
Guyana	2.90
Haiti	1.78
Honduras	2.47
Hungary	5.23
India	3.32
Indonesia	3.11
Israel	6.47
Italy	4.54
Jamaica	3.78
Kenya	2.11
Kiribati	4.60
Korea, Rep.	5.65
Kosovo	3.18
Kuwait	4.23

Competitive Particularism**	
Country Name	CoC Score 2012 (recoded)
Kyrgyz Republic	2.13
Latvia	4.94
Lebanon	2.64
Lesotho	4.85
Liberia	3.30
Libya	1.43
Lithuania	5.30
Macedonia, Fyr	4.64
Madagascar	3.22
Malawi	3.57
Malaysia	5.27
Maldives	3.59
Marshall Islands	4.27
Mauritius	5.35
Mexico	3.67
Micronesia, Fed. Sts.	4.35
Moldova	3.24
Mongolia	3.42
Montenegro	4.38
Morocco	3.66
Mozambique	3.26
Namibia	5.31
Nauru	4.70
Nepal	2.73
Nicaragua	2.84
Niger	3.04
Nigeria	2.03
Pakistan	2.20
Palau	3.95
Panama	3.72
Papua New Guinea	2.25
Paraguay	2.70
Peru	3.70
Philippines	3.27
Poland	5.92
Romania	3.98
Samoa	4.94
São Tomé And Principe	3.71

Competitive Particularism**	
Country Name	CoC Score 2012 (recoded)
Senegal	3.88
Serbia	3.90
Seychelles	5.35
Sierra Leone	2.48
Slovak Republic	4.75
Slovenia	6.43
Solomon Islands	3.59
South Africa	4.25
Sri Lanka	4.05
Suriname	3.76
Tanzania	2.67
Thailand	3.82
Timor-Leste	2.38
Togo	2.35
Tonga	4.43
Trinidad And Tobago	3.94
Tunisia	4.18
Turkey	4.97
Tuvalu	3.92
Uganda	2.44
Ukraine	2.27
Vanuatu	5.60
Venezuela, Rb	1.79
Zambia	3.78
109 Countries	

** Countries ranked as "free" or "partly Free" in Freedom House's Freedom in the World Index and with a recoded Control of Corruption score between 3.3 and 6.6.

Universalism***	
Country Name	CoC Score 2012 (recoded)
Denmark	10.00
New Zealand	9.84
Sweden	9.81
Norway	9.66
Finland	9.62
Switzerland	9.46
Netherlands	9.41
Luxembourg	9.39
Australia	9.10
Canada	8.94
Iceland	8.81
Liechtenstein	8.67
Germany	8.62
Barbados	8.35
United Kingdom	8.30
Japan	8.24
Chile	8.12
Belgium	8.10
Ireland	7.86
France	7.81
United States	7.71
Austria	7.64
Bahamas, The	7.63
Uruguay	7.58
Andorra	7.52
Antigua And Barbuda	7.52
Cyprus	7.40
Spain	6.96
St. Kitts And Nevis	6.82
St. Vincent And The Grenadines	6.82
Estonia	6.81
Malta	6.77
St. Lucia	6.77
Botswana	6.72
Portugal	6.69
35 Countries	

*** Countries ranked as "free" in Freedom House's Freedom in the World Index and with a recoded Control of Corruption score higher than 6.6.

References

Acemoglu, D. 1995. "Reward Structures and the Allocation of Talent." *European Economic Review* 39 (1): 17–33.

Acemoglu, D., S. Johnson, and J. A. Robinson 2001. "The Colonial Origins of Comparative Development: An Empirical Investigation." *American Economic Review* 91 (5): 1369–1401.

2003. "An African Success Story: Botswana." In D. Rodrik (ed.) *In Search of Prosperity: Analytic Narratives on Economic Growth*. Princeton University Press.

Acemoglu, D. and J. A. Robinson 2006. *Economic Origins of Dictatorship and Democracy*. Cambridge University Press.

2012. *Why Nations Fail: The Origins of Power, Prosperity, and Poverty*. Crown Business.

Adamolekun, L. and P. Morgan 1999. "Pragmatic Institutional Design in Botswana: Salient Features and an Assessment." *International Journal of Public Sector Management* 12 (7): 584–603.

Ades, A. and R. Di Tella 1997. "The New Economics of Corruption: A Survey and Some New Results." *Political Studies* 45 (3): 496–515.

1999. "Rents, Competition, and Corruption." *The American Economic Review* 89 (4): 982–94.

Ahmad, T. S. 2014. "What If Anti-Corruption Measures Aren't the Best Way to Fight Corruption?" Oxfam America, July 15. http://politicsofpoverty.oxfamamerica.org/2014/07/anti-corruption-measures-arent-best-way-fight-corruption/.

Aidt, T. S. 2003. "Economic Analysis of Corruption: A Survey." *The Economic Journal* 113: 632–52.

Alesina, A. and B. Weder 1999. "Do Corrupt Governments Receive Less Foreign Aid?" Working Paper 7108, National Bureau of Economic Research. www.nber.org/papers/w7108.pdf.

Ali, MA, and HS Isse. 2003. "Determinants of Economic Corruption: A Cross-Country Comparison." *Cato Journal* 22 (3): 449–66.

Al Jazeera. 2013. "Slovenian Parliament Ousts PM over Corruption." February 27. www.aljazeera.com/news/europe/2013/02/2013227231621128662.html.

Alsop, R. and N. Heinsohn 2005. *Measuring Empowerment in Practice: Structuring Analysis and Framing Indicators*. Policy Research Working Paper 3510. The World Bank. http://elibrary.worldbank.org/doi/pdf/10.1596/1813-9450-3510.

Alt, J. E. and D. D. Lassen 2003. "The Political Economy of Corruption in American States." *Journal of Theoretical Politics* 15 (3): 341–65.

Altman, D. 2008. "Collegiate Executives and Direct Democracy in Switzerland and Uruguay: Similar Institutions, Opposite Political Goals, Distinct Results." *Swiss Political Science Review* 14 (3): 483–520.

Anand, M. V., B. E. Ashforth, and M. Joshi 2004. "Business as Usual: The Acceptance and Perpetuation of Corruption in Organizations." *The Academy of Management Executive* 18 (2): 39–53.

Anderson, J. and C. Gray 2006. *Anticorruption in Transition 3: Who Is Succeeding and Why?* Washington, DC: The World Bank.

Andrews, M. 2008. "The Good Governance Agenda: Beyond Indicators Without Theory." *Oxford Development Studies* 36 (4): 379–407.

Andvig, J. C. and K. O. Moene 1990. "How Corruption May Corrupt." *Journal of Economic Behavior and Organization* 13 (1): 63–76.

Aquinas, T. 2006. *Summa Theologica Part I-II (Pars Prima Secundae)*. Complete American Edition. www.gutenberg.org/cache/epub/17897/pg17897.txt.

Ariu, A. and M. P. Squicciarini 2013. "The Balance of Brains: Corruption and Migration." *EMBO Reports*, no. 14: 502–4.

Armstrong, C. K. 2007. *Korean Society: Civil Society, Democracy, and the State*. Abingdon, Oxon: Routledge.

Arnold, P. E. 2003. "Democracy and Corruption in the 19th Century United States: Parties, Spoils, and Political Participation." In S Tiihonen (ed.) *The History of Corruption in Central Government*. Brussels: IOS Press.

Asch, S. E. 1955. "Opinions and Social Pressure." *Scientific American* 193 (5)31–35.

Asmerom, H. K. and E. P. Reis 1996. *Democratization and Bureaucratic Neutrality*. New York: St. Martin's Press.

Bac, M. 2001. "Corruption, Connections and Transparency: Does a Better Screen Imply a Better Scene?" *Public Choice* 107: 87–96.

Baer, D. 2007. "Voluntary Association Involvement in Comparative Perspective." In L. Trägårdh (ed.) *State and Civil Society in Northern Europe: The Swedish Model Reconsidered*. New York: Berghahn Books, 67–125.

Baker, R. and N. McKenzie 2012. "Labor Rejects Call for National Corruption Agency." *Sydney Morning Herald*, February. www.smh.com.au/opinion/political-news/labor-rejects-call-for-national-corruption-agency-20120214-1t468.html#ixzz1mt7chyqn.

Bandura, A. 1997. *Self-Efficacy: The Exercise of Control.* New York: W. H. Freeman.

1999. "Social Cognitive Theory of Personality." In L. Pervin and O. John (eds.) *Handbook of Personality*, 2nd edn. New York: Guilford Publications.

2002. "Selective Moral Disengagement in the Exercise of Moral Agency." *Journal of Moral Education* 31 (2): 101–19.

Banfield, E. C. 1958. *The Moral Basis of a Backward Society*. Glencoe, IL: The Free Press.

Banisar, D. 2006. *Freedom of Information Around the World 2006: A Global Survey of Access to Government Information Laws*. London: Privacy International.

Beck, T., G. Clarke, A. Groff, P. Keefer, and P. Walsh 2001. "New tools in comparative political economy: The Database of Political Institutions." *World Bank Economic Review* 15 (1) (September): 165–76.

Becker, G. 1968. "Crime and Punishment: An Economic Approach." *Journal of Political Economy* 76: 169–217.

Becker, G. and G. Stigler 1974. "Law Enforcement, Malfeasance, and the Compensation of Enforcers." *Journal of Legal Studies*, no. 3: 1–19.

Bertelsmann Stiftung 2009. *BTI 2010: Botswana Country Report.* Gütersloh:Bertelsmann Stiftung. www.bti-project.org/uploads/tx_itao_download/BTI_2010_Botswana.pdf.

Bexelius, A. 1967. "The Swedish Ombudsman." *The University of Toronto Law Journal* 17 (1): 170–76.

Birdsall, N. 2004. "Seven Deadly Sins: Reflections on Donor Failings." Working Paper 50. Center for Global Development. www.cgdev.org/files/2737_file_Working_Paper_50.pdf.

Birdsall, N. and W. D. Savedoff 2011. *Cash on Delivery: A New Approach to Foreign Aid.* Center For Global Development.

Boussard, C. 2003. *Crafting Democracy: Civil Society in Post-Transition Honduras.* Lund: Department of Political Science, Lund University.

Bozzini, A. 2014. *Background Report on Rwanda.* EU FP7 ANTICORRP project. http:/anticorrp.eu/publications/background-paper-on-rwanda/.

Braga, A. C. S. 2011. *Aid Selectivity and Anti-Corruption Policy. A Case Study of the Millennium Challenge Corporation.* Berlin: Hertie School of Governance.

Braun, M. and R. Di Tella. 2004. "Inflation, Variability, and Corruption." *Economics and Politics* 16 (1): 77–100.

Bräutigam, D. A. and S. Knack 2004. "Foreign Aid, Institutions, and Governance in Sub-Saharan Africa." *Economic Development and Cultural Change* 52 (2): 255–85.

Brazilian Ministry of Planning, Budget, and Management 2010. "Boletim Estatístico." www.servidor.gov.br/publicacao/boletim_estatistico/bol_estatistico_10/Bol176_Dez2010.pdf.

Broadman, H. G. and F. Recanatini 2000. "Seed of Corruption: Do Market Institutions Matter?" Policy Research Working Paper 2368. The World Bank.

Brown, A. J. and B. Head. 2004. "Ombudsman, Corruption Commission, or Police Integrity Authority? Choices for Institutional Capacity in Australia's Integrity Systems." Australasian Political Studies Association Conference. Adelaide.

Brown, D. S., M. Touchton, and A. B. Whitford 2005. *Political Polarization as a Constraint on Government: Evidence from Corruption*. SSRN. http://ssrn.com/abstract=782845.

Brunetti, A. and B. Weder 2003. "A Free Press Is Bad News for Corruption." *Journal of Public Economics* 87: 1801–24.

Buehn, A. and F. Schneider 2011. "Shadow Economies around the World: Novel Insights, Accepted Knowledge, and New Estimates." *International Tax and Public Finance* 19 (1). www.econ.jku.at/members/Schneider/files/publications/2012/BuehSchneider2.pdf.

Buquet, D. and R. Piñeiro 2014. *Background Report on Uruguay*. EU FP7 ANTICORRP project. http:/anticorrp.eu/publications/background-paper-on-uruguay/.

Burnside, C. and D. Dollar 2004. "Aid, Policies, and Growth: Revisiting the Evidence." Policy Research Working Paper 3251. The World Bank.

Carlyle, R. W. and A. J. Carlyle 1903. *A History of Medieval Political Theory in the West*. Vol. I. Edinburgh: Blackwood.

Carothers, T. 1998. "The Rule of Law Revival." *Foreign Affairs* 77 (March/April): 95–106.

Carr, I. M. and O. Outhwaite 2008. "The OECD Anti-Bribery Convention Ten Years Later." *Manchester Journal of International Law* 5 (1): 3–55.

Cerni, B. 2013. "Slovenia Ex-Premier Jansa Gets Two Years in Prison on Bribes." *Bloomberg News*. www.bloomberg.com/news/2013-06-05/slovenia-s-ex-premier-jansa-convicted-of-graft-in-military-deal.html.

Chang, E. C. C. and M. A. Golden 2003. "Electoral Systems, District Magnitude, and Corruption." Annual meeting of the American Political Science Association.

Charron, N. 2013. "European Perceptions of Quality of Government: A Survey of 24 Countries." In A. Mungiu-Pippidi (ed.) *The Anticorruption Report, Vol. 1: Controlling Corruption in Europe*. Opladen: Barbara Budrich Publishers, 99–120.

Cho-shui, L. 2011. "Civil Service Benefits Are among Best in the World." *Taipei Times*, January 14. www.taipeitimes.com/News/editorials/print/2011/01/14/2003493435.

Chumacero, R., R. Fuentes, R. Lüders, and J. Vial 2007. "Understanding Chilean Reforms." In J. M. Fanelli (ed.) *Understanding Market Reforms*. London: Palgrave Macmillan, 351–358.

Cicero, M. T. 1877. *Cicero's Tusculan Disputations; Treatises On The Nature Of The Gods; and On The Commonwealth*. 2005th edn. Project Gutenberg. www.gutenberg.org/dirs/1/4/9/8/14988/14988-h/14988-h.htm#FN-309.

1928. *De Re Publica, De Legibus*. Translated by C. W. Keyes. Loeb Classical Library.

Cingranelli, D. L. and D. L. Richards 1999. "Measuring the Level, Pattern, and Sequence of Government Respect for Physical Integrity Rights." *International Studies Quarterly* 43 (2): 407–17.

2010. "The Cingranelli and Richards (CIRI) Human Rights Data Project." *Human Rights Quarterly* 32 (2): 401–24.

Cohen, E. W. 1965. *The Growth of the British Civil Service, 1780–1939*. London: Frank Cass.

Collier, P. 1997. "The Failure of Conditionality." In C. Gwin and J. M. Nelson (eds.) *Perspectives on Aid and Development*. Washington, DC: Johns Hopkins University Press, 51–77.

1999. "Aid Dependency: A Critique." *Journal of African Economies* 8 (4): 528–45.

2011. *Wars, Guns, and Votes: Democracy in Dangerous Places*. London: Random House.

Collier, P. and D. Dollar 2002. "Aid Allocation and Poverty Reduction." *European Economic Review* 46: 1475–1500.

Collier, P., P. Guillaumont, S. Guillaumont, and J. W. Gunning 1997. "Redesigning Conditionality." *World Development* 25: 1399–1407.

"Corruption." 1989. *Oxford English Dictionary* 974. Oxford University Press.

Council of the European Union 2014. "Council Conclusions on the EU Anticorruption Report." www.gr2014.eu/sites/default/files/JHA%20ANTI%20CORRUPTION.pdf.

Cuervo-Cazurra, A. 2006. "Who Cares about Corruption?" *Journal of International Business Studies* 37 (6): 807–22.

2008. "The Effectiveness of Laws against Bribery Abroad." *Journal of International Business Studies* 39 (4): 634–51.

Damania, R., P. Fredriksson, and M. Muthukumara 2004. "The Persistence of Corruption and Regulatory Compliance Failures: Theory and Evidence." *Public Choice* 121: 363–90.

David-Barrett, L. and K. Okamura 2013. *Why Do Corrupt Countries Join EITI?* Working Paper 38. European Research Center for Anticorruption and State-Building (ERCAS).

Della Porta, D. 1996. "Actors in Corruption: Business Politicians in Italy." *International Social Science Journal* 48 (149): 349–64.

Della Porta, D. and A. Vannucci 1999. *Corrupt Exchanges: Actors, Resources, and Mechanisms of Political Corruption*. New York: Walter de Gruyter.

De Maria, W. 2010. "The Failure of the African Anticorruption Effort: Lessons for Managers." *International Journal of Management* 27 (1): 117–22.

De Sardan, J. O. 1999. "A Moral Economy of Corruption in Africa?" *The Journal of Modern African Studies* 37 (1): 25–52.

De Soto, H. 2002. *Listening to the Barking Dogs: Property Law against Poverty in the Non-West*. The Cato Institute. www.cato.org/pub_display.php?pub_id=5183.

Deutsch, M. 1985. *Distributive Justice*. New Haven, CT: Yale University Press.

Diamond, L. 1999. *Developing Democracy Towards Consolidation*. Baltimore, MD: Johns Hopkins University Press.

Dimulescu, V., R. A. M. Pop, and M. Doroftei 2013. "Bottom of the Heap: The Case of Romania." In A. Mungiu-Pippidi (ed.) *The Anticorruption Report, Vol. 1: Controlling Corruption in Europe*. Opladen: Barbara Budrich Publishers. http:/anticorrp.eu/publications/the-anticorruption-report-1-bottom-of-the-heap-the-case-of-romania/.

Disch, A., E. Vigeland, G. Sundet, and S. Gibson 2009. *Anti-Corruption Approaches: A Literature Review*. NORAD. www.norad.no/en/tools-and-publications/publications/publication?key=119213.

Djankov, S., C. McLiesh, T. Nenova, and A. Shleifer 2001. *Who Owns the Media?* Policy Research Working Paper 2620. The World Bank.

Doig, A., D. Watt, and R. Williams 2005. *Measuring "Success" in Five African Anti-Corruption Commissions: The Cases of Ghana, Malawi, Tanzania, Uganda, and Zambia*. U4 Report 2005:1. Bergen: Chr. Michelsen Institute. www.u4.no/publications/measuring-success-in-five-african-anti-corruption-commissions/downloadasset/2099.

Donchev, D. and G. Ujhelyi 2008. *What Do Corruption Indices Measure?* Working Paper. University of Houston Economics Department.

Dong, B., D. Uwe, and B. Torgler 2012. "Conditional Corruption." *Journal of Economic Psychology* 33 (3): 609–27.

Donsbach, W. 1995. "Lapdogs, Watchdogs, and Junkyard Dogs." *Media Studies Journal* 9: 17–30.

Dreher, A. 2006. "Does Globalization Affect Growth? Evidence From a New Index of Globalization." *Applied Economics* 38 (10): 1091–1100.

Dreher, A. and F. G. Schneider 2010. "Corruption and the Shadow Economy: An Empirical Analysis." *Public Choice* 144 (2): 215–77.

Easterly, W. and R. Levine 1997. "Africa's Growth Tragedy: Policies and Ethnic Divisions." *Quarterly Journal of Economics* 112 (4): 1203–50.

Economist, The 2014. "Planet Plutocrat", March 15. www.economist.com/news/international/21599041-countries-where-politically-connected-businessmen-are-most-likely-prosper-planet/comments?page=1.

Edwards, S. and D. Lederman 1998. *The Political Economy of Unilateral Trade Liberalization: The Case of Chile*. Working Paper 6510. National Bureau of Economic Research. www.anderson.ucla.edu/faculty/sebastian.edwards/W6510.pdf.

Eisenstadt, S. N. 1973. "Traditional Patrimonialism and Modern Neopatrimonialism." Research Papers in the Social Sciences. SAGE Publications Ltd.

Eisenstadt, S. N. and L. Roniger 1984. *Patrons, Clients, and Friends: Interpersonal Relations and the Structure of Trust in Society*. Cambridge University Press.

Elster, J. 1989. "Social Norms and Economic Theory." *Journal of Economic Perspectives* 3 (4): 99–117.

Erdmann, G. and U. Engel 2007. "Neopatrimonialism Reconsidered: Critical Review and Elaboration of an Elusive Concept." *Commonwealth and Comparative Politics* 45 (1): 95–119.

ERR News 2012. "New System Puts Local Government Spending Under Virtual Microscope." September 21. http://news.err.ee/Sci-Tech/7ee96ac8-05b8-43c9-b60b-38eb0cffc2dd.

Escresa, L. and L. Picci 2014. *A New Cross-National Measure of Corruption*. http://ssrn.com/abstract=2294477.

Etzioni-Halevy, E. 1989. "Exchanging Material Benefits for Political Support: A Comparative Analysis." In A. Heidenheimer, M. Johnston, and V. T. LeVine (eds.) *Political Corruption: A Handbook (rev. Edition)*. New Brunswick, NJ: Transaction Books,287–304.

European Commission 2012. Corruption. Special Eurobarometer 374. http://ec.europa.eu/public_opinion/archives/ebs/ebs_374_en.pdf.

European Council 2010. "The Stockholm Program: An Open and Secure Europe, Serving and Protecting Citizens." *Official Journal of the European Union* 23. http://eur-lex.europa.eu/legal-content/EN/TXT/PDF/?uri=CELEX:52010XG0504(01)andfrom=EN.

European Court of Auditors 2013. Press release. http://eca.europa.eu/portal/pls/portal/docs/1/22610783.PDF.

Evans, P. 1989. "Predatory, Developmental, and Other Apparatuses: A Comparative Political Economy Perspective on the Third World State." *Sociological Forum* 4 (4): 561–87.

2004. "Development as Institutional Change: The Pitfalls of Monocropping and the Potentials of Deliberation." *Studies in Comparative International Development* 38 (4): 30–52.

Falkner, G., O. Treib, and E. Holzleitner 2008. *Compliance in the Enlarged European Union. Living Rights or Dead Letters?* Aldershot: Ashgate.

Fazekas, M., J. Gutierréz Chvalkovská, J. Skuhrovec, I. János Tóth, and L. P. King 2014. "Are EU Funds a Corruption Risk? The Impact of EU Funds on Grand Corruption in Central and Eastern Europe." In A. Mungiu-Pippidi (ed.) *The Anticorruption Report, Vol. 2: The Anticorruption Frontline*. Opladen: Barbara Budrich Publishers, 68–89.

Fazekas, M., L. P. King, and I. J. Tóth 2013. "Hidden Depths. The Case of Hungary." In A. Mungiu-Pippidi (ed.) *The Anticorruption Report, Vol. 1: Controlling Corruption in Europe*. Opladen: Barbara Budrich Publishers. http:/anticorrp.eu/publications/the-anticorruption-report-1-hidden-depths-the-case-of-hungary/.

Fearon, J. and D. Laitin 1996. "Explaining Interethnic Cooperation." *The American Political Science Review* 90 (4): 715–35.

Feldbæk, O. 2000. "The Historical Role of the Nordic Countries in Europe." *European Review* 8: 123–28.

Felson, M. and R. L. Boba 2009. *Crime and Everyday Life*. SAGE Publications Inc.

Ferguson, A. 1996. *An Essay on the History of Civil Society*. Edited by F. Oz-Salzberger. Cambridge University Press.

Fisher, J. and H. Marquette 2014. *Donors Doing Political Economy Analysis: From Process to Product (and Back Again?)*. The Developmental Leadership Program (DLP), International Development Department, University of Birmingham. www.delog.org/cms/upload/pdf-pea/Donors_Doing_Political_Economy_Analysis_-_From_Process_to_Product_and_Back_Again.pdf.

Fisman, R. and E. Miguel 2007. "Corruption, Norms, and Legal Enforcement: Evidence from Diplomatic Parking Tickets." *Journal of Political Economy* 115 (6): 1020–48.

Fombad, C. M. 2001. "The Enhancement of Good Governance in Botswana: A Critical Assessment of the Ombudsman Act." *Journal of Southern African Studies* 27: 57–77.

Fott, D. 2002. "Preface to Translation of Montesquieu's 'Discourse on Cicero.'" *Political Theory* 30 (5): 728–32.

Frechette, G. R. 2001. "A Panel Data Analysis of the Time-Varying Determinants of Corruption." Annual Meeting of the European Public Choice Society.

Freedom House 2010. *Freedom in the World Country Report: Botswana.* https://freedomhouse.org/report/freedom-world/2010/botswana#.U8zaRrGnn-o.

2013. *Freedom of the Press Report: Botswana.* https://freedomhouse.org/report/freedom-press/2013/botswana#.U8yRMbuKCW8.

Freeland, C. 2012. *Plutocrats: The New Golden Age.* London: Random House LLC.

Friedman, E., S. H. Johnson, D. Kaufmann, and P. Zoido 1999. "Dodging the Grabbing Hand: The Determinants of Unofficial Activity in 69 Countries." The Nobel Symposium in Economics: The Economics of Transition, Stockholm. http://ssrn.com/abstract=194628.

Frisk Jensen, M. 2008. *Korruption Og Embedsetik: Danske Embedsmaends Korruption I Perioden 1800–1866.* Aalborg University.

Fukuyama, F. 2004. *State Building: Governance and World Order in the 21st Century.* Ithaca, NY: Cornell University Press.

2011. *The Origins of Political Order: From Prehuman Times to the French Revolution.* New York: Farrar, Straus and Giroux.

2012. "Acemoglu and Robinson on Why Nations Fail." *American Interest,* March.

2013. "What Is Governance?" *Governance* 26 (3): 347–68.

Galtung, F. 2006. "Measuring the Immeasurable: Boundaries and Functions of (Macro) Corruption Indices." In C. Sampford, A. Shacklock, C. Connors, and F. Galtung (eds.) *Measuring Corruption.* Aldershot: Ashgate, 101–30.

Gatti, R., S. Paternostro, and J. Rigolini 2003. *Individual Attitudes toward Corruption: Do Social Effects Matter?* Policy Research Working Paper 3122. The World Bank.

Gazmuri, C. 1999. "La via Familiar Y Cotidiana de Eduardo Frei Montalva Como Presidente de Chile." *Boletin de Historia Y Geografia, Santiago.*

Gazmuri, C., P. Arancibia, and A. Gongora 2000. *Eduardo Frei Montalva Y Su Epoca.* Santiago: Ed. Aguilar.

Geertz, C. 1963. *Peddlers and Princes: Social Development and Economic Change in Two Indonesian Towns.* University of Chicago Press.

Global Integrity 2010. "Poland," *Global Integrity Report.* www.globalintegrity.org/global/the-global-integrity-report-2010/poland/2010/.

Göbel, C. 2014. *Background Paper on Taiwan.* EU FP7 ANTICORRP project. http:/anticorrp.eu/publications/background-paper-on-taiwan/.

Gøbel, E. 2000. *De Styrede Rigerne: Embedsmænd I Den Dansk-Norske Civilecentraladministration, 1660–1814.* Odense Universitetsforlag.

Goetz, S. J., M. Partridge, and S. C. Deller 2009. "Evaluating Rural Entrepreneurship Policy." Rural Development Paper 46.

Golden, M. A. and C. C. Chang 2001. "Competitive Corruption: Factional Conflict and Political Malfeasance in Postwar Italian Christian Democracy." *World Politics* 53 (July): 588–622.

Gonzalez de Lara, Y. 2011. "The Protection of Investor Rights in Late Medieval Venice." In J. Koppell (ed.) *The Origins of Shareholder Advocacy*. New York: Palgrave MacMillan, 101–22.

Good, K. 1994. "Corruption and Mismanagement in Botswana: A Best-Case Example?" *Journal of Modern African Studies* 32 (3): 499–521.

GRECO 2003. *Evaluation Report on Hungary: First Evaluation Round.* www.coe.int/t/dghl/monitoring/greco/evaluations/round1/GrecoEval1(2002)5_Hungary_EN.pdf>.

2009. *Evaluation Report on Denmark on Incriminations (ETS 173 and 191, GPC 2).* www.coe.int/t/dghl/monitoring/greco/evaluations/round3/GrecoEval3%282008%299_Denmark_One_EN.pdf.

Greif, A. 1998. "Self-Enforcing Political Systems and Economic Growth: Late Medieval Genoa." In R. H. Bates, A. Greif, M. Levi, J.-L. Rosenthal, and B. R. Weingast (eds.) *Analytic Narratives*. Princeton University Press.

Grimes, M. 2008. "The Role of Civil Society Organizations in Combating Corruption." MPSA Annual National Conference, Chicago, IL. www.allacademic.com/meta/p266844_index.html.

Grzymała-Busse, A. 2007. *Rebuilding Leviathan: Party Competition and State Exploitation in Post-Communist Democracies*. New York: Cambridge University Press.

Gurgur, T. and A. Shah 2005. *Localization and Corruption: Panacea or Pandora's Box*. Policy Research Working Paper 3486. The World Bank.

Halévy, E. 1961. *History of the English People in the Nineteenth Century*. London: Ernest Benn.

Hall, R. E. and C. I. Jones 1999. "Why Do Some Countries Produce so Much More Output per Worker than Others?" *Quarterly Journal of Economics* 114: 83–116.

Hallin, D. C. and S. Papathanassopoulos 2002. "Political Clientelism and the Media: Southern Europe and Latin America in Comparative Perspective." *Media, Culture and Society* 24 (2): 175–96.

Hechler, H., G. F. Zinkernagel, L. Koechlin, and D. Morris. 2011. "Can UNCAC Address Grand Corruption? A Political Economy Analysis of the UN Convention Against Corruption and its Implementation in Three Countries." *U4 Report* 2011:2. www.cmi.no/publications/file/4226-can-uncac-address-grand-corruption.pdf.

Heeks, R. and H. Mathisen 2012. "Understanding Success and Failure of Anti-Corruption Initiatives." *Crime, Law and Social Change* 58 (5): 533–49. http://link.springer.com/article/10.1007%2Fs10611-011-9361-y.

Heidenheimer, A. J. 1989. "Perspectives on the Perception of Corruption." In A. J. Heidenheimer, M. Johnston, and V. T. LeVine (eds.) *Political Corruption: A Handbook*. New Brunswick, NJ: Transaction Books.

1996. "The Topography of Corruption: Explorations in a Comparative Perspective." *International Social Science Journal* 48 (149): 337–47.

Heilbrunn, J. R. 2004. *Anti-Corruption Commissions: Panacea or Real Medicine to Fight Corruption?* Working Paper 37234. World Bank Institute.

Hellman, J. S., G. Jones, and D. Kaufmann 2003. "Seize the State, Seize the Day: State Capture and Influence in Transition Economies." *Journal of Comparative Economics* 31 (4): 751–73.

Herzfeld, T. and C. Weiss 2003. "Corruption and Legal (In-)Effectiveness: An Empirical Investigation." *European Journal of Political Economy* 19: 621–32.

Hoff, K. and J. E. Stiglitz 2005. *The Creation of the Rule of Law and the Legitimacy of Property Rights: The Political and Economic Consequences of a Corrupt Privatization*. w11772. National Bureau of Economic Research. www.nber.org/papers/w11772.pdf.

Hofstede, G. 2011. "Dimensionalizing Cultures: The Hofstede Model in Context." *Online Readings in Psychology and Culture* 2 (1): 8.

Holmberg, S., B. Rothstein, and N. Nasiritousi 2009. "Quality of Government: What You Get." *Annual Review of Political Science* 12: 135–61.

Holmes, S. 2002. "Introduction." *East European Constitutional Review* 11: 1–2.

Hsueh, C.-Y. 2007. "Power and Corruption in Taiwan." *Issues and Studies* 43 (1): 1–39.

Huang, T. W. 2006. "The President Refuses to Cohabit: Semi-Presidentialism in Taiwan." *Pacific Rim Law and Policy Journal* 15 (2): 375–402.

Huntington, S. P. 1968. *Political Order in Changing Societies*. New Haven, CT: Yale University Press.

1993. "The Clash of Civilizations?" *Foreign Affairs* 72 (3): 22–49.

Husted, B. W. 1999. "Wealth, Culture, and Corruption." *Journal of International Business Studies* 3 (2): 339–59.

Huther, J. and A. Shah 2000. *Anticorruption Policies and Programs: A Framework for Evaluation*. Policy Research Working Paper 2501. The World Bank.

Inglehart, R. and C. Welzel 2009. "How Development Leads to Democracy: What We Know about Modernization." *Foreign Affairs* 88 (2): 33–48.

Islam, R. 2006. "Does More Transparency Go Along With Better Governance?" *Economics and Politics* 18 (2): 121–67.

ITAD 2011. "Joint Evaluation of Support to Anti-Corruption Efforts 2002–09." NORAD. www.norad.no/en/tools-and-publications/publications/publication?key=384730.

Jandieri, G. 2004. *New Anti-Corruption Governments: The Challenge of Delivery; Georgia Case Study*. Berlin: Transparency International.

John of Salisbury 1927. "Policraticus." In *The Statesman's Book of John of Salisbury*. New York: Alfred A. Knopf. www.fordham.edu/halsall/source/salisbury-poli4.html.

Johnson, D. and T. Zajonc 2006. "Can Foreign Aid Create an Incentive for Good Governance? Evidence from the Millennium Challenge Corporation." Working Paper 11. CID.

Johnsøn, J., N. Taxell, and D. Zaum 2012. "Mapping Evidence Gaps in Anticorruption: Assessing the State of the Operationally Relevant Evidence on Donors' Actions and Approaches to Reducing Corruption." *Chr. Michelsen Institute U4 Issue*, no. 7. www.u4.no/publications/mapping-evidence-gaps-in-anti-corruption-assessing-the-state-of-the-operationally-relevant-evidence-on-donors-actions-and-approaches-to-reducing-corruption.

Johnson, S., D. Kaufmann, and A. Shleifer 1997. "The Unofficial Economy in Transition." *Brookings Papers on Economic Activity* 2. http://scholar.harvard.edu/shleifer/files/unofficial_econ_transition.pdf.

Johnston, M. 2000. "The New Corruption Rankings: Implications for Analysis and Reform." International Political Science Association World Congress, Quebec City. http://departments.colgate.edu/polisci/papers/mjohnston/originals/JohnstonIPSA2000.pdf.

2005. *Syndromes of Corruption: Wealth, Power, and Democracy*. Cambridge University Press.

2006. "From Thucydides to Mayor Daley: Bad Politics and a Culture of Corruption." *P.S. Political Science and Politics* 39: 809–12.

2013. *Corruption, Contention, and Reform: The Power of Deep Democratization*. New York: Cambridge University Press.

Jones, P. J. 1997. *The Italian City-State: From Commune to Signoria*. Oxford: Clarendon Press.

Kantorowicz, E. 1939. *Federico II Di Svevia*. Milan: Garzanti.

Karklins, R. 2005. *The System Made Me Do It: Corruption in Post-Communist Societies*. New York: ME Sharpe.

Karl, T. L. 1999. "The Perils of the Petro-State: Reflections on the Paradox of Plenty." *Journal of International Affairs* 53 (1): 31–52.

Kasemets, A. 2012. *The Long Transition to Good Governance: The Case of Estonia. Looking at the Changes in the Governance Regime and Anti-Corruption Policy*. Working Papers 32. European Research Center for Anticorruption and State-Building (ERCAS). www.againstcorruption.eu/wp-content/uploads/2012/09/WP-32-Long-Transition-Estonia1.pdf.

Kasemets, A. and Ü. Lepp 2010. *Anti-Corruption Programs, Studies, and Projects in Estonia 1997–2009: An Overview*. Working Papers 5. European Research Center for Anti-Corruption and State-Building (ERCAS). www.againstcorruption.eu/reports/estonia/.

Kaufmann, D. 1997. "Corruption: The Facts." *Foreign Policy* no. 107: 114–31.

Kaufmann, D., A. Kraay, and M. Mastruzzi 2005. *Governance Matters IV: Governance Indicators for 1996–2004*. The World Bank Policy Research Group. http://papers.ssrn.com/sol3/papers.cfm?abstract_id=718081.

Kaufmann, D., A. Kraay, and P. Zoido-Lobatón 1999. *Aggregating Governance Indicators*. Policy Research Working Paper 2195. World Bank. http://info.worldbank.org/governance/wgi/pdf/govind.pdf.

Kaufmann, D. and P. C. Vicente 2011. "Legal Corruption." *Economics and Politics* 23: 195–219.

Keefer, P. 2004. *What Does Political Economy Tell Us about Economic Development and Vice Versa?* Vol 3250. World Bank Publications.

Khan, M. H. 1998. "Patron-Client Networks and the Economic Effects of Corruption in Asia." *European Journal of Development Research* 10 (1): 15–39.

Khatib, L. 2014. *Background Report on Qatar*. EU FP7 ANTICORRP project. http:/anticorrp.eu/publications/background-paper-on-qatar/.

Kitschelt, H., K. Hawkins, J. P. Luna, G. Rosas, and E. Zechmeister 2010. *Latin American Party Systems*. Cambridge University Press.

Kleemann, K. 2010. *The European Neighborhood Policy: A Reality Check. How Effective Is the European Neighborhood Policy in Promoting Good Governance?* www.againstcorruption.eu/uploads/rapoarte_finale_PDF/The-%20European-Neighbourhood-Policy-A-Reality-Check.pdf.

Klitgaard, R. 1988. *Controlling Corruption*. Berkeley, CA: University of California Press.

1998. "International Cooperation Against Corruption." *Finance and Development* 35 (1): 3–6.

2000. "Subverting Corruption." *Finance and Development* 37 (2): 2–3.

Knack, S. 2001. "Aid Dependence and the Quality of Governance: Cross-Country Empirical Tests." *Southern Economic Journal* 68 (2): 310–29.

2004. "Does Foreign Aid Promote Democracy?" *International Studies Quarterly* 48 (1): 251–66.

2006. *Measuring Corruption in Eastern Europe and Central Asia: A Critique of the Cross-Country Indicators*. Policy Research Working Paper 3968. The World Bank.

Knudsen, T. 2006. *Fra Enevælde Til Folkestyre: Dansk Demokratihistorie Intil 1973*. Copenhagen: Akademisk Forlag.

Kocaoglu, N. and A. Figari 2006. *Using the Right to Information as an Anti-Corruption Tool*. Berlin: Transparency International.

Kolstad, I. and A. Wiig 2009. "Is Transparency the Key to Reducing Corruption in Resource-Rich Countries?" *World Development* 37 (3): 521–52.

Kunicova, J. and S. Rose-Ackerman 2005. "Electoral Rules and Constitutional Structures as Constraints on Corruption." *British Journal of Political Science* 35 (4): 573–606.

Kupatadze, A. 2011. "Similar Events, Different Outcomes: Accounting for Diverging Corruption Patterns in Post-Revolution Georgia and Ukraine." *Caucasus Analytical Digest* 26: 2–4.

Lambsdorff, J. 2008. *The Organization of Anticorruption: Getting Incentives Right!* University of Passau.

Ledeneva, A. 2006. *How Russia Really Works: The Informal Practices That Shaped Post-Soviet Politics And Business*. Ithaca, NY: Cornell University Press.

Lederman, D., N. Loayza, and R. Soares 2005. "Accountability and Corruption: Political Institutions Matter." *Economics and Politics* 17: 1–35.

Leite, C. A. and J. Weidmann 1999. *Does Mother Nature Corrupt?: Natural Resources, Corruption, and Economic Growth*. Working Paper WP/99/85. International Monetary Fund.

Lerner, D. 1964. "The Transformation of Institutions." In W. B. Hamilton (ed.) *The Transfer of Institutions*. Durham, NC: Duke University Press, 3–26.

Levitz, P. and G. Pop-Eleches 2010. "Monitoring, Money and Migrants: Countering Post-Accession Backsliding in Bulgaria and Romania." *Europe-Asia Studies* 62 (3): 461–79.

Lindsay, W. M. 1911. *Isidore of Seville: The Etymologies (or Origins)*. Oxford University Press. http://penelope.uchicago.edu/Thayer/E/Roman/Texts/Isidore/home.html.

Lipset, S. M. 1981. *Political Man: The Social Bases of Politics*. Baltimore, MD: The Johns Hopkins University Press.

Lipset, S. M. and G. S. Lenz 2000. "Corruption, Culture, and Markets." In L. E. Harrison and S. P. Huntington (eds.) *Culture Matters*. New York: Basic Books, 112.

Lutz, D. 1984. "The Relative Importance of European Writers in Late Eighteenth-Century American Political Thought" *189–97 American Political Science Review* 189 (1984): 189–97

Macfarlane, A. 1978. *The Origins of English Individualism: The Family, Property and Social Transition*. Oxford: Blackwell.

Machiavelli, N. 2009. *Discourses on Livy*. University of Chicago Press.

Mancini, P. 2009. *Elogio Della Lottizzazione*. Bari: Laterza.

March, J. G. 1994. *Primer on Decision Making: How Decisions Happen*. New York: Simon and Schuster.

Marquette, H., R. Flanary, S. Rao, and D. Morris 2012. *Supporting Anticorruption Reform in Partner Countries: Concepts, Tools, and Areas for Action*. Concept Paper 2. Europe Aid. http://capacity4dev.ec.europa.eu/sites/default/files/file/02/02/2012_-_1358/ade_1111_anti-corruption_full_low.pdf.

Marshall, M. G. and K. Jaggers 2002. *POLITY IV PROJECT: Political Regime Characteristics and Transitions, 1800–2002; Dataset Users' Manual*. Center for International Development and Conflict Management, University of Maryland, College Park. www3.nd.edu/mcoppedg/crd/PolityIVUsersManualv2002.pdf.

Mauro, P. 1995. "Corruption and Growth." *The Quarterly Journal of Economics* 110 (3): 681–712.

Mauss, M. 1990. *The Gift: The Form and Reason for Exchange in Archaic Societies*. London: Routlege.

McCoy, J. and H. Heckel 2001. "The Emergence of a Global Anticorruption Norm." *International Politics* 38: 65–90.

McMullan, M. 1961. "A Theory of Corruption Based on a Consideration of Corruption in the Public Services and Governments of British Colonies and Ex-Colonies in West Africa." *The Sociological Review* 9 (2): 181–201.

McNeil, M. and C. Malena 2010. *Demanding Good Governance: Lessons from Social Accountability Initiatives in Africa*. Washington, DC: World Bank Publications.

Meagher, P. and C. Voland 2006. *Anticorruption Agencies (ACAs): Office of Democracy and Governance Anticorruption Program Brief*. USAID. http://pdf.usaid.gov/pdf_docs/PNADM208.pdf.

Messick, D. M. and K. Sentis 1983. "Fairness, Preference, and Fairness Biases." In D. M. Messick and K. S. Cook (eds.) *Equity Theory: Psychological and Sociological*. New York: Praeger Publishers, 52.

Messick, R. E. 1999. "Judicial Reform and Economic Development: A Survey of the Issues." *The World Bank Research Observer* 14 (1): 117–36.

Migdal, J. S. 1988. *Strong Societies and Weak States: State-Society Relations and State Capabilities in the Third World*. Princeton University Press.

Millennium Challenge Corporation 2006. *Annual Report of International Finance Corporation Highlights Reform Incentives Created by Millennium Challenge Corporation*. Press release, September 6. Millennium Challenge Corporation. www.mcc.gov/pages/press/release/release-090606-annualreportifc.

2010. *Summary of Compacts Signed to Date*. Fact sheet, October 26. Millennium Challenge Corporation. www.mcc.gov/documents/press/factsheet-2010002016503-summaryofcompacts1.pdf.

Miller, N. 1996. *Stealing from America: A History of Corruption from Jamestown to Whitewater*. New York: Marlowe and Co.

Montecinos, V. 2003. *Economic Policy Making and Parliamentary Accountability in Chile*. Working Paper 11. Democracy, Governance, and Human Rights Program, UNRISD. www.unrisd.org/unrisd/website/document.nsf/462fc27bd1fce00880256b4a0060d2af/afa3585f2764bf98c1256f010023b686/$FILE/montecin.pdf.

Montinola, G. R. and R. W. Jackman 2002. "Sources of Corruption: A Cross-Country Study." *British Journal of Political Science* 32: 147–70.

Moore, B. Jr. 1966. *Social Origins of Dictatorship and Democracy*. Boston: Beacon Press.

Moore, J. and J. Smith 2007. *Corruption in Urban Politics and Society. Britain 1780–1950*. Aldershot: Ashgate.

Morrisson, C. and F. Murtin 2009. "The Century of Education." *Journal of Human Capital* 3 (1): 1–42.

Moscovici, S. 2001. "Why a Theory of Social Representations?" In K. Deaux and G. Philogène (eds.) *Representations of the Social*. Oxford: Blackwell, 8–35.

Mosley, P., J. Hudson, and A. Verschoor 2004. "Aid, Poverty Reduction, and the New Conditionality." *The Economic Journal* 114: F217–43.

Mousnier, R. 1969. *Les Hierarchies Sociales de 1450 a Nos Jours*. Paris: Presses Universitaires de France.

Mungiu-Pippidi, A. 2006a. "Deconstructing Balkan Particularism: The Ambiguous Social Capital of Southeastern Europe." *Southeast European and Black Sea Studies* 5 (1): 49–68.

2006b. "Corruption. Diagnosis, and Treatment." *Journal of Democracy* 17 (3): 86–99.

2010. *A Case Study in Political Clientelism: Romania's Policy-Making Mayhem*. http://ssrn.com/abstract=1686617.

2012. "Freedom Without Impartiality: The Vicious Circle of Media Capture." In P. Gross and K. Jakubowicz (eds.) *East European Media Twenty Years After*. New York: Lexington Books,49–66.

2013a. *Global Comparative Trend Analysis Report*. EU FP7 ANTICORRP project. http:/anticorrp.eu/publications/global-comparative-trend-analysis-report-1.

2013b. "The Widening Implementation Gap: The Impact of EU Accession on Governance in the Western Balkans." In E. Prifti (ed.) *The European Future of the Western Balkans: Thessaloniki@10*. European Institute for Security Studies, 35–44. www.iss.europa.eu/publications/detail/article/the-european-future-of-the-western-balkans-thessaloniki10/.

2013c. "Controlling Corruption by Collective Action." *Journal of Democracy* 24 (1): 101–15.

2014. "Becoming Denmark: Historical Designs of Corruption Control." *Social Research* 80 (4): 1259–86.

Mungiu-Pippidi, A., M. Loncaric, B. Vaz Mundo, A. C. Sponza Braga, M. Weinhardt, A. Pulido Solares, A. Skardziute, M. Martini, F. Agbele, M. F. Jensen, C. von Soest, and M. Gabedava (NORAD) 2011. *Contextual Choices in Fighting Corruption: Lessons Learned*, NORAD, Report 4/2011. www.norad.no/globalassets/import-2162015-80434-am/www.norad.no-ny/filarkiv/vedlegg-til-publikasjoner/contextual-choices-in-fighting-corruption-lessons-learned.pdf.

2014. *Quantitative Report: Why Do Some Societies Manage to Establish Control of Corruption and Others Not?* EU FP7 ANTICORRP project. http:/anticorrp.eu/news/quantitative-report-why-do-some-societies-manage-to-establish-control-of-corruption-and-others--not/.

Murphy, K. M., A. Shleifer, and R. W. Vishny 1991. "The Allocation of Talent: Implications for Growth." *The Quarterly Journal of Economics* 106 (2): 503–30.

Neild, R. R. 2002. *Public Corruption: The Dark Side of Social Evolution*. London: Anthem Press.

Neumann, F. 1986. *The Rule of Law: Political Theory and the Legal System in Modern Society*. Heidelberg: Berg.

Norris, P. (ed.) 2010. *Public Sentinel: News Media & Governance Reform*. World Bank Publications.

2012. *Making Democratic Governance Work: The Impact of Regimes on Prosperity, Welfare, and Peace*. Cambridge University Press.

North, D., J. J. Wallis, and B. R. Weingast 2009. *Violence and Social Orders: A Conceptual Framework for Interpreting Recorded Human History*. New York: Cambridge University Press.

Nye, J. S. 1967. "Corruption and Political Development: A Cost-Benefit Analysis." *American Political Science Review* 61 (2): 417–27.

O'Donnell, G. 1996. "Illusions about Consolidation." *Journal of Democracy* 7 (2): 34–51.

O'Dwyer, C. 2006. *Runaway State-Building: Patronage Politics and Democratic Development*. Baltimore, MD: Johns Hopkins University Press.

O'Leary, C. 1962. *The Elimination of Corrupt Practices in British Elections, 1868–1911*. Oxford: Clarendon Press.

Öhler, H., P. Nunnenkamp, and A. Dreher 2010. "Does Conditionality Work? A Test for an Innovative US Aid Scheme." Working Paper 1630. Kiel Institute for the World Economy.

Okada, K. and S. Samreth 2012. "The Effect of Foreign Aid on Corruption: A Quantile Regression Approach." *Economics Letters* 115 (2): 240–43.

Olken, B. 2008. *Corruption Perceptions vs. Corruption Reality*. Working Paper 12428. NBER.

Olowu, B. 1999. "Combating Corruption and Economic Crime in Africa. An Evaluation of the Botswana Directorate of Corruption and Economic Crime." *International Journal of Public Sector Management* 12 (7): 604–14.

Olson, M. 1965. *The Logic of Collective Action: Public Goods and the Theory of Groups*. Cambridge, MA: Harvard University Press.

Park, H. 2003. "Determinants of Corruption: A Cross-National Analysis." *The Multinational Business Review* 11 (2): 29–48.

Parker, G. 1978. *Philip II*. London: Open Court.

Parsons, T. 1997. *Introduction to Max Weber. The Theory of Social and Economic Organization*. New York: The Free Press.

Peck, L. L. 1990. *Court Patronage and Corruption in Early Stuart England*. London: Unwin Hyman.

Persson, A., B. Rothstein, and J. Teorell 2013. "Why Anticorruption Reforms Fail – Systemic Corruption as a Collective Action Problem." *Governance* 26 (3): 449–71.

Persson, T. and G. E. Tabellini 2003. *The Economic Effects of Constitutions*. Cambridge, MA: MIT Press.

2004. "Constitutions and Economic Policy." *The Journal of Economic Perspectives* 18 (1): 75–98.

Piattoni, S. 2001. *Clientelism, Interests, and Democratic Representation: The European Experience in Historical and Comparative Perspective*. Cambridge University Press.

Polity IV 2010. *Country Report: South Korea*. www.systemicpeace.org/polity/rok2.htm.

Pope, J. 2000. *Confronting Corruption: The Elements of a National Integrity System. Sourcebook*. Transparency International. www.transparency.org/publications/sourcebook.

PREM Network, The World Bank 1997. "Helping Countries Combat Corruption: The Role of the World Bank." www1.worldbank.org/publicsector/anticorrupt/corruptn/cor06.htm.

Pritchett, L. and M. Woolcock 2004. "Solutions When the Solution Is the Problem: Arraying the Disarray in Development." *World Development* 32 (2): 191–212.

Radelet, S. 2005. "Supporting Sustained Economic Development." *Michigan Journal of International Law* 26 (4): 1203–22.

Rauch, J. E. and P. B. Evans 2000. "Bureaucratic Structure and Bureaucratic Performance in Less Developed Countries." *Journal of Public Economics* 75 (1): 49–71.

Renouard, Y. 2009. *Les Hommes D'affaires Italiens Du Moyen Age*. Paris: Éditions Tallandier.

RISO 2012. "State Information System, eProcurement." www.riso.ee/en/node/102/.

Roberts, M. 1986. *The Age of Liberty: Sweden 1719–1772*. Cambridge University Press.

Rosanvallon, P. 1990. *L'Etat en France de 1789 à nos Jours*. L'Univers Historique. Paris: Le Seuil.

1992. *Le Sacre du Citoyen. Histoire Du Suffrage Universel en France*. Paris: Éditions Gallimard.

Rose-Ackerman, S. 1999. *Corruption and Government: Causes, Consequences, and Reform*. Cambridge University Press.

Rotberg, R. I. 2014. "Good Governance Means Performance and Results." *Governance* 27 (3): 511–18.

Rothstein, B. 2011. *The Quality of Government: Corruption, Social Trust, and Inequality in International Perspective*. The University of Chicago Press.

Rothstein, B. and J. Teorell 2008. "What Is Quality of Government? A Theory of Impartial Government Institutions." *Governance* 21 (2): 165–90.

2011. *The Quality of Government: Corruption, Social Trust, and Inequality in International Perspective*. The University of Chicago Press.

2012. "Defining and Measuring Quality of Government." In S. Holmberg and B. Rothstein (eds.) *Good Government: The Relevance of Political Science*. Cheltenham: Edward Elgar, 6–26.

Rothstein, B. and E. M. Uslaner 2005. "All for All: Equality and Social Trust." *World Politics* 58 (1): 41–72.

Sah, R. K. 2007. "Corruption Across Countries and Regions: Some Consequences of Local Osmosis." *Journal of Economic Dynamics and Control* 31: 2573–98.

Salamon, L. M. and S. W. Sokolowski 2011. "Measuring Civil Society: The Johns Hopkins Global Civil Society Index." In J. S. Ott and L. A. Dicke (eds.) *The Nature of the Nonprofit Sector*. Boulder, CO: Westview Press, 31–57.

Samuelsson, K. 1968. *From Great Power to Welfare State: 300 Years of Swedish Social Development*. London: George Allen und Unwin.

Sandholtz, W. and R. Taagepera 2005. "Corruption, Culture, and Communism." *International Review of Sociology* 15 (1): 109–31.

SAR (Romanian Academic Society) 2011. *Beyond Perception. Has Romania's Governance Improved after 2004?* www.sar.org.ro/files/Corruption.pdf.

Sartori, G. 1976. *Parties and Party Systems: A Framework for Analysis*. Cambridge University Press.

1994. *Comparative Constitutional Engineering: An Inquiry into Structures, Incentives, and Outcomes*. New York University Press.

Sasse, G. 2008. "The European Neighborhood: Conditionality Revisited for the EU's Eastern Neighbors." *Europe-Asia Studies* 60 (2): 295–316.

Schimmelfennig, F. and H. Scholz 2008. "EU Democracy Promotion in the European Neighborhood: Political Conditionality, Economic Development and Transnational Exchange." *European Union Politics* 9 (2): 187–215.

Schneider, F. 2007. "Shadow Economies and Corruption All over the World: New Estimates for 145 Countries." *Economics: The Open-Access, Open-Assessment E-Journal* 9: 1–66. www.economics-ejournal.org/.

Schudson, M. 1998. *The Good Citizen: A History of American Public Life*. New York: The Free Press.

Scott, J. C. 1969. "Corruption, Machine Politics, and Political Change." *American Political Science Review* 63 (4): 1142–58.

1972. *Political Corruption*. Englewood Cliffs, NJ: Prentice-Hall.

Sebudubudu, D. 2014. *Background Report on Botswana*. EU FP7 ANTICORRP project. http://anticorrp.eu/publications/background-paper-on-botswana/.

Sedelmeier, U. 2008. "After Conditionality: Post-Accession Compliance with EU Law in East Central Europe." *Journal of European Public Policy* 15 (6): 806–25.

Segal, P. 2006. "Coming Clean on Dirty Dealing: Time for a Fact-Based Evaluation of the Foreign Corrupt Practices Act." *Florida Journal of International Law* 18: 169–204.

Seldadyo, H. and J. De Haan 2006. "The Determinants of Corruption: A Literature Survey and New Evidence." Annual Meeting of the European Public Choice Society, Turku.

Sen, A. 1999. *Development as Freedom*. New York: Alfred A. Knopf.

Sharafutdinova, G. 2010. *Political Consequences of Crony Capitalism inside Russia*. University of Notre Dame Press.

Shepsle, K. A. and B. R. Weingast 1981. "Political Preferences for the Pork Barrel: A Generalization." *American Journal of Political Science* 25 (1): 96–111.

Sherif, M. and C. Hovland 1961. *Social Judgment: Assimilation and Contrast Effects in Communication and Attitude Change*. New Haven, CT: Yale University Press.

Shin, D. C. and Y.-H. Chu 2004. *The Quality of Democracy in South Korea and Taiwan: Subjective Assessment from the Perspective of Ordinary Citizens*. Working Paper Series 25. Asian Barometer. www.asianbarometer.org/newenglish/publications/workingpapers/no.25.pdf.

Siebert, F. S., T. Peterson, and W. Schramm 1956. *Four Theories of the Press*. Urbana, IL: University of Illinois Press.

Simon, H. 1997. *Administrative Behavior: A Study of Decision-Making Processes in Administrative Organization*. New York: Free Press.

Skinner, Q. 1989. "Ambrogio Lorenzetti: The Artist as Political Philosopher." In H. Belting and D. Blume (eds.) *Malerei Und Stadtkultur in Der Dantezeit: Die Argumentation Der Bilder*. Munich: Hirmer, 85–103.

Spector, B. I. (ed.) 2005. *Fighting Corruption in Developing Countries: Strategies and Analysis*. Bloomfield, CT: Kumarian Press.
Stapenhurst, R. 2000. *The Media's Role in Curbing Corruption*. The World Bank Institute. http://siteresources.worldbank.org/INTWBIGOVANTCOR/Resources/media.pdf.
Stoyanov, A., R. Stefanov, and B. Velcheva 2014. "Bulgarian Anti-Corruption Reforms: A Lost Decade?" In A. Mungiu-Pippidi (ed.) *The Anticorruption Frontline, Vol. 2*. Opladen: Barbara Budrich Publishers, 25–39.
Sung, H.-E. 2003. "Fairer Sex or Fairer System? Gender and Corruption Revisited." *Social Forces* 82 (2): 703–23.
2004. "Democracy and Political Corruption: A Cross-National Comparison." *Crime, Law, and Social Change* 41 (2): 179–93.
Svensson, J. 2000. "Foreign Aid and Rent Seeking." *Journal of International Economics* 51: 437–61.
2003. "Who Must Pay Bribes and How Much? Evidence From a Cross-Section of Firms." *Quarterly Journal of Economics* 118 (1): 207–30.
Swart, K. W. 1949. *Sale of Offices in the Seventeenth Century*. The Hague: Martinus Nijhoff.
Tajfel, H. 2004. *The Social Identity Theory of Intergroup Behavior*. New York: Psychology Press.
Tanzi, V. 1994. *Corruption, Governmental Activities, and Markets*. Working Paper 94/99. International Monetary Fund.
Tanzi, V. and H. R. Davoodi 1997. *Corruption, Public Investment, and Growth*. Working Paper 97/139. International Monetary Fund.
Tarullo, D. K. 2003–2004. "Limits of Institutional Design: Implementing the OECD Anti-Bribery Convention." *Virginia Journal of International Law* 44, March: 665–708.
Tavares, J. 2003. "Does Foreign Aid Corrupt?" *Economics Letters* 79 (1): 99–106.
Thomas, M. A. 2009. "What Do the Worldwide Governance Indicators Measure?" *European Journal of Development Research* 22 (1): 31–54.
Tisne, M. and D. Smilov 2004. *From the Ground Up: Assessing the Record of Anticorruption Assistance in Southeast Europe*. Budapest: Central European University Press.
Tocqueville, A. 2006. *Democracy in America*. Project Gutenberg. www.gutenberg.org/ebooks/816.
Transparency International 2007. *National Integrity Systems. Country Study Report: Botswana*. http://archive.transparency.org/policy_research/nis/nis_reports_by_country/africa_middle_east.
2009. *Global Corruption Barometer 2009*. www.transparency.org/policy_research/surveys_indices/gcb/2009.
2010/2011. *Global Corruption Barometer 2010/11* www.transparency.org/gcb201011.

2011. *Strategy 2015*. www.transparency.org/files/content/ourorganisation/TI_Strategy_2015.pdf.

2012. *Corruption Perceptions Index 2012: An Updated Methodology*. http://cpi.transparency.org/cpi2012/in_detail/.

2013. *Global Corruption Barometer 2013*. www.transparency.org/gcb2013.

Treisman, D. 2000. "The Causes of Corruption: A Cross-National Study." *Journal of Public Economics* 76 (3): 399–457.

2007. "What Have We Learned about the Causes of Corruption from Ten Years of Cross-National Empirical Research?" *Annual Review of Political Science* 10: 211–44.

Tsie, B. 1996. "The Political Context of Botswana's Development Performance." *Journal of Southern African Studies* 22 (4): 599–616.

Tsitsishvili, D. 2010. *Georgia: Corruption Developments and Anti-Corruption Activities Since 1990s*. Working Papers 6. European Research Center for Anticorruption and State-Building (ERCAS). www.againstcorruption.eu/reports/georgia-corruption-developments-and-anti-corruption-activities-since-1990s/.

Tuchman, G. 1972. "Objectivity as Strategic Ritual: An Examination of Newsman's Notions of Objectivity." *American Journal of Sociology* 77: 662–66.

UNDP 1997. *Reconceptualizing Governance*. Discussion Paper 2. ftp://pogar.org/LocalUser/pogarp/other/undp/governance/reconceptualizing.pdf.

2005. *Institutional Arrangements to Combat Corruption – A Comparative Study*. http://asia-pacific.undp.org/content/dam/rbap/docs/Research%20and%20Publications/democratic_governance/RBAP-DG-2005-Institutional-Arrangements-Combat-Corruption.pdf.

US Congress 2007. Hearing before the Subcommittee on Asia, the Pacific, and the Global Environment, Committee on Foreign Affairs. 154th US House of Representatives.

Uslaner, E. and B. Rothstein 2012. *Mass Education, State-Building, and Equality*. Working Paper Series 5. QoG.

Valenzuela, A. 1977. *Political Brokers in Chile: Local Government in a Centralized Polity*. Durham, NC: Duke University Press.

1989. "Chile: Origins, Consolidation, and Breakdown of a Democratic Regime." In L. Diamond, J. Linz, and S. M. Lipset (eds.) *Democracy in Developing Countries, Vol. 4: Latin America*. Boulder, CO: Lynne Rienner, 159–206.

Van de Walle, N. 2001. *African Economies and the Politics of Permanent Crisis, 1979–1999*. Cambridge University Press.

Van Rijckeghem, C. and B. Weder 1997. *Corruption and the Rate of Temptation: Do Low Wages in the Civil Service Cause Corruption?* Working Paper. International Monetary Fund.

Von Soest, C. 2007. "How Does Neopatrimonialism Affect the African State? The Case of Tax Collection in Zambia." *Journal of Modern African Studies* 45 (4): 621–45.

2009. *Stagnation of a Miracle: Botswana's Governance Record Revisited.* Working Paper 99. German Institute of Global and Area Studies (GIGA).

Wallace, C. and C. W. Haerpfer 2000. *Democratisation, Economic Development, and Corruption in East-Central Europe.* Sociological Studies 44. Institute for Advanced Studies (IHS), Vienna. www.ihs.ac.at/publications/soc/rs44.pdf.

Wallis, J. J., P. V. Fishback, and S. E. Kantor 2006. "Politics, Relief, and Reform: Roosevelt's Efforts to Control Corruption and Political Manipulation during the New Deal." In E. L. Glaeser and C. Goldin (eds.) *Corruption and Reform: Lessons from America's Economic History*. University of Chicago Press, 343–72.

Weaver, D. H., J. M. Buddenbaum and J. E. Fair, 1985. "Press Freedom, Media, and Development, 1950–1979: A Study of 134 Nations." *Journal of Communication* 35 (2): 104–17.

Weber, M. 1968. *Economy and Society: An Outline of Interpretive Sociology*. Edited by G. Roth and C. Wittich. Vols. I–III. New York: Bedminster Press.

1976. *General Economic History*. London: Unwin Paperbacks.

Wedel, J. R. 2009. *Shadow Elite: How the World's New Power Brokers Undermine Democracy, Government, and the Free Market.* New York: Basic Books.

White, G. 1995. "Civil Society, Democratization and Development (II): Two Country Cases." *Democratization* 2 (2): 56–84.

Wilson, J. Q. 1993. *The Moral Sense*. New York: Free Press.

World Bank 1994. *Governance: The World Bank's Experience. Development in Practice.* Washington, DC: The World Bank. http://documents.worldbank.org/curated/en/1994/05/698374/governance-world-banks-experience.

2001. "Making Aid More Effective in Reducing Poverty." In *World Development Report 2000–01: Attacking Poverty*, Chapter 11. New York: Oxford University Press. https://openknowledge.worldbank.org/bitstream/handle/10986/11856/9780195211290_ch11.pdf?sequence=17.

2011. *Country-Level Engagement on Governance and Anti-Corruption: An Evaluation of the 2007 Strategy and Implementation Plan.* Independent Evaluation Group, The World Bank. http://ieg.worldbank.org/Data/reports/Final_GAC_Eval_Approach_Paper_to_CODE_6-8–10.pdf.

Wulf, A. 2012. "Audit Slams Effectiveness of EU's Kosovo Mission." *Deutsche Welle*, October 31. www.dw.de/audit-slams-effectiveness-of-eus-kosovo-mission/a-16343948.

You, J.-S. 2006. "A Comparative Study of Income Inequality, Corruption, and Social Trust: How Inequality and Corruption Reinforce Each Other and Erode Social Trust." Harvard University, Kennedy School of Government.

You, S.-J. 2012. "Transition from a Limited Access Order to an Open Access Order: The Case of South Korea." In D. C. North, J. J. Wallis, S. B. Webb, and B. R. Weingast (eds.) *In the Shadow of Violence: Politics, Economics, and the Problems of Development*. Cambridge University Press, 293–327.

Young, J. 2013. "Tear Gas and Pointed Guns: Inside Protests at Confederations Cup." *Sports Illustrated Online*, June. www.si.com/soccer/2013/06/24/brazil-protests-confederations-cup.

Youngs, R. 2010. *The European Union and Democracy Promotion: A Critical Global Assessment*. Baltimore, MD: Johns Hopkins University Press.

Yu, C., C.-M. Chen, W.-J. Juang, and L.-T. Hu 2008. "Does Democracy Breed Integrity? Corruption in Taiwan during the Democratic Transformation Period." *Crime Law Society Change*, no. 49: 167–84.

Zola, E. 1898. "J'accuse." *L'Aurore*. www.cahiers-naturalistes.com/jaccuse_lettre_au_presidentdelar.html.

Index

Page numbers in *italic* denote figures; those in **bold** denote tables.

For EU product safety concerns, contact us at Calle de José Abascal, 56–1°, 28003 Madrid, Spain or eugpsr@cambridge.org.

www.ingramcontent.com/pod-product-compliance
Ingram Content Group UK Ltd.
Pitfield, Milton Keynes, MK11 3LW, UK
UKHW020354060825
461487UK00008B/655

* 9 7 8 1 1 0 7 1 1 3 9 2 3 *